ACTA UNIVERSITATIS UPSALIENSIS
Studia Anglistica Upsaliensia
51

Birgit Bramsbäck

Folklore and W. B. Yeats

The Function of Folklore Elements in Three Early Plays

Uppsala 1984

Distributor:
Almqvist & Wiksell International
Stockholm

Printed with a grant from The Swedish Council for Research
in the Humanities and Social Sciences

Abstract

Bramsbäck, Birgit, 1984. *Folklore and W. B. Yeats: The Function of Folklore Elements in Three Early Plays.* Acta Universitatis Upsaliensis. *Studia Anglistica Upsaliensia* 51. xii + 178 pp. Monograph. Uppsala. ISBN 91-554-1502-4.

This monograph deals with three of Yeats's early plays, *The Countess Cathleen* (*CC*), *The Land of Heart's Desire* (*LHD*), and *The Shadowy Waters* (*SW*), and is the first full-scale study of the *function* of folklore elements in Yeats's work. My critical approach is a synthesis of historical, comparative and close-reading methods. Yeats, who firmly believed in the vital interaction of folklore and literature, explored the living tradition of his own time as well as traditional lore of countless generations. Although there is some overlap, three major folklore categories, i.e. traditional tales, traditional popular belief, and folk poetry (including ballads and folk music), can be distinguished. The first category provides subject matter, some themes and motifs as well as certain symbols. From the second spring a large number of symbols, one of the key concepts being the multiform Otherworld. Between this invisible world and the visible one there is a continuous conflict which is enacted by the protagonists. The third category sets or changes the mood or tone of an act or a scene, intensifies emotions and passions, and heightens the conflict. Other key concepts are rebirth and transformations. Numerous symbols like fairies, ghosts, demons, birds, animals, sacred flowers and trees, fire, natural phenomena, musical instruments, etc., create an arcane world of taboos and magic. Specific attributes denote the supernatural quality of birds and animals, e.g. the human faces and voices of the grey horned owls and of the ash-grey sea-birds, the silver feet and the crest of gold of the white bird, the one red ear of the white hound, etc. In *SW* there is an almost ritual use of a wake and the traditional keening for the dead. A folk ballad inspired the Sailors' ale-song, and Dectora's lament over her dead king and husband recalls the *marbhna* or learned elegy. This study shows how successful Yeats was in enriching his drama by using folklore elements.

Birgit Bramsbäck, The Department of English and the Celtic Section, Uppsala University, Box 513, S-751 20 Uppsala, Sweden

ISBN 91-554-1502-4
ISSN 0562-2719

Printed in Sweden by Borgströms Tryckeri AB, Motala 1984

"In Ireland this world and the world we go to after death are not far apart"

To the Memory of
My Parents

Preface

This study has been motivated by the richness of folklore material enshrined in Yeats's works, especially in the early plays, *The Countess Cathleen (CC), The Land of Heart's Desire (LHD),* and *The Shadowy Waters (SW),* and the later revised versions of them. It should, however, be stressed that my investigation concerns, not folklore *per se,* but the function of folklore elements in Yeats's plays.

The book grew out of two lectures, one delivered at the International Yeats Summer School, Sligo, Ireland, in August 1971, another at the English Department, Connecticut University, Storrs, in November 1972. My warmest thanks for these arrangements go to the former Swedish Ambassador to Ireland, Dr. Sven-Eyvind Bratt, Dublin, Professor A. Norman Jeffares, now at Stirling University, and Professor G. B. Saul, now Emeritus Professor, University of Connecticut, Storrs.

The Introduction to the present study appeared in a somewhat different form as an article entitled "William Butler Yeats and Folklore Material", published in *Béaloideas: Journal of the Folklore of Ireland Society,* Vol. 39–41, 1971–73 (Dublin: 1975), 56–68, and in *Hereditas: Essays and Studies presented to Professor Séamus Ó Duilearga,* ed. Bo Almqvist, Breandán Mac Aodha and Gearóid Mac Eoin (Dublin, 1975), pp. 56–68. This article is one of the first to point to Yeats's lifelong use of folklore in his work, and my warm thanks are due to the editors and publishers of *Béaloideas* and *Hereditas* for permission to print it in its present form. Apart from listing important folklore material, oral and written, which Yeats drew upon, the Introduction is intended to show that one of Yeats's aims was to bring about a creative interchange between folklore and literature.

The three main chapters of my study will investigate the function of three categories of folklore in the three plays concerned, Chapter I traditional prose tales underlying the plays, Chapter II popular belief as it functions in the plays, and Chapter III the impact of folk poetry and music on the songs written into the plays at various times.

I should like to express my sincere thanks to Professor Claes Schaar, Lund, for having provided me with the idea of dividing the folklore elements in the plays into some kind of categories. Likewise to Ailbhe

Ó Corráin, B.A., Lecturer in Celtic Languages at Uppsala University, for suggesting some stylistic revisions.

It is a pleasure to acknowledge my debt of gratitude to the staffs of Uppsala University Library, the National Library of Ireland, Dublin, and the British Library, London, for their never-failing courtesy.

I wish to express my gratitude to Statens Humanistisk-Samhällsvetenskapliga Forskningsråd and to Acta Universitatis Upsaliensis for financing the printing of this monograph.

I am also grateful to Uppsala University for a number of travel grants which have facilitated my research, as well as for a year's sabbatical leave in 1982 which enabled me to complete this work.

Grateful acknowledgement is made to Miss Anne Yeats and Senator Michael B. Yeats for permission to print four musical illustrations [Appendix II].

Uppsala, August–December 1983
Birgit Bramsbäck

Contents

Preface vii

Contents ix

Abbreviations xi

Introduction: W. B. Yeats and Folklore Material 1

Chapter I. Traditional Tales, or Stories, Underlying
The Countess Cathleen, The Land of Heart's Desire, and
The Shadowy Waters 14

   The Countess Cathleen and Traditional Stories 15
   The Land of Heart's Desire and Traditional Stories 27
   The Shadowy Waters and Traditional Stories 29
   The Wooing of Étain—A Traditional Tale Explored in
   All Three Plays 35
   Concluding Remarks 46

Chapter II. The Function of Popular Belief in the Three Plays 48

   The Irish-Celtic Otherworld 48
   The Countess Cathleen—Three Otherworlds 49
   The Land of Heart's Desire—A Fairy Otherworld 59
   The Shadowy Waters—An Otherworld Vision in the Western Sea 69
   Bird Lore and Associated Beliefs in the Three Plays 85
   Concluding Remarks 100

Chapter III. Impact of Folk Poetry and Music on the Songs in the
   Three Plays 102

   Yeats on Popular Poetry 102
   The Poet/Musician in *The Countess Cathleen* 105
   Songs in *The Countess Cathleen* 110
   Fairy Song and Fairy Music in *The Land of Heart's Desire* 129
   Songs in *The Shadowy Waters* 135
   Concluding Remarks 143

Afterword 145

Appendix I 151

Three versions of a ballad:

  1 *An Gruagach Uasal* 151
  2 *Oro! A Lionn-dubh Buidhe!* 152
  3 *O the Brown and the Yellow Ale!* 152

Appendix II 154

Musical Illustrations:

  1 *Impetuous heart, be still, be still* 154
  2 *The Wind Blows out of the Gates of the Day* 155
  3 *[The Sailors' Song]* 155
  4 *[Dectora's Lament]* 156

Bibliography 157

A. Works of W. B. Yeats Quoted or Referred To 157
B. Swedish Translations of the Works of W. B. Yeats Referred To ... 159
C. Other Works Quoted or Referred To 160

Index 171

Abbreviations

Best 1	Best, R. I., *Bibliography of Irish Philology*
Best 2	— *Bibliography of Irish Philology 1913—1941*
Bran I	Meyer, Kuno, *The Voyage of Bran* Vol. I
Bran II	— *The Voyage of Bran* Vol. II
CC	Yeats, W. B., *The Countess Cathleen*
CRC	Cultural Relations Committee of Ireland
Frayne, I	Frayne, John P., ed., *Uncollected Prose by W. B. Yeats,* I
Frayne, II	Frayne, John P. and Colton Johnson, ed., *Uncollected Prose by W. B. Yeats,* II
IACI	Irish-American Cultural Institute
IGE	Yeats, W. B., *Ideas of Good and Evil*
ITS	Irish Texts Society
IUP	Irish University Press
LHD	Yeats, W. B., *The Land of Heart's Desire*
OUP	Oxford University Press
PQ	Philological Quarterly
RC	Revue Celtique
RIA	Royal Irish Academy
SW	Yeats, W. B., *The Shadowy Waters*
VP	*The Variorum Edition of the Poems of W. B. Yeats*
VPl	*The Variorum Edition of the Plays of W. B. Yeats*
Wade	Wade, Allan, *A Bibliography of the Writings of W. B. Yeats*
WR	Yeats, W. B., *The Wind Among the Reeds*
ZCP	Zeitschrift für Celtische Philologie
Yeats: CH	Jeffares, A. N., ed., *W. B. Yeats.* The Critical Heritage Series

(For full bibliographical details consult Bibliography.)

Introduction

W. B. Yeats and Folklore Material

As early as 1934, almost fifty years ago, in a stimulating essay "Den unge Yeats och den gamle" [Yeats Young and Old], the famous Swedish poet Anders Österling (d. 1981) stated that Yeats's "reverence for popular lore is far more than just an aesthetic mania", and must to a large extent be attributed to his "fundamental susceptibility to every kind of mystical suggestion."[1] Undoubtedly, Yeats, especially in the 1880s and 1890s, worked for the preservation and cultivation of folklore, and its communication to a larger number of people, as well as for the artistic use of it in creative writing. One of his dreams was that folklore should function as a living organism in a country's literature, and he loved to point out that Irish poets had at their disposal a rich Celtic tradition, "an untouched marble block" from which stories, myths and legends could be cut and passed on by Irish poets to avid listeners all over the world. As stated in the Preface, the present work will investigate some of the ways in which Yeats made folklore function in his early plays. If, in the final pages of this introductory chapter, the enumeration of a large number of folklore sources available to Yeats and other Irish authors at the end of last and the beginning of this century, may seem a little tedious, my excuse is that these lists will comprise background material significant not only for this investigation but also for other studies of Yeats and folklore.

For a long time, folklore material in Yeats's prose and verse was a somewhat neglected field in Yeatsian research. There are, it is true, an ever-growing number of works—articles, books and parts of books—which treat of various aspects of the appropriation, adaptation and interpretation by Yeats of myths and legends, and of his creation of a mythology and philosophy of his own.[2] It is also generally agreed that popular lore, especi-

---

[1] *Horisonter* (Stockholm: Albert Bonniers Förlag, 1939), pp. 205–221, esp. 210 (my trans.).

[2] One of the earliest examples on the use by Yeats and other writers of legendary material is William Larminie's "Legends as Material for Literature", first published in the *Daily Express*, 19 November 1893, then included in *Literary Ideals in Ireland*, by John Eglinton and others (London, 1899), pp. 57–65. For full bibliographical details of critical works on Yeats up to 1965, see K. G. W. Cross and R. T. Dunlop, *A Bibliography of Yeats Criticism, 1887–*

ally Irish, was a vital source of inspiration for Yeats and other writers of the Celtic Revival, and many critics and scholars have touched on this subject, especially on Yeats's use of fairy lore, stressed, as just stated, for example by Anders Österling. Likewise, in an obituary article in March 1939, the late Professor J. J. Hogan emphasized that "Fairy lore, local and from books, supplied. . . symbol and metaphor to a poetry of suggestion which is Celtic in demanding the suspension of disbelief to a degree other poets do not ask for."[3] Mention should also be made of some pioneering works, Elsbeth Schweisgut's *Yeats' Feendichtung,*[4] Russell K. Alspach's article "The Use by Yeats and Other Irish Writers of the Folklore of Patrick Kennedy",[5] and Michael B. Yeats's fine article "W. B. Yeats and Irish Folk Song."[6] Simultaneously with my own "William Butler Yeats and Folklore Material", mentioned in the Preface, appeared Sheila O'Sullivan's thought-provoking article "W. B. Yeats's Use of Irish Oral and Literary Tradition", in *Béaloideas* (Dublin, 1975) and in *Hereditas* (Dublin, 1975), pp. 266–279. Articles which should not be forgotten are Bruce A. Rosenberg's "Irish Folklore and 'The Song of Wandering Aengus' ", in the *Philological Quarterly,* 46 (October 1967), 527–535, and Ole Munch-Pedersen's "Crazy Jane: A Cycle of Popular Literature", in *Éire: Ireland* (Spring 1979), 56–73.[7]

In her *W. B. Yeats and Irish Folklore* (Dublin; Totowa, 1980)—a landmark in the field of Yeats and folklore—Professor Mary Helen Thuente remarked (p. 2) that in my essay in *Hereditas,* I had pointed out (p. 57) the lack of a "full-scale comprehensive investigation of the rôle played by folklore in the Yeats canon." Her study, which is acknowledged at appropriate points in the present work, certainly fills this gap and provides us, for the first time, with a study of "the broad range of oral traditions which belonged to the nineteenth-century Irish peasantry—narratives, songs, beliefs, customs—which Yeats studied so thoroughly in both oral and written form during the 1880s and 1890s" (p. 2), and also shows how "narrative traditions of Irish folklore, in particular legends, influenced Yeats in subject, theory, and style" (p. 3).

1965. (London and Basingstoke: Macmillan, 1971); hereafter Cross-Dunlop; up to 1978, K. P. S. Jochum, *W. B. Yeats: A Classified Bibliography of Criticism* (Urbana, Chicago, London: Univ. of Illinois Press, 1978); hereafter Jochum; K. P. S. Jochum, "A Yeats Bibliography for 1981", *Yeats: An Annual of Critical and Textual Studies,* ed. Richard J. Finneran, I (1983), 155–173.

[3] "W. B. Yeats", *Studies* (March 1939), pp. 35–48, esp. 36.
[4] Diss. Ludwigs-Universität zu Giessen (Darmstadt: K. F. Bender, 1927). 55 pp.
[5] *Journal of American Folk-Lore,* 59 (October–December 1946), 404–412.
[6] *Southern Folklore Quarterly,* 31 (June 1966), 153–178. Hereafter Michael Yeats.
[7] (Spring 1979), pp. 56–73.

Just as the present work was ready for the press, F. Kinahan's stimulating article "Armchair Folklore: Yeats and the Textual Sources of *Fairy and Folk Tales of the Irish Peasantry*", in *Proceedings of the Royal Irish Academy,* 83 C 10 (Dublin: RIA, 1983), 255—267, came to hand.

However, a good deal still remains to be written about how folklore enriches Yeats's essays and stories, poems and plays, and I hope that the present study of the function of folklore elements in three of his early plays, *The Countess Cathleen (CC), The Land of Heart's Desire (LHD)* and *The Shadowy Waters (SW),* will reveal how Yeats's use of folklore informs his plays, throws new light on the contents, the characters of the plays and their real and visionary worlds, provides subject-matter and symbols, and affects the moods of the plays.

Before proceeding, I should like to say a few words about the term 'folklore', notoriously difficult to define, and also unfortunately often misunderstood as something chiefly dealing with fairy lore and "such things". The lexical definition, "The beliefs, legends and customs current among the common people; the study of these",[8] reflects a view[9] no longer generally accepted since it is too narrow. For the purpose of this study it is not necessary to enter into a discussion of the various controversial definitions of the term folklore which have appeared since the coining of the term in 1846 by the English antiquarian, William John Thoms. Suffice it to say that there seems to be no general agreement as to the exact meaning of the word—at least twenty different definitions are to be found in the *Standard Dictionary of Folklore, Mythology and Legend,*[10] a title which in itself, as pointed out by J. Hautala in his article "Folkminnesforskningen som vetenskapsgren" [Folklore as a Discipline], illustrates some of the difficulties involved.[11] However, most specialists agree that, to quote Stith Thompson, "The common idea in all folklore is that of tradition, something handed on from one person to another either by memory or practice rather than written record" (Funk and Wagnalls, p. 403).

Today most folklorists favour a comprehensive view, that is, they tend to regard folklore as one immense field including both spiritual and mate-

---

[8] *Shorter Oxford English Dictionary* (1959 ed.), under "Folk-Lore".

[9] Andrew Lang (1844—1912), for example, gives the following definition: "properly speaking, folklore is only concerned with the legends, customs, beliefs, of the classes which have least been altered by education, which have shared least in the progress." *Custom and Myth* (London, 1884; 1885), p. 11.

[10] Funk and Wagnalls *Standard Dictionary of Folklore, Mythology and Legend,* ed. Maria Leach (London: Funk & Wagnalls, 1972 [1949]), pp. 398—403; hereafter Funk and Wagnalls.

[11] In *Folkdikt och folktro* [Folk Literature and Folk Belief], ed. Anna Birgitta Rooth (Lund: Gleerups, 1971), pp. 33—63.

rial folk culture and folk life, yet the traditional division into a spiritual and material sphere is retained for convenience sake, and perhaps also because the field is so immense. This is how the well-known American folklorist, Richard Dorson, puts it in his article "Is Folklore a Discipline?"

. . . I would say they [folklorists today] are concerned with the study of traditional culture, or the unofficial culture, or the folk culture, as opposed to the elite culture. . .

At one pole the oral genres of folk narrative, folk poetry, and smaller forms seem clear cut. At the other end the categories of material culture, ranged under the relatively new term 'folk life', do not so readily fall into place. Folk art, folk crafts, and folk architecture seem to hang together as all involving traditional handiwork, while the performing arts of folk music, folk dance, folk drama, and folk festival appear to form another cluster. Folk costume and folk cuisine belong somewhere in the material culture area, while folk religion and folk medicine, involving belief, ritual, and custom, spread over the genres and material culture in ways not easily classified.[12]

Another rather similar definition is that afforded by Francis Lee Utley in his introductory essay to the inspiring volume, *American Folklore,* where he states that "Folklore as a whole is not", as he once thought, "merely 'literature orally transmitted',"[13] even if folk literature, in all its major and minor genres, such as folktales, fables, legends, ballads, folk lyrics and songs, nursery songs, riddles, proverbs, and weather sayings, etc., forms a central area of folklore; equally important areas are folk customs, popular belief, magic and superstitions, as are folk music, folk dance and folk festivals, etc. Art and craft certainly belong to folklore, for why exclude from that discipline "the vital aspect of material culture and folklife", to which American schools of folklore "are beginning to pay more attention" than has hitherto been the case?[14]

Yeats would have agreed with both Dorson and Utley, for he was firmly convinced that folklore in all its manifestations was a living force, a power which should be used to vitalize literature. To Yeats, the 'folk' meant above all the largely illiterate people of the Irish countryside—peasants, farmers, fishermen, especially in Connacht, but also in other parts of Ireland. It was to the potency and vitality of the visionary imagination of the folk that the early Yeats gave pride of place: "No conscious invention

[12] *Folklore,* 84 (Autumn 1973), 177—205, esp. 197, 199.

[13] "A Definition of Folklore", *American Folklore* (Voice of America Forum Lectures), ed. Tristram Coffin (1968), pp. 3—14.

[14] Ibid., p. 7.

can take the place of tradition...", he stated in 1893.[15] Accordingly, like today's folklore specialists, he stressed the role of tradition, and held that, for example Shakespeare and Keats, who "had the folklore of their own day", were greater poets than Shelley, who "had but mythology".[16]

That Irish authors should explore their own native traditions was a literary tenet which Yeats clung to throughout his long career, and that Irish writers ought to choose Irish subjects was something he stressed again and again. They should unfold and develop their own traditions as did William Carleton, who "came from the heart of Gaelic Ireland, and found there the symbols of his art", Yeats wrote in 1896.[17]

An excellent example of Yeats's appreciation of popular imaginative tradition is found in "By the Roadside", the last prose piece in *The Celtic Twilight* (1893). Yeats describes his going one night to "a wide place on the Kiltartan road to listen to some Irish songs."[18] Here in the open he heard— as he must have done on many other occasions—Irish traditional singing and saw folk dancing being performed. Among songs sung that night was the well-known love song

Eiblín a Rúin, that glad song of meeting which has always moved me more than other songs, because the lover who made it sang it to his sweetheart under the shadow of a mountain I looked at every day through my childhood.[19]

The song inspired in Yeats a mood in which he saw himself transferred "to the roots of the Trees of Knowledge and of Life", and he adds:

There is no song or story handed down among the cottages that has not words and thoughts to carry one as far, for though one can know but a little of their ascent, one knows that they ascend like mediæval genealogies through unbroken dignities to the beginning of the world. Folk-art is, indeed, the oldest of the aristocracies of thought, and because it refuses what is passing and trivial, the merely clever and pretty, as certainly as the vulgar and insincere, and because it has gathered into

---

[15] "The Message of the Folk-lorist", in *Uncollected Prose by William Butler Yeats,* vol. I, ed. John P. Frayne (London: Macmillan; New York: Columbia UP, 1970), pp. 283–288, esp. 288; hereafter Frayne, I. The article was first printed in the *Speaker* (August 19 1893), under the title, "A Literary Causerie", and is a review of Thistelton Dyer's *The Ghost World* (London, 1893).

[16] Frayne, I, p. 288

[17] Ibid., p. 395.

[18] *Mythologies* (London: Macmillan, 1959), p. 138.

[19] Ibid., p. 138. The phrase "that glad song of meeting" refers to the last stanza of the poem, in which the lover says to his beloved: "A hundred thousand welcomes, Eileen a Roon! A hundred thousand welcomes, Eileen a Roon! Oh! welcome evermore, With welcomes yet in store, Till love and life are o'er, Eileen a Roon!" Irish text, and Thomas Furlong's trans. in James Hardiman, *Irish Minstrelsy,* 2 vol. (London, 1831), I, pp. 264–267; hereafter *Hardiman,* I and II.

itself the simplest and most unforgettable thoughts of the generations, it is the soil where all great art is rooted.[20]

Folk art—used here in a wide sense by Yeats—"spoken by the fireside", "sung by the roadside", "carved upon the lintel", is, in Yeats's words, "the soil where all great art is rooted". A poet, Yeats claimed, should listen to the old storytellers and, in order to be able to express "subjective moods", he must have access to symbols, types and stories embedded in folk imagination.

In early reviews and articles Yeats expressed many of his opinions on folklore and literature. Of absorbing interest are a number of articles in which he tries to assess the value of such works, as Lady Wilde's *Ancient Cures, Charms, and Usages of Ireland* (1890),[21] Douglas Hyde's *Beside the Fire* (1890),[22] and *Love Songs of Connacht* (1893),[23] William Larminie's *West Irish Folk-Tales* (1893).[24] A series of articles on "Irish National Literature" published in the London *Bookman* (July—October 1895) reveals Yeats's belief in the development and growth of a native Irish literature.[25] In his review of Hyde's *Beside the Fire* he stated that "Our new-awakened interest in the impossible has been of the greatest service to Irish folk-literature."[26] He pays homage to T. Crofton Croker (1798—1854) and Patrick Kennedy[27] (1801—1873) as precursors, yet finds fault with their imperfect methods of collecting folklore, and he blames Croker for being too rationalistic. Actually, Crofton Croker's *Fairy Legends and Traditions of the South of Ireland,* published anonymously in 1825 (sixty-three years before the publication of Yeats's own *Fairy and Folk Tales of the Irish*

---

[20] *Mythologies,* pp. 138–139.
[21] The review first appeared in the *Scots Observer,* 1 March 1890. Frayne, I, pp. 169–173.
[22] The *National Observer,* 28 February 1891. Frayne, I, pp. 186–190.
[23] The *Bookman,* London, October 1893. Frayne, I, pp. 292–295.
[24] The *Bookman,* London, June 1894. Frayne, I, pp. 326–328.
[25] Ibid., pp. 359–364; 366–373; 375–387.
[26] Ibid., p. 187.
[27] Kennedy's six volumes containing folklore and semi-folklore are *Legends of Mount Leinster* (Dublin, 1855, written under the pen-name of Harry Whitney), *Legendary Fictions of the Irish Celts* (London, 1866), *The Banks of the Boro* (Dublin, 1867), *Evenings in the Duffrey* (Dublin, 1869), *The Fireside Stories of Ireland* (Dublin, 1870), and *The Bardic Stories of Ireland* (Dublin, 1871). The use made of these stories by Yeats has been dealt with by Russell K. Alspach in his article "The Use by Yeats and Other Irish Writers of the Folklore of Patrick Kennedy", *Journal of American Folk-Lore,* 59 (October–December 1946), 404–412. Another of these early collectors of folklore was Jeramiah Curtin (1835–1906), an Irish-American who, to quote S. Ó Duilearga, collected and edited "three outstanding collections of Irish folk- and fairytales, (1) *Myths and Folk-Lore of Ireland* (Boston: London, 1890 and 1911); (2) *Hero-Tales of Ireland* (Boston: London, 1894) and (3) *Tales of the Fairies and the Ghost World, collected from oral tradition in Southwest Munster* (Boston: London, 1895)." See *Irish Folk-Tales* Collected by Jeremiah Curtin, ed. S. Ó Duilearga (Dublin: Talbot; 1956), p. ix.

6

Peasantry)[28] appears to be the very first collection of oral tales to have been gathered in the British Isles.[29]

Eager to make Irish folk literature better known to his own countrymen Yeats edited several collections of stories, the first of which was the one already mentioned, *Fairy and Folk Tales of the Irish Peasantry.* Brought out in 1888 it was followed in 1889 by an edition of *Stories from Carleton,* in 1891 by a two-volume collection of *Representative Irish Tales,* and in 1892 by *Irish Fairy Tales* delightfully illustrated by his brother, Jack B. Yeats. These books are of enduring importance not only because of their intrinsic value but also because of their linking up with Yeats's own poems and plays. At least two of the stories were dramatized by Yeats, "The Priest's Soul", which is the source of *The Hour-Glass* and "The Countess Kathleen O'Shea", the source of *The Countess Cathleen.*[30] "Hy-Brasail—The Isle of the Blest", one of Gerald Griffin's poems,[31] seems to be one of the sources of *The Shadowy Waters,* and some of the other stories and poems included, notably Sir Samuel Ferguson's "The Fairy Thorn: An Ulster Ballad",[32] deal with the same theme as *The Land of Heart's Desire,* the abduction of a human being into fairyland.

Hyde's *Love Songs of Connacht* and Yeats's *The Celtic Twilight* both appeared in 1893. They are both deeply rooted in Irish folklore, yet very different in kind. Unlike Hyde, unlike Lady Gregory—who in her collections of folklore from County Galway, notably *Visions and Beliefs in the West of Ireland* (1920), set down the bare stories without any comments of her own woven into the text—Yeats intermingled his material with his own commentary. This may be the reason why the folklorist has, until quite recently, tended to dismiss Yeats's *Celtic Twilight* stories as mere fiction, mere playing with fairies and ghosts. Whereas *Irish Fairy and Folk Tales* is largely made up of material gleaned from other folklore collectors, the stories in *The Celtic Twilight,* as well as some early articles of his, such as "Irish Fairies",[33] "Invoking the Irish Fairies",[34] or "Michael Clancy, the

---

[28] (New York, 1888); also in the Modern Library Ed., under the title, *Irish Fairy and Folk Tales* (n.d. [1918]), to which my quotations refer).

[29] See R. Dorson's Foreword, *Folktales of Ireland,* ed. and trans. Sean O'Sullivan (London: Routledge & Kegan Paul, 1966; 3rd impression, 1969), p. v.

[30] The two stories are found in *Irish Fairy and Folk Tales,* pp. 230−235, and 248−251.

[31] Ibid., pp. 226−227. Gerald Griffin (1803−1840), whose *Tales of the Munster Festivals* (in three series, 1827, 1829, and 1832), and other works, are full of folk customs, tales and legends.

[32] *Irish Fairy and Folk Tales,* pp. 40−42.

[33] First published in the *Leisure Hour,* London, October 1890. Yeats had begun this article as early as July 1887. See Frayne, I, pp. 175−182.

[34] First published in the first issue of *The Irish Theosophist,* October 1892. Frayne, I, pp. 245−247.

Great Dhoul, and Death''[35] are chiefly based on material which Yeats himself collected in the field. He preserved a good deal of material from County Sligo as well as from other counties, e.g. Dublin, Donegal, Galway, Leitrim, and Mayo. Unfortunately he seldom gave exact information as to who his informant was—something that even Lady Gregory often failed to do for fear of irritating or embarrassing her informants—but he always gave the location, sometimes in detail, as for example when describing a well-known fairy haunt: "At Howth, for instance, ten miles from Dublin, there is a 'fairies path' . . . from the hill to the sea . . . also a field . . . a cholera shed . . .'' or, in more general terms, "down westward among the deep bays and mountains valleys of Sligo'' where he had "heard the best tales and found the most ardent belief'',[36] or "a western village'', or even "at sea, when the nets are out and the pipes are lit''.[37] One of his informants was "one Paddy Flynn, a little bright-eyed old man, who lived in a leaky and one-roomed cabin in the village of Ballisodare'', and is stated by Yeats to have told many of the tales in *The Celtic Twilight*.[38] Another person referred to is "an old Martin Roland, who lived near a bog a little out of Gort'',[39] others are "the people of Rosses'',[40] a woodcutter and his old wife, a Mayo woman, a boy who had heard stories in Irish told by his grandparents, and so on. From his autobiography we learn that Yeats also heard stories told by servants, by Sligo relatives, by his own mother. It is important to remember that in Yeats's childhood and youth the majority of the old country people in Sligo and neighbouring counties would, to a large extent, still have been bilingual.[41] Even though Yeats himself "had no Gaelic'', he picked up many Irish words and phrases.

Yeats knew intuitively how, where and from whom to get the best stories: in a country village, from children, old farmers, old fishermen, old

---

[35] This story was, as Yeats states in a note, "founded upon a legend [he] heard down in Sligo'', and was printed in *The Old Country*, a Christmas Annual for 1893. Frayne, I, pp. 310–317. Michael Clancy is a tinker, who meets the Dhoul, that is, the Devil. In a letter to Standish James O'Grady [published Christmas, 1898] Yeats relates this tale to "stories and poems written about Reynard the Fox in the Middle Ages'', and to a Russian tale he had come across (*Letters of W. B. Yeats*, ed. Allan Wade [London, 1954], pp. 307–308); hereafter Wade, *Letters*.

[36] Frayne, I, pp. 175–176.

[37] *Irish Fairy and Folk Tales*, pp. x–xi.

[38] *Mythologies*, p. 5. Cf. *Irish Fairy and Folk Tales*, p. xii.

[39] *Mythologies*, p. 117.

[40] *Ibid.*, p. 95.

[41] Rodenberg, a German traveller describes, in *Die Insel der Heiligen* (Berlin, 1860), I, p. 185, the Kerry people as talking Irish among themselves. Douglas Hyde in his *Literary History of Ireland* (London, 1901), states that in 1891 over three quarters of a million people were bilingual, and 66,140 could speak only Irish.

women, and so on. Yeats's own phrase "some ancient hoarder of tales" conjures up the image of a story-teller, a real tradition bearer, in whom centuries of oral lore have been preserved.[42] Yeats's interest in folklore was aroused in his childhood. In the absence of definite proof, it is not really possible to say how much of the folklore he drew upon later, had already filtered through his mind in some form or other during his childhood summers in Sligo. But we do know that he started to collect folklore more methodically when he was about twenty and that he actually kept records, for his own use, of folklore gathered by himself in the field. In 1890, for example, he speaks of "quite a number of records . . . picked up at odd times from the faithful memories of old peasants."[43]

Consequently it may be stated that Yeats drew folklore from two main sources:

1. From his personal work in the field, that is from informants he himself interviewed.

2. From material already adapted, arranged, commented on, or treated in a popular, literary, or scholarly way in newspapers, periodicals, magazines, journals, books, etc. Here—although sometimes overlapping—at least four subdivisions can be distinguished:

(a) Other people's collections containing the kind of material he needed in the form of tales, legends (sagas), fables, songs and ballads, sayings and proverbs, customs, beliefs and superstitions, etc. Apart from works by Crofton Croker, Jeremiah Curtin, Douglas Hyde, William Larminie, and Lady Wilde already referred to, we may mention a variety of sources, such as Sir Jonah Barrington's *Personal Sketches and Recollections of his Own Times* (1827–32)[44]—a veritable mine of information, although sometimes both bizarre and grotesque—Giraldus Cambrensis, *Topographia Hibernica (The Historical World of Giraldus Cambrensis containing the Topography of Ireland, and the History of the Conquest of Ireland*, trans. Thomas Forester, London, 1863); Lady Henrietta Georgiana Chatterton's *Rambles in the South of Ireland during the year 1838* (1839); Anna Maria and Samuel Hall's *Ireland: Its Scenery, Character*, etc., 3 vol. (1842–43); James Hardiman's *Irish Minstrelsy;* P. W. Joyce's *Old Celtic Romances*

---

[42] *Irish Fairy and Folk Tales,* p. xi.

[43] Frayne, I, p. 177.

[44] 3 vol. (London: H. Coburn & R. Bentley, 1827–32; Glasgow and London: Cameron, Ferguson & Co., n.d. [1867]); generally referred to as Barrington's *Recollections.* Sir Jonah Barrington (1760–1834) worked against the Union between Ireland and England and in his *Rise and Fall of the Irish Nation* (Paris: G. G. Bennis, 1833) expressed his disapproval of methods used to bring about the Union of 1800.

(1879), *The Origin and History of Irish Names of Places*,[45] and *Social History of Ancient Ireland* (1903); Geoffrey Keating's *The General History of Ireland*;[46] Samuel Lover's *Legends and Stories of the Irish Peasantry* (1832; 1834; 1899); John O'Donovan's Introduction to the *Annals of the Four Masters*;[47] Edward Walsh, *Irish Popular Songs* (1847);[48] Lady Wilde's *Ancient Legends, Mystic Charms, and Superstitions of Ireland* (1888); Sir William Wilde's *Irish Popular Superstitions* (1852), and numerous others.[49]. Douglas Hyde's *Beside the Fire* (1890) can perhaps, as Stephen Brown puts it in his *Ireland in Fiction*, be said to be "the first really scientific treatment of Irish folklore"[50] and as is well known, Hyde's works, not least *Love Songs of Connacht* and *Religious Songs of Connacht* were of importance to both Yeats and other writers of the Irish Renaissance.[51] One could also mention works like *Reliquiae Celticae*, 2 vol., ed. by Alexander Cameron (Inverness, 1892), and *Leabhar na Feinne: Heroic Gaelic Ballads collected in Scotland chiefly from 1512 to 1871*, arranged by J. F. Campbell (London, 1872).

(b) Purely fictional or semi-fictional works, such as Charlotte Brooke's *Reliques of Irish Poetry* (1789);[52] novels and stories by Michael Banim (1796–1874) and his brother John (1798–1842); William Carleton's novels and stories, especially *The Black Prophet* (1847) and *Tales and Sketches of the Irish Peasantry*;[53] Maria Edgeworth's novels (Yeats particularly praised her *Castle Rackrent*);[54] Sir Samuel Ferguson's *Lays of the Western*

---

[45] 3 vol. (1869, 1870, 1913); hereafter Joyce, *Irish Names of Places*.

[46] Trans. from the original Irish by Dermod O'Connor (Westminster, 1726). Several subsequent translations.

[47] *Annals of the Kingdom of Ireland by the Four Masters, from the earliest period to the year 1616*. Ed. John O'Donovan. 7 vol. (Dublin, 1848–51).

[48] Michael Yeats (p. 156) states that from this source Yeats took much of his information about the Gaelic poets, such as William Heffernan (1715–1802) and Owen Roe O'Sullivan (1748–1784), and that he based some of his early ballads on poems gleaned from this book. According to Frayne, I (p. 146), Yeats used the 2nd ed. of 1883.

[49] In *Irish Fairy and Folk Tales* (p. 351) Yeats refers to chap-books, *Hibernian Tales, Royal Fairy Tales*, and *Tales of the Fairies*, etc.

[50] (Dublin and London, 1919), p. 143.

[51] See e.g. Lester Conner, "The Importance of Douglas Hyde to the Irish Renaissance", in *Modern Irish Literature: Essays in Honor of William York Tindall*, ed. R. J. Porter and J. D. Brophy (New York: Iona College Press, Twayne, 1972), pp. 95–114.

[52] Consisting of *heroic poems, odes, elegies, and songs translated into English verse* (Dublin, 1789).

[53] For its full title see Bibliography, infra. Cf. M. H. Thuente, *W. B. Yeats and Irish Folklore*, p. 76.

[54] (New York: Pratt, 1800; rpt. New York: Century, 1903; OUP, 1964; OUP Paperback, 1969). Cf. Frayne, I, pp. 168f.

Gael (1865), and *Congal* (1872); Gerald Griffin's *Tales of the Munster Festivals* (1827), *Tales of the Jury Room* (1842) and *The Duke of Monmouth* (1842); Charles Kickham's *Knocknagow* (1879); novels and stories by Emily Lawless (1845–1913), Charles Lever (1806–1872), Sheridan Le Fanu (1814–1873), and Samuel Lover (1797–1868); Standish James O'Grady's *History of Ireland* (1878–1880), *Early Bardic Literature: Ireland* (1879), *Finn and his Companions* (1892), *The Chain of Gold* (1895); ballad poetry by eighteenth-century Gaelic writers, such as Michael Comyn, Torlough O'Carolan, William Dall O'Heffernan, Egan O'Rahilly, Owen Roe O'Sullivan, and the nineteenth-century poet Anthony Raftery (d. 1835); poetry by James Clarence Mangan (1803–1849)[55] and William Allingham (1824–1889)[56] as well as *Ballads and Poems of Young Ireland,* an anthology published in 1888. Two well-known sources are Lady Gregory's *Cuchulain of Muirthemne*[57] and *Gods and Fighting Men.*[58] The list could be extended, for the number of works inspired by the rich heritage of Gaelic-speaking Ireland is considerable. To some of these writers, notably S. J. O'Grady, Sir Samuel Ferguson, and Lady Gregory, Yeats freely acknowledged his debt.

(c) Newspapers, magazines, learned and popular periodicals and journals, in which Irish tales and legends (sagas) were transcribed, edited, translated, analysed and commented on. Some of the more important of these are *Atlantis;*[59] *Dublin and London Magazine* for 1825–1828 (referred to by Sir William Wilde as "the best collection of Irish folklore in existence");[60] *Dublin Penny Journal* (1832–36); *Dublin University Magazine* (1833–77), the *Folk-Lore Record*[61] and *Folk-Lore;*[62] *Revue Celtique;*[63] *Transactions of the Gaelic Society* (1808); *Transactions of the Kilkenny Archeological Society* Vol. 1—2, 1849–53 (Dublin, 1856); *Transactions of the Ossianic*

---

[55] Notice especially *The Poets and Poetry of Munster: a selection of Irish songs by the poets of the last century* (Dublin, 1849).

[56] *Irish Songs and Poems* (London, 1887).

[57] (London, 1902; 2nd ed., Coole Ed., Gerrards Cross: Colin Smythe, 1970); hereafter *Cuchulain of Muirthemne.*

[58] (London, 1904; 2nd ed., Coole Ed., Gerrards Cross: Colin Smythe, 1970); hereafter *Gods and Fighting Men.*

[59] *The Atlantis* . . . (Dublin, London, 1858–1870). Suspended during the years 1864–69.

[60] Quoted by Yeats, *Irish Fairy and Folk Tales,* p. 351.

[61] First appeared in February 1879 as an annual, the periodical of the London Folk-Lore Society.

[62] A quarterly, the continuation of the *Folk-Lore Record.*

[63] Vol. 1 published in Paris, 1870.

Society for 1853—58, 6 vol. (Dublin 1854—61);[64] *Zeitschrift für Celtische Philologie,*[65] and others.[66] The publications of the Irish Texts Society, whose first volume appeared in 1899, should also be mentioned.

(d) Scholarly works published in book form by scholars, such as Eugene O'Curry, whose *On the Manners and Customs of the Ancient Irish,* 3 vol. (1873), and other works, can hardly be overestimated as source material; the same applies to H. d'Arbois de Jubainville, *Essai d'un catalogue de la littérature épique de l'Irlande* (1883) and *Le cycle mythologique irlandais et la mythologie celtique* (1884), translated into English by Richard Best as *The Irish Mythological Cycle and Celtic Mythology* (1903); John Rhŷs, *Lectures on the Growth of Religion as Illustrated by Celtic Heathendom* (1888); Alfred Nutt and Kuno Meyer,[67] *The Voyage of Bran Son of Febal to the Land of the Living,* 2 vol. (1895—1897); and Andrew Lang, *Custom and Myth* (1884; new ed. 1893, 1898, 1904), and *Myth, Ritual and Religion* (1887; new ed. 1899). Perhaps of lesser influence on Yeats were Edward B. Tyler, whose major works appeared in the years 1865—71, and Max Müller, to whose etymological and solar theories Lang objected fiercely. On the other hand Sir James Frazer's *The Golden Bough: A Study in Comparative Religion,*[68] and Standish Hayes O'Grady's *Silva Gadelica,* 2 vol. (1892) are standard works whose significance for the Irish Renaissance can hardly be overestimated. Eleanor Hull's *The Cuchullin Saga in Irish Lite-*

[64] Scholars who edited texts were e.g. Eleanor Hull, W. H. Hennessy, J. O'Beirne Crowe, Standish Hayes O'Grady, Brian O'Looney, Eugene O'Curry and John O'Donovan.

[65] Vol. I published in Tübingen, 1896.

[66] E.g. *All the Year Round,* a weekly conducted by Charles Dickens. With which is incorporated *Household Words,* 20 vol. (London 1859—60. N. S., 1869—88. 3rd Series, 1889—95); *Duffy's Fireside Magazine.* A monthly miscellany containing original tales, etc. 4 vol. (Dublin, 1851 [50]—54); *Duffy's Hibernian Magazine,* 3 vol. (Dublin, 1860, 61). N.S. 5 vol. (Dublin, 1862—69).

[67] Kuno Meyer (1885—1919), a noted Celtic scholar, whose translations of ancient Irish poetry are particularly fine. It should be mentioned that at the end of the eighteenth century there were a number of Celtophiles in Ireland who took an interest in the Gaelic culture. The most important and colourful of these was Charles Vallancey (1721—1812), whose somewhat fanciful theories about the Irish language led to a more critical study of the Celtic Languages in the following centuries. J. K. Zeuss laid down the principles for further scholarship in his monumental *Grammatica Celtica* (1853). His work was carried on by a number of scholars in Ireland, Germany, France and Scandinavia. Some of the more important early names are Whitley Stokes, John Strachan, Ernst Windisch, Edward O'Reilly, Julius Pokorny, George Vendryes, W. Haliday, Heinrich Zimmer, Sir John Rhŷs, Arbois de Jubainville, Georges Dottin, Henri Gaidoz, Rudolf Thurneysen, Carl Marstrander, Osborn Bergin, Richard Best, and many others could be included.

[68] 2 vol. (London, 1890); 3rd enl. ed., 12 vol. (1907—1915). Mention should also be made of John B. Vickery's " 'The Golden Bough': Impact and Archetype", *Virginia Quarterly Review,* 39 (Winter 1963), 37—57.

rature (1898), and *A Text Book of Irish Literature,* 2 vol. (1906–1908) may also have had some influence on Yeats.

It is not possible to enumerate every single work that could have served as a source for Yeats and other Irish Renaissance writers, but the account given above shows that an abundance of material was at their disposal. There is no denying that Irish traditional prose tales (folktales as well as legends), Irish traditional belief, and Irish traditional folk poetry served as basic material for Yeats, and inspired his creative writing. Hennig Cohen's words "Literature nourishes folklore, and folklore nourishes literature"[69] might well have been uttered by Yeats himself.

•

[69] "American Literature and American Folklore", in *American Folklore,* Voice of America Forum Lectures, ed. Tristram Coffin (March 1968), pp. 269–278, esp. 269.

Chapter I

Traditional Tales, or Stories, Underlying *The Countess Cathleen, The Land of Heart's Desire,* and *The Shadowy Waters*

Our first task in this chapter will be to examine more closely the traditional tales concerned and their importance for the three plays investigated in this study, for example which elements Yeats used or rejected, or what additions or changes he made when creating his dramas. Since *The Wooing of Étain* is the only one of the stories to have been explored in all three plays, this tale will be dealt with in a section of its own towards the end of the chapter.

A few words should perhaps first of all be said about some of the terms used in the present chapter.[1] The term 'tale' is generally a very broad one and can refer to any prose story, oral or literary. The term 'folktale' in its broadest sense is used to refer to every kind of traditional prose story, but it is often used in a more limited sense about the 'household tale', or 'fairy tale', as pointed out by Stith Thompson, who in his work *The Folktale* uses the word in its widest possible sense.[2] For our purposes, traditional tales fall into two main categories, fairy tales and legends.[3] Even if it may sometimes be difficult to differentiate between the two, there is nevertheless a commonly accepted distinction which, however general it may be, undoubtedly serves a purpose. The fairy tale, set in an unreal world, is believed by the folk to be pure invention, whereas the legend is believed by the folk to be true, or at least to be based on reality since it is associated with a real place and with a person who exists, has existed, or is believed to have existed. Paradoxically, however, a fairy tale need not necessarily be concerned with fairies (though it often is) and a traditional tale may in one variant be a fairy tale, in another a legend. It should also be noted that, as shown by Stith Thompson, legends have a strong tendency "to make new

---

[1] Definitions are based chiefly on Stith Thompson's and C. W. von Sydow's terminology.

[2] *The Folktale* (New York: The Dryden Press, 1964), p. 4.

[3] "Legend" must of course be distinguished from a "saint's legend" (Sw. "helgonlegend").

14

attachments which may even drive out all memory of the original person or place" (*The Folktale*, p. 270). Furthermore, legends, like fairy tales, may be brief or long, have a simple structure, or a more complex one with a multiplicity of motifs and episodes. Also of great interest to the Irish material is C. W. von Sydow's distinction between brief one-episode legends and longer multi-episode legends.[4] The latter are particularly important from our point of view, for a large number of Irish sagas may be said to be multi-episodic legends, within which there are often a number of references to place names. The Irish legendary or saga material can be divided into numerous sub-categories—the old story-tellers had their own traditional division according to the type of story told, such as cattle-raids, battles, destructions, visions, voyages, adventures, deaths (or tragedies), etc., but later, Irish tales or sagas were divided into cycles, the Mythological, the Red Branch, the Fenian, and the Historical Cycles. One of the stories relating Ossian's adventures in the Happy Otherworld was the first to be explored by Yeats in his long narrative poem *The Wanderings of Oisin* (1889). The emphasis in this study is not on how folklore developed among the Irish people, but what role it plays in Yeats's creative writing, notably the three plays here singled out for analysis. As made clear in the Introduction, Yeats explored the living tradition of his own time as well as traditional lore gathered during countless generations.

The Countess Cathleen and Traditional Stories

The story "The Countess Kathleen O'Shea" on which *CC* is based, was at first erroneously taken by Yeats to be indigenous west-of-Ireland folklore.[5] It relates how, long ago, Ireland was devastated by a great famine. Shiploads of food are expected to arrive within eight days. Two rich unknown merchants, magnificently dressed, and wearing gloves to hide their claws, are staying at an inn where they attract people's attention by their mysterious behaviour and the yellow pieces of gold which they count again and again while waiting for the famished people to come and offer them their souls. Different souls bring in different prices. To prevent this soul-trading, the Countess Cathleen sells a large part of her earthly goods and asks her

---

[4] See "Prosa-folkdiktningens kategorier" [The Categories of Prose Folk Literature], in *Folkdikt och Folktro*, ed. Anna Birgitta Rooth (Lund: Gleerups, 1971), pp. 110–111. My thanks are due to Professor Phebe Fjellström, Uppsala and Umeå, for drawing my attention to this source.

[5] Included in *Irish Fairy and Folk Tales*, pp. 248–251. In the first version of his play Yeats spelt Kathleen with a "K", then with a "C".

butler to distribute the money among the poor. Her treasury is still full of money, but the merchants who want her soul, break in and rob her of it all. After a twelve-hour struggle with herself, she desperately decides to sell her own soul for 150 000 pieces of gold. Like Faustus, she signs the fatal document, though not in order to gain omnipotence and omniscience, but to save her starving people from eternal damnation. Three days later she dies of grief, and the legend says: "But the sale of this soul, so adorable in its charity, was declared null by the Lord; for she had saved her fellow-citizens from eternal death." The two Satanic traders vanish for ever, nobody knows where: "But the fishermen of the Blackwater pretend that they [the traders] are enchained in a subterranean prison by order of Lucifer, until they shall be able to render up the soul of Kathleen, which escaped from them."[6]

It is well known that the story is not, as first surmised by Yeats, a folktale from the west of Ireland, but a translation of a tale taken down in French by Léo Lespès, and first published in *Les Matinées de Timothée Trimm*.[7] Apparently Yeats had put too great trust in his first source, "a London-Irish newspaper",[8] something that left him open to severe criticism, but on learning the truth, he published the French original in an explanatory note to one of the revised versions of *CC*.[9] A textual comparison between the two versions of the tale, i.e. the original, as written down in French, and the English translation, shows that the translator deviated somewhat from the original. The main differences are as follows:

(1) In the French version as reproduced by Yeats, the Countess's name is Ketty O'Connor,[10] in the English Kathleen O'Shea.

(2) The English version omits the seven opening lines, in which the narrator introduces his story as an Irish Lenten tale—known by the blind, the

[6] *Irish Fairy and Folk Tales*, p. 251.

[7] Lespès, Antoine, Joseph-Napoléon (Léo) (pseud.: Timothée Trimm, Mme Vieuxbois, 1815—1875), a French writer whose work *Les Matinées de Timothée Trimm*, Illustrées par H. de Montaut, was published in the Librarire du Petit Journal (Paris, n.d. [1865]). This rare book (a copy of which I have consulted in the Bibliothèque Nationale at Paris) contains 74 short prose pieces, stories and essays of a mixed character. Our particular story is illustrated with a picture called "Les Marchands d'Ames" showing two demons seated at a table opposite the Countess Ketty O'Donnor, the name used by Léo Lespès, of whom a bibliographical note is included in E. de Mirecourt (pseud. for Ch. J. B. Jacquot), *Timothée Trimm*, Histoire Contemporaine, 16 (Paris, 1867). (Story entitled "Les Marchands d'Ames".)

[8] *Irish Fairy and Folk Tales*, p. 248n.

[9] Quoted in *The Variorum Edition of the Plays of W. B. Yeats*, ed. R. V. Alspach (London: Macmillan, 1966), pp. 170—173; hereafter *VPl*.

[10] This form is sometimes used by Yeats.

lame and the paralysed in Dublin and Limerick, told by shepherds on the banks of the river Blackwater and taught to every Catholic girl in Ireland who is being prepared for Holy Communion.[11]

(3) After the initial description of the two rich unknown merchants, who have just come to Ireland, the English version omits three and a half lines which relate that at the time Ireland was in the throes of a famine because there had been little sun and hardly any harvest. The poor did not know which saint to turn to in their need, and their misery was getting worse and worse.[12]

(4) Also omitted in the English version are the narrator's concluding lines, stating that this is the legend as he knows it; that it has been told by the poor from one generation to another, and that there is a ballad about Ketty O'Connor, two stanzas of which he quotes, a ballad said to be sung at that time [in the 1860s] by the children of Cork and Dublin. The final rhetorical question as to whether the story, nourished by the imagination of Green Erin's poets, is not a true Lenten tale is also omitted in the English version.[13]

(5) "des pays d'Orient" (*VPl*, p. 171) is erroneously or perhaps purposely translated as "from the western lands",[14] "Leurs griffes s'allongèrent..." (*VPl*, p. 172) as "Their claws were clutched . . .",[15] and "le démon" (*VPl*, pp. 171, 172), which occurs twice, is translated as "the demon"[16] although the context makes it quite clear that the word should mean "Satan" in both cases, *le démon* being a common denomination for Satan in French.

---

[11] In French the lines omitted in the English text are: "Ce que je vais vous dire est un récit du carême irlandais. Le boiteux, l'aveugle, le paralytique des rues de Dublin, ou de Limerick, vous le diraient mieux que moi, cher lecteur, si vous alliez le leur demander, un sixpence d'argent à la main.—Il n'est pas une jeune fille catholique à laquelle on ne l'ait appris pendant les jours de préparation à la communion sainte, pas un berger des bords de la Blackwater qui ne le puisse redire à la veillée." Quoted in *VPl*, p. 170.

[12] The French text: "Or, à cette époque, comme aujourd'hui, l'Irlande était pauvre, car le soleil avait été rare, et des récoltes presque nulles. Les indigents ne savaient à quel saint se vouer, et la misère devenait de plus en plus terrible." Quoted in *VPl*, p. 170.

[13] The French text: "Je vous dis la légende telle que je la sais. − Mais les pauvres l'ont raconté d'âge en âge et les enfants de Cork et de Dublin chantent encore la ballade dont voici les derniers couplets:—Pour sauver les pauvres qu'elle aime /Ketty donna/ Son esprit, sa croyance même: /Satan paya/ Cette âme au dévoûment sublime, /En écus d'or,/ Disons pour racheter son crime, /Confiteor./ Mais l'ange qui se fit coupable /Par charité/ Au séjour d'amour ineffable /Est remonté./ Satan vaincu n'eut pas de prise /Sur ce coeur d'or;/ Chantons sous la nef de l'église, /Confiteor./ N'est ce pas que ce récit, né de l'imagination des poètes catoliques de la verte Érin, est un véritable récit de carême?" Quoted in *VPl*, pp. 172–173.

[14] *Irish Fairy and Folk Tales*, p. 250.

[15] Ibid., p. 251.

[16] Ibid., pp. 249, 251.

The narrator in the French version refers to the story as being Irish. The tradition-bearers are stated to be shepherds tending their sheep on the banks of the river Blackwater and fishermen fishing in the same river, so it would seem that the story may have had its centre around the river Blackwater which runs partly through Co. Kerry, partly through Co. Limerick. From there the story then could have spread to the poor in the cities of Cork, Limerick and Dublin where every Catholic girl is said to have known it. The ballad on the same theme is said to be known by the Cork and Dublin children and even though this tale, a folk legend, thus seems to have been firmly rooted in Ireland, certain features nevertheless point to its having originally been a religious story spread among the Catholic poor. Since no study of this aspect of the story has, as far as I know, been undertaken and can hardly be said to lie within the scope of the present study, the question must be left open.[17] The story as presented in French is a legend well attached to a real place in Ireland, the river Blackwater and the Blackwater valley, and to a person believed to have once existed, that is Ketty O'Connor.[18] At different times Yeats himself refers to the story as a folk tale, a legend, and a parable comparable to the Greek Alcestis legend, one difference being that the Greek heroine sacrificed herself for her husband, Cathleen for her people.

If the question of the origin and circulation of the Kathleen legend is complicated, the story of Yeats's play is even more complex. As is well known, when first performed in Dublin on May 8, 1899, it caused a riot in the theatre, and its alleged blasphemous nature inspired a prolonged controversy. Yeats revised it both before and after its first performance, and Peter Ure, who examines the growth of the play and the differences between it and its source, analyses five major versions of the play.[19] One might, however, say that there are as many as eleven versions—1892, 1895, 1899, 1901, 1907, 1908, 1912, 1913, 1921, 1923, 1934 (1952)—although after 1913 with but slight differences.[20] The editors of *VPl* refer to at least

[17] One could perhaps ask if the Cathleen legend which Yeats drew upon may possibly have its roots in the many versions existing of the legend about Saint Catherine of Alexandria, who, as a result of her protests against the persecutions of Christians, was tied to a wheel and beheaded. Her historicity (early 4th c.) is doubted, but her dead body is believed to have been carried by angels "to Mt. Sinai, where it was discovered about A.D. 800." She is the patron saint, not only of wheelwrights, but also of virgins and scholars. See *Encyclopaedia Britannica* (1964 ed.), 5, p. 76b.

[18] Yeats used both "O'Donnor", and "O'Connor".

[19] "A Counter-Truth: *The Countess Cathleen*", in *Yeats the Playwright* (London, Routledge & Kegan Paul, 1963), pp. 9–30; hereafter Peter Ure.

[20] Cf. M. Sidnell, Photographic Copy of a typed essay by Michael J. Sidnell and the MS versions of "The Countess Cathleen" by W. B. Yeats. MS 12,076, National Library of Ireland.

nine different versions (some with only minor alterations) and print two complete versions, that of 1892, and the final text of 1952 with collations of all other printings from 1895–1934.[21]

Although *CC* was revised so many times, its main themes—starvation and the buying of souls—remain unchanged throughout. As in the legend, unknown demon traders—advocates of the Devil—go about buying souls from starving peasants in a hunger-stricken Ireland. Their antagonist is the Countess Cathleen, who, in order to prevent them from buying the souls of the poor, first sells most of what she owns, then while waiting for shiploads of food, is robbed by the demons, appearing now as Oriental merchants, now as horned owls. Cathleen, after much praying, sells her own soul at a very high price, but only on condition that the other souls be set free. When she comes to the demons, they address her as "saint with the sapphire eyes" (*VPl*, pp. 144, 149)—an echo of the words of the legend, in English, "saint, with eyes of sapphire",[22] in French, "sainte aux yeux de saphir".[23] Cathleen dies soon after the signing of the contract, but her soul goes straight to heaven. Deprived at the last moment of their prey, the demonic traders who were about to clutch Cathleen's soul in their claws, disappear, apparently, like demons of the air.[24]

The most salient difference between Yeats's play and the folk legend is Yeats's introduction of a number of characters not found in the tale. In the

---

[21] *VPl*, p. xiii. See Allan Wade, *A Bibliography of the Writings of W. B. Yeats* (London: Rupert Hart-Davis, 1951); hereafter Wade. The play was first printed in *The Countess Kathleen and Various Legends and Lyrics* (Boston, London, 1892); the play was rev. and rpt. as *The Countess Cathleen* in *Poems* (London, 1895; rev. and rpt. London, 1899, and London, 1901, etc.); in *The Poetical Works of William B. Yeats in Two Volumes*, II: *Dramatical Poems* (New York and London: Macmillan, 1907; rpt. 1909, 1911; rev. and rpt. New York and London, 1912; 1914); in *The Collected Works in Verse and Prose*, III (Stratford-on-Avon: Shakespeare Head Press, 1908); printed separately as *The Countess Cathleen* (London: Fisher Unwin, 1912; rpt. 1916, 1920, 1922; 1924); in *A Selection from the Poetry of W. B. Yeats* (Leipzig: Tauchnitz, 1913); in *Selected Poems* (New York: Macmillan, 1921); in *Plays and Controversies* (London: Macmillan, 1923; 1927; New York: Macmillan, 1924); in *Collected Plays of W. B. Yeats* (London: Macmillan, 1934; New York: Macmillan, 1935; rev. with additional plays, London: Macmillan, 1952; New York: Macmillan, 1953; several rpts.). The play was first written as a five-scene play in 1892, changed in 1895 to a play with a three-act structure, then turned into a four-act play in 1899. In 1912 Yeats restored the original five-scene arrangement—retained throughout further revisions of the play. By 1913, when published in the Tauchnitz ed., the play was almost in its final form. Yet there were further slight revisions up to 1934. (The 1895 version has 3, not 4 acts, as stated in *VPl*, p.xii.)

[22] *Irish Fairy and Folk Tales*, p. 250.

[23] *VPl*, p. 172.

[24] In the tale *The Death of the Children of Lir*, the evil stepmother Aoife, after transforming Lir's children into swans, is herself transformed by Lir into a demon of the air, a severe punishment because, as the legend states, she can never resume her human shape again. See P. W. Joyce, *Old Celtic Romances* (London, 1879).

group centring around the Countess we have her old nurse Oona, and her other dependents, a gardener, a herdsman, a treasurer, a porter—in the tale there is only her butler or majordomo. Furthermore, Yeats introduces the starving cottagers in the wood, Shemus Rua,[25] a poor farmer (in the 1892 version of the play an innkeeper, whose inn is called "The Lady's Head"), his wife Mary and their fourteen-year-old son Teigue (spelt Teig in the 1892 version). The most important addition is undoubtedly the young poet Aleel (in the 1892 version called Kevin), whom Cathleen and her foster-mother Oona meet in the wood. He sings to the accompaniment of a harp—in some versions a lute, in some both a lute and a harp. As Peter Ure has shown, the poet's role is becoming more and more significant with every revision.[26] In the 1892 version, Kevin appears twice in Scene IV (first when trying to sell his soul, and again when snatching the parchment from Kathleen as she is signing it) and he is also mentioned in Scene V by one of the peasants; in the 1895 version—which has three acts—his name has become Aleel and he appears in two acts (Acts I and III); in the 1901 version he appears in Acts I, II and III (a new love scene between the Countess and him). When in 1912 Yeats restored the five-scene structure, he made Aleel appear in all scenes except in Scene IV, and in the final version in all five scenes. Apart from the two demons, there are also, as the stage directions inform us, *"Angelical beings, spirits and fairies"* (*VPl*, p. 4); in the 1912 version the spirits were retained in the robbery scene and also introduced into the new scene IV (Demon-Merchants, Peasants, and six Spirits *"carrying bags"*, pass by on their way to the market). In the 1913 Tauchnitz version the spirits were taken out of the play and the robbery scene was reduced to "a few words and actions".[27] The numerous revisions, which are certainly somewhat confusing, show that Yeats was all the time working towards an expansion of Aleel's role and a reduction or abbreviation of other elements.

All the elements in Shemus Rua's cottage are invented by Yeats. Although suggested in the original tale, the episode of Sc. V, in which Teigue and Shemus arrive with their gold, is also chiefly Yeats's own invention. On the other hand the next episode in Sc. V, in which the country-people sell their souls to the demons for gold, can be traced to the passage in the

---

[25] Shemus Rua (Red James) occurs in a story by Patrick Kennedy, "The Witches' Excursion", first printed in *Legendary Fictions of the Irish Celts* (London, 1866) and rpt. in Yeats's *Irish Fairy and Folk Tales*, pp. 179–182.

[26] Peter Ure, pp. 14–15. Ure gives a table of the various revisions of the play.

[27] Ibid., p. 14. See Ch. III below for my list of the songs written into the play at various times.

legend which describes how the traders charge different prices for different souls, the soul of a young maiden being the most expensive.[28] The tableau-like Sc. IV, in which a number of peasants tell one another that they have seen bags and bags of gold, can be traced to the passage in the legend which states that the merchants "did nothing but count over and over again out of their money-bags pieces of gold, whose yellow brightness could be seen through the windows of their lodging" (*Irish Fairy and Folk Tales,* p. 248). The moral of Yeats's play is similar to that of the legend, that is, God's charity surpasses Cathleen's. Because of the sacrificial nature of her sin, she is forgiven. However, the climax of the legend may be said to be the sale of Cathleen's soul, whereas in the play the nodal point is the moment when demonic and angelic powers clash in a battle over Cathleen's soul. The defeat of the demons by the heavenly powers, seen in a vision by Oona in the first version, and by Aleel—who also sees a vision of hell—in the later versions, is the real climactic moment. Their aims having been frustrated, the demons disappear for ever. The farmers, with their souls restored, and Aleel and Oona, are left as if standing on a visionary mountain grieving for their Countess, "the great white lily of the world" (*VPl,* p. 163), as one of the peasants says, thereby referring to Cathleen's innocence and her role as almost a world saviour. One character, an Old Man, gloomily declares that we must die for our sins, but Aleel forces one of the stern-looking armed Angels to speak, and Cathleen's apotheosis is depicted: she is passing through "the gates of pearl" to "the floor of peace" (*VPl,* p. 167). The play has many features in common with the miracle plays,[29] and in several respects it also recalls Marlowe's *Doctor Faustus,* even though at the end of the play Cathleen is not torn to pieces by devils like Faustus. The foster-mother Oona is given the final word. In the first version she selfishly asserts her right above everybody else to keen Kathleen and then "go die" (*VPl,* p. 168). In the later version we see her crushed under the burden of grief and old age:

[28] See *Irish Fairy and Folk Tales,* p. 249.

[29] The sub-title of the first version is *An Irish Drama,* a title stressing the Irish character of the play, which was denounced as heretic by Cardinal Logue. The programme of the first performance at the Antient Concert Rooms, Dublin, on 8 May, 1899, refers to the play as *A Miracle Play in Four Acts.* See *Beltaine* (May 1899—April 1900), ed. W. B. Yeats; rpt. in English Little Magazines, No. 15, ed. B. C. Bloomfield (London, 1970), p. 2. See R. Ellmann, *The Man and the Masks* (New York: Macmillan, 1948; London: Macmillan, 1949), p. 131, and Liam Miller, *The Noble Drama of W. B. Yeats* (Dublin: The Dolmen Press, 1977), pp. 33—43; hereafter Miller. The Abbey Theatre put on a revised version of the play on 14 December 1911.

The years like great black oxen tread the world,
And God the herdsman goads them on behind,
And I am broken by their passing feet.

VPl, p. 169; cf. p. 158

Here Yeats has introduced the traditional image of black oxen symbolizing human misery and suffering, and these concluding lines are certainly more gripping than those of the first version, not only because the image used is more universal, but also because Oona—very much like old Maurya in Synge's *Riders to the Sea*—is stoically resigned to her fate. She no longer egoistically demands to be the only keener who has the right to express her grief, but now symbolizes the whole suffering mankind—the feet of God's "great black oxen" have crushed her.

Thus, even though Yeats kept within the framework of the old legend, he took his imagery from other sources as well. The visionary light, the kneeling farmers, the stern-looking angels, the old woman broken under the feet of the black oxen—all these images bring to mind an old world of Biblical hardship and simplicity—a rural landscape, whether Ireland or elsewhere, threatened by demonic powers, but watched over by God and his angels. Death awaits everybody, but at the end of time the heavenly light will shine.

An analysis of one special part of *CC*, that is, Aleel's Hell vision, will show that it derives from a number of stories. Kevin/Aleel is the first visionary in Yeats's plays, but not the last. The most complex of Yeats's visionary dramatic characters is probably Martin Hearne in *The Unicorn from the Stars* (1908; first performed at the Abbey Theatre on 23 November, 1907). In him we have a visionary of a violent kind: in his vision, he and his army are riding on horses which suddenly turn into unicorns, a sign that the destruction is brought on from above by a divine force, the unicorn, the divine beast.[30] Martin Hearne himself becomes a tool for this destruction on earth, but is manipulated by a number of rebels who are carrying on a struggle against the landlords. In one of his frenzies Martin Hearne sets fire to a landlord's house thinking that he is carrying out the work of the sacred unicorn. When the police are about to catch him, one of the rebels, as if by accident, shoots Martin in order to save him from the death on the gallows. The priest, quite confused by all this, blames the rebel for shooting a man who has just seen a vision of Heaven. Before dying, Martin Hearne says that "It is a long climb to the vineyards of

---

[30] See Giorgio Melchiori, *The Whole Mystery of Art* (London: Routledge & Kegan Paul, 1960), pp. 35–72, esp. p. 53.

Eden" (*VPl*, p. 710). This play dramatically depicts a character, who is not only a madman but is also a social rebel, a visionary and a martyr, depending on the point of view taken. Aleel is a far less complicated character, who sees a vision of a Celtic Hell.[31]

In the first version of *CC* in which Kevin reveals at the end of Sc. IV that he has had a vision, there is no idea of a Celtic Hell. The vision seen here by Kevin "under a green hedge" is limited to Satan:

> − men yet shall hear
> Archangels rolling over the high mountains
> Old Satan's empty skull.
>
> *VPl*, p. 150

This is an almost realistic way of introducing the theme of severed, often speaking, heads so typical of many Celtic saga tales.[32]

Kevin and to an even larger extent Aleel are characteristic of the numerous visionary figures Yeats delights in creating, for example Aedh, Mongan, Red Hanrahan, Owen Aherne, Michael Robartes, who appear in his stories and poems. His *Celtic Twilight* stories are also full of peasant visionaries with tales of the Otherworld and other supernatural phenomena. Aleel, the poet, becomes a much more important character than Kevin, the bard, and the development of this character can be studied both in the songs he composes and in the vision he conjures up. Let us turn to the latter and see how Yeats, when expanding the poet's role, also makes him more Irish-Celtic, something that may also be said to reveal Yeats's own growing interest in Irish gods and goddesses.

After Cathleen's signing of the document, Aleel takes over the scene completely. His vision begins in the same spectacular way as Kevin's, with Satan's empty skull seen rolling over the mountain tops. A rising thunderstorm (*VPl*, p. 155) forms a suitable background for the Celtic Hell to which Aleel fears that Cathleen's soul will eventually be taken. The vision falls into three major parts, the first depicting Balor and his demon crew, the second Orchil and her female long-taloned devils, and the third a battle

---

[31] Could Yeats have been inspired by [James Farewell's] *The Irish Hudibras, OR Fingallian Prince, Taken from the Sixth Book of Virgil's Aeneids, and Adapted to the Present Times* (London, 1689)? This is a satirical poem placing many of the Fenian heroes such as Finn Mac-Heuyle (Mac Cumhaill), Oscar and Oisin, in a Hell approached "by way of St. Patrick's Purgatory in Lough Derg." Of course Yeats's purpose is quite different from that of *The Irish Hudibras*, a book attributed to James Farewell. Alan Bliss in *Spoken English in Ireland 1600− 1740* (Dublin, 1979, p. 57) states that James Farewell "might have edited it for the English market."

[32] See e g. Georges Dottin, *The World of the Celts*, trans. David Macrae (Genève: Minerva, 1979), p. 9. For Yeats's use of a severed head singing, see Ch. III, n. 57 below.

in which Balor is killed by Lug. This is Aleel's description of the hell of Balor of the Evil Eye:

> The brazen door stands wide, and Balor comes
> Borne in his heavy car, and demons have lifted
> The age-weary eyelids from the eyes that of old
> Turned gods to stone;[33] Barach, the traitor, comes
> And the lascivious race, Cailitin,
> That cast a druid weakness and decay
> Over Sualtim's and old Dectora's child;
> And that great king Hell first took hold upon
> When he killed Naoise and broke Deirdre's heart;
> And all their heads are twisted to one side,
> For when they lived they warred on beauty and peace
> With obstinate, crafty, sidelong bitterness.[34]

VPl, p. 155

When Oona enters, Aleel, still experiencing his vision, says: "Crouch down, old heron, out of the blind storm", thus alluding to her as if she were an ancient druidess able to change herself into a heron. Balor (or Balar) of the Evil Eye, who, according to T. F. O'Rahilly may have been a sun-god like Lug, is the Satan of this Hell.[35] In Irish legend he is also the king of "the Fomoroh" or the Fomorians, who, as Yeats explains in a note are "powers of night and death and cold" (*Poems*, 1901, p. 304), and who fight a battle with "the Tuatha De Danaan", "the powers of light and life and warmth" (pp. 303–304), gods and goddesses who finally became the fairies of folk belief. Balor's companions in Hell are Barach, Conchubar, and the witchlike Cailitin and his seven sons, who are all murderers. Barach helped to bring about the death of Deirdre and Naoise and his two brothers when he invited King Fergus to a banquet which the latter could not refuse, thus leaving Deirdre and Naoise without protection against King Conchubar, who was subsequently able to carry out his murderous plan; and Cailitin and his seven sons caused the death of Cuchulain, "Sualtim's and old Dectora's child". (According to one saga version, Cailitin, or *Gaile Dána*, i.e. the brave one, had 27 sons, who struck Cuchulain's head off.)

If Balor is the Satan of this hell, then Orchil is its goddess of death. Frantically pointing downwards, Aleel tells Oona of the frightening vision he sees of Orchil and her realm:

---

[33] Notice that Yeats here deviates from the traditional one-eyed Balor.

[34] Cf. Dante's *Inferno*, which places those who are punished for fraud in the eighth and ninth circles of Hell.

[35] *Early Irish History and Mythology* (1946; rpt. Dublin: Dublin Institute for Advanced Studies, 1971), pp. 313–314.

24

First Orchil, her pale, beautiful head alive,
Her body shadowy as vapour drifting
Under the dawn, for she who awoke desire
Has but a heart of blood when others die;
About her is a vapoury multitude
Of women alluring devils with soft laughter;
Behind her a host heat of the blood made sin,
But all the little pink-white nails have grown
To be great talons.

VPl, pp. 157, 159

Aleel, dragging Oona into the middle of the room, *"points downward with vehement gestures"* (*VPl*, p. 159), while to a roaring wind the song of Orchil's "vapoury multitude" is resounding. Yeats here uses the word "blood" in the sense of passion. Orchil's companions are all governed by their lust, and the whole scene reminds us somewhat of Dante's *Inferno*. Where could Yeats have come across Orchil and her function as the death goddess? In a note he calls her a "Fomorah" and a "sorceress" and also says that he has forgotten what he once knew about her (*Poems,* 1901, p. 303). Orchil also turns up in "The Madness of King Goll" where she symbolizes night, and like the Queen of Night she shakes her long, dark hair. But in *CC* she has a much more sinister role as the long-taloned goddess of a Celtic Hell, and is actually more akin to the vampire-like women of Baudelaire and Swinburne than for example to the Celtic death goddess Badhbh, i. e. Morrígan or Morrígu, the carrion crow who appears in Yeats's last play, *The Death of Cuchulain*.

My search for Orchil led me, perhaps not surprisingly, to one of Yeats's early favourites, Standish James O'Grady, in whose novel *The Chain of Gold* (1895) Orchil figures. The protagonist of this novel of adventure, set, partly in Brittany, partly on the west coast of Ireland, finds a manuscript written by a former king, who after the loss of his kingdom lives in various disguises and ends up as a hermit famous for his ascetic life. This is also a disguise, for he has not given up the thought of his kingdom. In his decision to find enough gold to win back his kingdom, he has learnt magic and one day he is "let down into the Cave of the Demons" (p. 261), "the vestibule of the great cave *(ingens speluncula)* of Orchil, *quae fuit dea subterranea gentium Hibernorum,* i.e. Orchil, the earth-goddess of the Pagan Irish" (p. 262). This temple of the earth- or death-goddess with two caves and two openings, both once closed by St. Brendan the Navigator, for some time becomes the abode of the king-magician, who through his magic is able to "overleap" the barriers of time and project himself into the future. He finally comes across a large gold treasure consisting of Irish ring money and five links of a mysterious gold chain from which the novel takes its name. That this novel about a Prospero-like king should have lingered in Yeats's mind, is hardly strange, but in his own work he restricts his use of Orchil to *CC* and "The Madness of King Goll". (However, she does turn up in the MSS of *SW* as well.) Orchil is of Balor's Fomorian clan and is used by Yeats for the obvious purpose of intensifying the horror of Aleel's vision of the hell that he is afraid might swallow up Cathleen.[36]

The third part of the vision comes after Cathleen's farewell speech to Oona and Aleel ("Bend down your faces . . ." *VPl*, p. 163). Now Aleel sees "the clamorous war / Of angels upon devils" (p. 165):

> Angels and devils clash in the middle air,
> And brazen swords clang upon brazen helms.
> [*A flash of lightening followed immediately by thunder.*
> Yonder a bright spear, cast out of a sling,
> Has torn through Balor's eye, and the dark clans
> Fly screaming as they fled Moytura of old.
> [*Everything is lost in darkness.*

In the first part of his vision Aleel sees demons holding up Balor's eyelids. But in the latter part of the vision Balor's power is broken, for Lug's bright spear is driven through his single huge eye. Angels and devils are seen taking part in the battle from which "the dark clans", that is, the Fomorians and the Fir Bolg (Balor's people), "fly screaming". The imaginary battle, in which Balor's people are seen as demons and Lug's as angels, is based on the *Second Battle of Moytura (Mag Tured)* which deals with the mythical duel between Balor and Lug. This tale and the *First Battle of Moytura* partly derive from the story in *Lebor Gabála Érenn (The Book of the Taking of Ireland)* of how the Túatha Dé Danann when arriving in Ireland vanquished the Fir Bolg and the Fomorians, and were in their turn driven away by the sons of Mil or the Milesians (supposed to be the ancestors of the present Gaels).[37] In his poetic version of the battle between Lug and Balor, Yeats followed Irish popular belief about battles over the souls of the dead or dying people (see Ch. II below), but also modern folk versions of the Lug-Balor myth, for example tales collected by Jeremiah Curtin in Connemara and Donegal, especially "Balor of the Evil Eye and Lui Lavada, his Grandson".[38]

---

[36] Fiona MacLeod also makes use of Orchil in "The Washer of the Ford", in *At the Turn of the Year: Essays and Nature Thoughts* (Edinburgh: Turnbull and Speirs, 1913), pp. 147—216.

[37] For these tales, see *Ancient Irish Tales*, ed. T. P. Cross and C. H. Slover (London: Harrap, n.d.). For *The Second Battle of Mag Tured* see also Wh. Stokes's ed. in *RC*, 12 (1891), pp. 52—130. In the old tale Lug used a sling-stone, not a sword, to destroy Balor's poisonous eye. (*Cath Maige Tuired*, new ed., ITS, 52, 1982.)

[38] *Irish Hero-Tales* (London, 1894), pp, 296—311. Cf. *Gods and Fighting Men*, p. 66.

As can be deduced from the previous examination of Aleel's Hell vision, Yeats here makes allusive use of certain ancient Irish tales, that is, *The Tragic Death of the Sons of Uisnech, The Death of Cuchulain,* and the two *Battles of Moytura* as well as other stories from *Lebor Gabála* dealing with the Fomorians and the Túatha Dé Danann. Yet characters and features from these tales are so closely intermingled in Aleel's vision that they could be said to make a new tale in which a vision of Hell is the central theme or motif. Aleel's vision comes to an end with the arrival of the angels.

The Land of Heart's Desire and Traditional Stories

Yeats says quite rightly that neither *LHD* nor *SW* is based on one particular story;[39] the two plays are, however, based on a number of stories with similar themes. *LHD,* a play of great simplicity, is woven around a story of how a newly-married bride is carried away to fairyland. There are, in Ireland, "thousands" of folk tales and legends about fatal meetings between fairies and mortals,[40] and ever since his childhood Yeats had heard many such stories, and was familiar with popular traditions about the Irish fairies. The luring away of a newly-married bride to fairyland was an exceedingly popular theme in Yeats's youth and was used in poems by many nineteenth-century writers, such as J. C. Mangan, William Allingham and Samuel Ferguson, not to mention English poets like Keats and Shelley.

LHD, which exists in two major versions, one of 1894 and one of 1912, was first performed at the Avenue Theatre in London on March 29 1894. According to Yeats himself this play contains most of his early experiments in blank verse, but it also produced some of his finest early lyrics.

In *Irish Fairy and Folk Tales,* Yeats—apart from making many of his own observations on different kinds of fairies, such as the trooping fairies, the solitary fairies, etc.—also preserved a number of stories dealing with fairy enchantments, stories of how human beings are stolen by fairies, particularly brides just after marriage, or babies just after birth. Also in *The Celtic Twilight* there are many such tales, for example "Kidnappers", which Yeats himself refers to as the source of one of the ballads in *The*

[39] *VPl,* p. 1283.
[40] See e.g. Sean O'Sullivan, ed., *Folktales of Ireland* (London: Routledge & Kegan Paul, 1969), p. 273. Cf. Funk and Wagnalls, under "abduction", and T. P. Cross, *Motif-Index of Early Irish Literature* (Bloomington: Indiana Univ. Publ., 1952).

Wind Among the Reeds.[43] The poem referred to is "The Host of the Air",[42] which first appeared, under the title "The Stolen Bride", in the *Bookman* (Nov. 1893), and related the story of how the newly-wed Bridget was tempted away by dancing fairy pipers. As recorded by Yeats (*Mythologies,* pp. 73—74), this story taking place near the Heart Lake, "some five miles southward of Sligo", may be said to be typical, and is therefore quoted here:

A little way from this lake I heard a beautiful and mournful history of faery kidnapping. I heard it from a little old woman in a white cap, who sings in Gaelic, and moves from one foot to the other as though she remembered the dancing of her youth.

A young man going at nightfall to the house of his just-married bride, met on the way a jolly company, and with them his bride. They were faeries and had stolen her as a wife for the chief of their band. To him they seemed only a company of merry mortals.[43] His bride, when she saw her old love, bade him welcome, but was most fearful lest he should eat the faery food, and so be glamoured out of the earth into that bloodless dim nation, wherefore she set him down to play cards with three of the cavalcade; and he played on, realising nothing until he saw the chief of the band carrying his bride away in his arms. Immediately he started up, and knew that they were faeries, for all that jolly company melted into shadow and night. He hurried to his house, and as he drew near heard the cry of the keeners and knew that his wife was dead.

[41] *Mythologies,* p. 74 n 1.

[42] *The Wind Among the Reeds* (London: Elkin Mathews, 1899; New York and London: John Lane, 1899; 1902), pp. 7—9; hereafter *WR.*

[43] In Irish folk belief, fairies are often thought to be the same size as human beings, one of the greatest differences between them and English fairies, who are small, as are also sometimes Irish fairies. Yeats tried imaginatively rather than scientifically to explain the varying sizes and shapes of the fairies in his article "Irish Fairies, Ghosts, Witches, etc.", first printed in *Lucifer* (a theosophical review), 15 January 1889. Here he wrote that the Sheogues (i.e. the little fairies) "are usually of small size when first seen, though seeming of common human height when you are once glamoured. It sometimes appears as if they could take any shape according to their whim" (see Frayne, I, p. 133). Yeats also distinguishes between sea fairies and land fairies. In *Researches in the South of Ireland* (London, 1824), Ch. V, "Fairies and Supernatural Agency", Crofton Croker mentions that the fairies "are exceedingly diminutive in their stature, having an arch and malicious expression of countenance." Lady Gregory in *Visions and Beliefs in the West of Ireland* (1920; rpt. 1970), p. 10, writes: "There are two races among the Sidhe. One is tall and handsome, gay, and given to jesting and to playing pranks . . . These ride on horses through the night-time in large companies and troops, or ride in coaches . . . The people of the other race are small, malicious, wide-bellied, carrying before them a bag. When a man or woman is about to die, a woman of the Sidhe will sometimes cry for a warning, keening and making lamentation. At the hour of death fighting may be heard in the air or about the house—that is, when the man in danger has friends among the shadows . . ."

Even though the parallel between the story quoted above and Yeats's play is not complete, the theme of abduction is there in a particularly imaginative form, that of fairy pipers inciting a human being to a life of love in fairyland. Fairy music plays a great part in *LHD*, and in the story as in the play, abduction by the fairies involves death. In *Visions and Beliefs in the West of Ireland*, in the section "Away" (Coole Ed., 1, 1970, pp. 104–147), Lady Gregory recorded a large number of short abduction stories in which people taken by the fairies die on their return home.

It is only to be expected that a play dealing with a fairy theme should be set in Yeats's own County Sligo, more particularly, as the stage directions inform us, *"in the Barony of Kilmacowen"*... *"and at a remote time"* (*VPl*, p. 180). As in *CC*, Yeats introduces a farmer's family, Maurteen and Bridget Bruin, and their son Shawn, recently married to Maire (Mary in the later version), a young woman already losing interest in the hard cottage life. Her curiosity about the Otherworld has been aroused by old fairy stories which she reads in spite of her mother-in-law's disapproval. She falls easy prey to the mysterious powers in the forest outside. The stage directions help to increase the dreamy mood: *"...the moon or a late sunset glimmers through the trees and carries the eye far off into a vague, mysterious world"* (*VPl*, p. 180). The non-human beings become particularly powerful on May Eve, and two worlds—the human and the non-human—meet in a conflict which engages the audience from the very first. Apart from the four family members, there is also a priest, Father Hart. The only other character is the Faery Child, whose voice is heard in the wind. The child first sends her forerunners to the cottage but finally she herself—an enticing figure in green—enters the cottage and casts an enchantment on everybody there, even the priest, who removes the crucifix and in so doing loses his power over the non-human child. The whole troop of invisible fairy dancers and pipers rushes into the cottage. Mary dies, but her soul, in the shape of a white bird, soars to the fairy realm, while her dead body is taken by her mother-in-law to be a mere image, a fairy changeling with neither substance nor soul. Various beliefs firmly established among Irish country people have been woven into the play as will be demonstrated in Ch. II of this study.

The Shadowy Waters and Traditional Stories

Compared with *LHD, SW* is a much more complicated play. One must distinguish between the dramatic poem of 1900, revised in 1906, and the Acting Version written in both prose and verse and first printed in 1907, after its performance in 1906, then further revised for the 1908 *Collected*

Works version and printed as the final Acting Version of 1911.[44] The differences in detail between the early and the later versions are so considerable that the editors of the *Variorum Poems* found collation confusing and printed both versions in full (the 1900 version, *VP*, pp. 746–769, and the 1906 version, *VP*, pp. 217–252).

The plot of the final Acting Version can be summarized as follows. The play begins with a dream which Forgael, the voyager, has had about a beautiful woman whom he thinks he has known in a former life when he himself seems to have been a god. He sets out across the waters in search of his visionary woman believed by him to be one of the Ever-living, one

---

[44] *SW* has a most complicated history of composition and stage production. Yeats began this work in the early 1880s when he was still a boy. The first printed version—the dramatic poem —appeared in the *North American Review* (May 1900), and, with but slight revisions, also in book form in 1900. See Wade, Nos. 30 and 31. This version was first performed on 14 January 1904, by the National Theatre Society at the Molesworth Hall in Dublin—with Yeats's permission—while he was in the US. Later, there was also a performance directed by Florence Farr, before the members of an International Theosophic Conference, at the Court Theatre, London, on 8 July 1905. Maurice Maeterlinck was among those present. This version, included in *The Collected Poems* (1933; 2nd enl. ed., 1950; several rpts.), was revised after the performance and first printed in that form in *Poems, 1899–1905* (London: A. H. Bullen, 1906); it should not be confused with the Acting Version, first performed on 8 December 1906 and first printed separately in 1907 (Wade, No. 66). This version was also further revised and printed in *The Collected Works*, II (1908); then again revised as the Acting Version of 1911 (included in *The Collected Plays*); in Peter Allt and Russell K. Alspach, ed., *The Variorum Edition of the Poems of W. B. Yeats* (New York: Macmillan, 1957); hereafter *VP*. Collation is done in *VP* of 14 printings of the rev. version of 1906 and 9 printings of the Acting Version of 1907. See also *VPl*, pp. 317–343. Much excellent work has been done on *SW*, as will be seen from the following selected list of references: Peter Ure; Thomas Parkinson, *W. B. Yeats Self-Critic: A Study of his Early Verse* (Berkeley: Univ. of California Press, 1951), pp. 59–65; Richard Ellmann, *The Identity of Yeats* (London: Macmillan, 1954), pp. 64–65; 80–85 (deals exclusively with the dramatic poem); hereafter Ellmann, *Ident.;* Leonard E. Nathan, *The Tragic Drama of W. B. Yeats* (New York and London, 1965); S. B. Bushrui, *Yeats's Verse Plays: The Revisions 1900–1910* (Oxford: Clarendon Press, 1965), pp. 1–38; hereafter Bushrui, *Revisions;* Harold Bloom, *Yeats* (New York: OUP, 1970); David R. Clark, ed., "Half the Characters had Eagles' Faces: W. B. Yeats' unpublished 'Shadowy Waters'," *The Massachusetts Review*, 6 (Autumn 1964–Winter 1965); David R. Clark and George P. Mayhew, ed., *A Tower of Published Black Stones: Early Versions of The Shadowy Waters* (Dublin: The Dolmen Press, 1971); Michael J. Sidnell, George P. Mayhew, and David R. Clark, ed., *Druid Craft: The Writings of The Shadowy Waters* (Amherst: Univ. of Massachusetts Press, 1971); hereafter *Druid Craft;* Miller; George Mills Harper, *Yeats's Golden Dawn* (London: Macmillan, 1974); A. Norman Jeffares, *A Commentary on the Collected Poems of W. B. Yeats* (London: Macmillan, 1968); hereafter Jeffares, *Commentary Poems;* A. Norman Jeffares and A. S. Knowland, *A Commentary on the Plays of W. B. Yeats* (London: Macmillan, 1975); hereafter Jeffares and Knowland, *Commentary Plays;* G. B. Saul, *Prolegomena to the Study of Yeats's Poems* (Philadelphia: Univ. of Pennsylvania Press, 1957; rpt. New York: Octagon Books, 1971), and *Prolegomena to the Study of Yeats's Plays* (Philadelphia: Univ. of Pennsylvania Press, 1958); A. Norman Jeffares, ed., *W. B. Yeats:* The Critical Heritage Series (London: Routledge & Kegan Paul, 1977); hereafter Jeffares, *Yeats: CH*. See also Wade, Cross/Dunlop, and Jochum.

who casts no shadow. He is accompanied by his friend Aibric and some sailors whom he has paid well. When the latter start plotting against his life, his miraculous instrument, a magic harp, fills them with fear and awe and prevents them from killing him. Grey sea-birds with human faces and human voices—messengers of the Ever-living—circle around the ship and guide it across the Ocean. Suddenly, when the sailors are beginning to get desperate, a merchant ship laden with spices and other riches turns up. Aibric and the sailors board the strange ship and murder "golden-armed Iollan", a king of a foreign country, and capture Dectora, his Queen, who turns out to be the woman of Forgael's dream. At first Forgael is, however, disappointed to find that she is an ordinary mortal. Dectora's first impulse is to slay Forgael with Aibric's sword, in revenge for her husband's death, but the magic music of the harp makes her change her mind. All of a sudden the sailors, also lulled by the music of the harp, decide to have a wake on board the captured ship, and during their rollicking ale-song, Dectora, remaining on board Forgael's ship, starts keening and lamenting her dead husband. Then, to the changing tunes of the harp—Forgael now plays the laughing tune—she suddenly starts laughing and addresses a love song to Forgael. Passing through a mood of grief to one of joy, she decides to accompany Forgael to the land of the Ever-living. Aibric, who also falls in love with Dectora, is jealous of Forgael (in some early manuscript versions his jealousy is more marked), but he is likewise mastered by the harp. Dectora cuts the rope which joins the two ships, Aibric and the sailors, who are now rich, turn homewards on the captured ship, whereas Forgael and Dectora drift on towards the land of beauty and ideal love, the land of immortality.[45]

The most radical differences between the early and the later printed versions are not so much in the plot as in the setting and the use of fewer symbols (see Bushrui, *Revisions,* p. 33), and Yeats's acceptance of "the limitations of stage-production" (ibid., p. 36), as well as the style and the language. He also, with every revision, made the characters more realistic, particularly the sailors, which was pointed out as early as 1950 by Thomas

---

[45] Yeats himself asking his audience of 1906 to take his play as a fairy tale, made a summary of the play in *The Arrow,* No. 2, 24 November 1906, pp. [3–4]. There was no Abbey Theatre performance on 9 July 1905, but on July 8 1905 (see *Druid Craft,* p. 302, n. 25), Florence Farr was in charge of a performance at the Court Theatre, London, in connection with the International Theosophic Congress then in session in London". For contemporary impressions of *SW* see, e.g. Fiona MacLeod, "The Later Work of Mr. W. B. Yeats", *North American Reviw,* 551, October 1902, 477 ff., and Horatio S. Krans, *William Butler Yeats and the Irish Literary Revival,* Contemporary Men of Letters Series (London: Heinemann, 1905), p. 132. See also Jeffares, *Yeats: CH.*

Parkinson in *W. B. Yeats Self-Critic,* who comments that "The sailors of 1905 are ordinary men with a normal endowment of sensuality... They are sensual men with a common-sense view of life" (p. 70).

Yeats found the illusion of a harp burning of itself difficult to achieve on the stage. For the 1905 London performance he had to use the term "stringed instrument" instead of harp and make other textual changes as well. He himself stated (*VPl*, p. 341) that

the stage carpenter found it very difficult to make the crescent-shaped harp that was to burn with fire; and besides, no matter how well he made the frame, there was no way of making the strings take fire. I had, therefore, to give up the harp for a sort of psaltery, a little like the psaltery Miss Farr speaks to, where the strings could be slits covered with glass or gelatine on the surface of a shallow and perhaps semi-transparent box; and besides, it amused one to picture, in the centre of a myth, the instrument of our new art.

In the 1908 version (*Collected Works*, II, pp. 178–229, esp. 183–187), Yeats reintroduced his favourite symbol, the harp, although it was no longer crescent-shaped. The detailed stage directions with, e.g. a striking colour-scheme of dark green, tints of blue, copper, etc., devised by Yeats himself, are retained (*VPl*, pp. 317–318, under line; see also *Collected Works*, II, p. 185, and IV, p. 131), but in the final Acting Version of 1911, stage directions are greatly simplified and leave many details to the imagination (*VPl*, p. 317).

In the first printed version of *SW* (the dramatic poem of 1900), Forgael is a pirate captain, Aibric a mountain robber gone to sea, and Dectora a Queen from Lochlann married to an elderly Lochlann king with whom she has had to flee from her own country. Their ship is attacked by Forgael's pirate sailors and the king and all his men are killed, and Dectora is taken prisoner and brought over to Forgael's galley. She wants Forgael to sail with her to Lochlann and help her recapture her country and crown, but Forgael's determination to sail to the country of the gods cannot be shaken. He is under the special protection of the perfect lovers, the love god Aengus and his lover Edaine (spelt Edain in the later versions), who has been called the Aphrodite of Celtic myth. In this first version the White Fool, a special messenger from Aengus, has come out of the wood and given Forgael a magic harp, the harp of Aengus, which is actually the harp of the great and good god, the Dagda. The sailors are planning mutiny from the very start but their plan to kill Forgael is frustrated by the magic harp, as is Dectora's attempt to make Forgael's sailors murder him and join her.

Yeats worked for decades on *SW;* it took him about seventeen years to complete the first printed version of the play, as the editors of *Druid Craft* have shown (pp. 3f). He began it as early as 1883 when studying the habits of sea-birds. Early pre-publication drafts of the play show that it contained figures of horror like the eagle-headed Fomorians or the "Seabars" (or Siavras).[46] It was an extremely violent play to start with, but in the printed versions, violence is more or less restricted to the murder by the sailors of the king on the meeting ship. The attempted murder of Forgael himself by the sailors as well as by Dectora is averted by the agency of the magic harp. Originally, in early manuscripts, Dectora's lover, the poet Aleel, was crudely stabbed on the open stage by Forgael, a druid and pirate, who as a practising magician had to soothe the Seabars with human sacrifices. The murder committed on a voyage is a motif also in e.g. *Hamlet,*[47] but Yeats could have taken this idea from many other sources, especially stories about the Fomorians, who appear, if not as pirates, as a kind of Irish Titans in many tales. At some stage in the course of the compositon of the play, the poet is eliminated, and King Iolan or Iollan, a character drawn either from the Deirdre legend, in which he is one of Fergus's sons, or from a Fenian tale, appears as Dectora's husband.

Early drafts and the 1900 printed version show clearly that a number of Irish legendary tales greatly influenced Yeats when he was writing the play. A good deal of what seems to be mostly contemporary oral lore, figures even more prominently in the drafts than in the published versions, as does his dabbling in certain forms of black magic. Two classes of tales are, however, of particular interest, voyages (Ir. *immrama*), and visions *(aislingi)*. Professor Bushrui has pointed out the resemblance of the play to *The Voyage of Bran.*[48] This, the earliest of the Irish voyages, probably going back to a seventh-century original, abounds in beautiful descriptions of the Otherworld.[49] As happens to Forgael, a woman of great beauty (and with a "branch of music" in her hand), appears to Bran in a dream, and in a long poem she entreats him to come to her country, a happy Silverland, a

---

[46] For an explanation of Yeats's "Sheavra" or "Seabar", see Joyce, *Irish Names of Places, I,* where it is stated that *"siabhra* [sheevra]" is a word "now very frequently employed to denote a fairy" (p. 190) and that the *siabhra* were perhaps the Túatha Dé Dananns (p. 181), according to "The History of Cemeteries" found in MS. 3.17., Trinity College, Dublin. See also Crofton Croker, *Fairy Legends and Traditions in the South of Ireland,* 3 vol. (London, 1925–28), I, p. 162, where a distinction is made between "the Cluricaune and the Shefro." Quoted by Edward Hirsch, in "The Poet as Folklorist", in *The Genres of the Irish Literary Revival,* ed. Ronald Schleifer (Oklahoma: Pilgrim Books; Dublin: Woolfhound Press, 1980), p. 15.

[47] For the first comprehensive investigation of the influence of Shakespeare on Yeats, see Rupin W. Desai, *Yeats's Shakespeare* (Evanston: Northwestern UP, 1971).

[48] *Revisions,* p. 4.

[49] Kuno Meyer, ed., *The Voyage of Bran Son of Febal to the Land of the Living,* 2 vol. (London, 1895–97), I, p. xvi; hereafter Bran I and Bran II.

great plain, a land of apple blossoms and beautiful horses, a Land of Promise.

From various statements of his, we know that Yeats read not only *The Voyage of Bran,* but all voyage stories that were available to him, the *Voyage of Maeldún,* of *St. Brendan,* of *the Uí Chorra,* as well as *The Adventures of Connla,* which is sometimes also referred to as a voyage.[50] Not only did he find in these tales a structure and a theme for his play—a hero setting out in quest of a distant happy land, or in search of marvellous strange islands—he also found ample material from which to create a beautiful and esoteric symbolic language. The sea is of course not only a setting but above all a symbol.[51] In a note to one of the poems in *WR* (p. 90), Yeats draws a parallel between Neo-Platonic thought and Celtic voyages:

Some neo-platonist, I forget who, describes the sea as a symbol of the drifting indefinite bitterness of life, and I believe there is like symbolism intended in the many Irish voyages to the islands of enchantment, or that there was, at any rate, in the mythology out of which these stories have been shaped.

A mythological tale which also underlies *SW* is *The Dream of Óengus (Aislinge Óenguso),* in which is found the same theme of a woman appearing to the hero in a dream. Moreover, the bird symbolism of this tale has also left its traces not only on *SW* but also on other plays of Yeats and on many of his poems. Yeats's original attempts to incorporate a number of mytholocigal stories about the Fomorians could hardly have proved very successful on Yeats's kind of stage. Making Forgael a Fomorian (in early drafts) is, however, in keeping with one tradition according to which Forgaill (Yeats's Foregael or Forgael) was a king of Tethra, i.e. the Underworld, in other words, the ruler of the regions of death.

In *The Adventures of Connla,* the Otherworld beings are referred to as the people of Tethra *(doíni Tethrach).*[52] Yeats retained Forgael as the name of his hero throughout all the revisions of his play, but from being a murderous young pirate-magician, he was turned into a mysterious voyager and owner of a miraculous harp with seven strings woven out of the long hair of the love god Aengus. Both Forgael and Dectora (a variation of *Deichtire,* older *Deichtine*) are famous names in Irish legend, Forgaill being the father of Emer, Cuchulain's wife, and Deichtire, the mother of

---

[50] For a discussion of "The Voyages", see e.g. Myles Dillon, *Early Irish Literature* (Chicago: Univ. of Chicago Press, 1948), pp. 124—131.

[51] Bushrui, *Revisions,* pp. 4—38, has compared the various printed versions and made a detailed study of the symbols, primary and secondary. See also Ellmann, *Ident.,* pp. 82—83.

[52] *ZCP,* 17 (1927), 193—205 esp. 199. German trans. by J. Pokorny.

Cuchulain, yet neither of them figuring as such in the play. As for Aibric,[53] a name replacing an earlier Aleel, a poet—Yeats must first have come across this name in the well-known story "The Fate of the Children of Lir", as told e.g. in P. W. Joyce's *Old Celtic Romances*.[54] In the Lir tale, Aibric is the young man who listens to the sad story of the speaking swans and tells it to the world after their death. As Aibric in the tale listens to the musical speech of the swans, Yeats's Aibric listens to Forgael's harp, the instrument which helps him to reach the land of ideal love.

The Wooing of Étain — A Traditional Tale Explored in All Three Plays

The Irish legend of rebirth and love called *The Wooing of Étain (Tochmarc Étaíne)* fascinated Yeats for many years, perhaps all his life. He actually began to explore this tale in the early 80s when working on his first drafts of *SW*, and it also absorbed him when he was composing his first version of *The Countess Kathleen*.[55] He wove this legendary material into both *SW* and *CC* as well as into *LHD*, and later also into *Deirdre*. He also based a long narrative poem "The Two Kings" on one part of the Étain legend.[56] For convenience sake the saga will be summarized as follows: According to one version Midir and Aengus, both gods, are rivals for Étain, daughter of Ailill, a king living in the North-east. Midir wins her and Aengus steals her from him and puts her in a "glass bower" which he carries about with him wherever he goes. According to another tradition Aengus woos Étain on behalf of Midir. Fuamnach, Midir's first wife, who is jealous of Étain, and her chief magician transform her into a purple fly "as big as a man's

---

[53] See *Druid Craft*, p. 277, for the first introduction of this character into the MSS of the play.

[54] (London, 1879, 2nd ed. 1894; rpt. Dublin, 1961), pp. 19 and 316. Joyce spells the name "Ebric" in the text and gives the Gaelic form as "Aibhric" in his list of names. Lady Gregory in her version of "The Children of Lir" in *Gods and Fighting Men*, pp. 123–136, uses the form "Aibric" (p. 134).

[55] Yeats often began by writing a prose sketch. This is the case with many of his plays, e.g. *Deirdre*, and many of his longer poems. A complete prose version is preserved of *The Countess Kathleen*. J. M. Sidnell—in his article "Yeats's First Work for the Stage: The earliest Versions of 'The Countess Kathleen'", in *W. B. Yeats 1865–1965: Centenary Essays*, ed. D. F. S. Maxwell and S. B. Bushrui (Ibadan: Ibadan Univ. Press, 1965, pp. 167–188)—examines the unpublished prose version of the play and clarifies several points concerning its origins; hereafter *Centenary Essays*. See also J. M. Sidnell's "Manuscript Versions of Yeats's *The Countess Cathleen*", in *Papers of the Bibliographical Society of America*, 56, (1962).

[56] *Collected Poems* (London, 1950), pp. 503–510. See G. B. Saul, *Prolegomena to the Study of Yeats's Poems*, pp. 187–188.

head, the comeliest in the land. Sweeter than pipes and harps and horns was the sound of her voice and the hum of her wings."[57] In her jealousy Fuamnach stirs up a magic storm which hurls the fly across land and sea until—after having spent some time in the sunny bower of Aengus—she lands on the roof of the King's palace in Ulster and falls into the cup of the Queen (considering the size of the fly, the cup must have been enormous), is swallowed by her, and in due time reborn as Étain, daughter of Étar, 1012 years after her first birth. According to one tradition Midir and Aengus have Fuamnach's head struck off for what she has done to Étain.

In her new life as Étain, daughter of Étar, she is wooed and won by Eochaid, King of Tara. His rival is Midir, Étain's former husband, who woos her through Eochaid's brother Ailill, whose love-sickness takes up most of this part of the saga. Midir fails, however, for Étain refuses to desert the King of Ireland for an unknown stranger whose lineage she does not know. Étain's honour is saved, and Ailill is restored to health. (This is the part of the saga on which Yeats based his poem "The Two Kings".)

In the third part we are told how Midir, eager to retrieve Étain, goes in his own shape to Tara, plays chess with Eochaid for her and wins her from him. Against his will Eochaid has to allow his rival to kiss and put his arms around Étain. A transformation takes place and Midir and Étain disappear in the shape of two white swans.

Determined to win back his wife, Eochaid attacks all the fairy mounds in Ireland, Midir's Brí Leith included. Midir mocks him by placing fifty women, all like Étain, on the plain of Tara. Instead of his wife he chooses his own daughter, Midir's stepdaughter, by whom he begets another daughter. When the truth is revealed to him, he orders the child to be cast out. He then returns to Brí Leith and manages to find his wife, with whom he returns to Tara. Midir brings Étain, together with Eochaid's severed head, back to his mound, and it is only then that Étain remains with him for ever.

Numerous motifs are present in this mythological tale—rebirth, metempsychosis, supernatural wooing, transformation of supernatural wooer and lover into swans, beauty, love, love-sickness and divine possession, incest, destruction of a fairy mound, magic storm, magic sleep, etc. Étain,

---

[57] O. J. Bergin and R. I Best, ed, "Tochmarc Étaíne", *Ériu*, 12 (1938), 137–196, esp. 153. This ed. contains text, trans. and a critical analysis of the two versions of the saga. See also R. Thurneysen, *Die irische Helden- und Königsage* (Halle: Max Niemeyer, 1921), pp. 589 ff.; Myles Dillon, *Early Irish Literature* (Chicago: Univ. of Chicago Press, 1948), pp. 54–58; Eugene O'Curry, *On the Manners and Customs of the Ancient Irish*, 3 vol. (London, 1873), III, pp. 190–191; hereafter *Manners and Customs*.

the central figure, is loved by Midir, Aengus, and Eochaid, and hated by Fuamnach. Étain—who according to one tradition is a fairy woman herself—is not pictured as longing to return to Midir's supernatural world. She does not even recognize her former husband when he comes in search of her. Midir, on the other hand, never forgets her and never gives up his quest for her. These are conventions typical of such tales. It is hardly strange that this beautiful and rather complex story should have excited Yeats's imagination for a number of years. Yeats associated the Otherworld not only with fairies but also with definite characters of rank like kings, queens and princesses, and Adene (Edain) was identified by Yeats as "a famous legendary queen who went away from the world and dwelt among the 'shee'."[58] In the early version of *The Countess Kathleen*, Adene (Edain) is also clearly associated with the fairy realm, and Kathleen herself claims to be descended from this legendary queen. In the first prose version, however, Kathleen traces her ancestry to Morna, whom Yeats mentions as a woman who "went away with her lover into a cavern that leads down to fairyland."[59] (Morna is also a character in James Macpherson's poem *Fingal*.)

Although rebirth will be dealt with in Ch. II of this investigation, it is convenient to deal with it also here since rebirth was used by Yeats as an underlying by-motif recurring in the three plays, and in all three plays this motif is closely associated with the lovely Adene (Edain). Kathleen, saddened by stories of the famine related to her by her Herdsman, is impressed by a song ("Who will go drive with Fergus now...?") composed by Kevin (or Aleel in later versions), the poet who loves her, and sung by Oona. She is filled with longing for a peace to be found neither in this world nor among the "brazen cars" of Fergus. The horn of Fergus—with its erotic allusion—appeals to her heart, and, tempted by its alluring tune, she says nostalgically to Oona:

---

[58] *VPl*, pp. 1284–1285. In the early version of *The Countess Kathleen* Yeats spells the name "Adene"; later he uses "Edain", sometimes other spellings. As stated by him in a note (*Collected Poems*, p. 523), he followed Lady Gregory's spellings of all Gaelic names with the exception of "Edain" and "Aengus" (which he preferred to "Angus"). Yeats was fully aware of the difficulties involved in the spelling and the pronunciation of Irish names. He also knew that modern pronunciation and spelling differ from earlier usage, as is shown by what he wrote in 1895: "The modern pronunciation, which is usually followed by those who spell the words phonetically, is certainly unlike the pronunciation of the time when classical Irish literature was written, and, so far as I know, no scholar who writes in English or French has made that minute examination of the way the names come into the rhythms and measures of the old poems which can alone discover the old pronunciation" (*VPl*, p. 1282).

[59] Quoted by M. J. Sidnell, "Yeats's First Work for the Stage", *Centenary Essays*, p. 177.

O, I am sadder than an old air, Oona;
My heart is longing for a deeper peace
Than Fergus found amid his brazen cars:
Would that like Adene my first forebear's daughter,
Who followed once a twilight piercing tune,
I could go down and dwell among the shee
In their old ever-busy honeyed land.

VPl, pp. 60, 62

In these lines Adene's (Edain's) happy land is contrasted to Kathleen's sorrowful world which makes her sadly wish to follow the same "twilight piercing tune" as her alleged ancestor Adene whom she sees depicted on a tapestry—"The image of young Adene on the arras" (*VPl,* p. 62). Here Yeats gives a strong pastoral colouring to his play. Like a shepherdess the Countess hears her lover's call:

> . . .
> *For Fergus rules the brazen cars,*
> *And rules the shadows of the wood,*
> *And the white breast of the dim sea*
> *And all dishevelled wandering stars.*

VPl, p. 56

This linking of the Adene motif with Fergus is typical of Yeats's manner of adaptation. As he explains in a note, "Fergus, poet of the Conorian age, had been king of all Ireland, but gave up his throne that he might live at peace hunting in the forest", and in another note: "He was the poet of the Red Branch cycle as Usheen (. . .) was of the Fenian. . . ." (*VPl,* p. 1285). Fergus's hunting horn tempts Kathleen, but she resists its sound and rejects Kevin's world out of duty to her people. Although Kathleen would have liked to join "the unending dance", to become one of the invisible dancers, to sing their "wild song", she feels she will have to fulfil her mission. In fact, Kathleen could never have accepted life among the Shee. When she signs the contract, her heart is consumed, which is a rather Oriental way of making the gates of Heaven swing open. At this time Yeats was greatly influenced by Brahmaism, and there is a strange mixture of Christian, Oriental, and Celtic ideas in the play. It seems only proper for Kathleen, who can claim descent from a supernatural woman but is nevertheless unable to follow the siren voices of the Shee, to ascend to Heaven at the end of the play.

In making Kathleen refer to herself as a late descendant of "Adene", Yeats evidently wanted to claim a major place for her in Irish legend. In the final version of the play, however, he omitted the passage in which the Countess speaks of her legendary forebear. His having realized that the

Kathleen story was not an indigenous West-of-Ireland folk tale as well as his wish to make his play what he called "more realistic" may have contributed to this change. And again to an audience unfamiliar with the Irish legend, Edain would have been just a name which did not convey the desired connotations, and to those familiar with the legend, the time-gap between Kathleen and Edain would perhaps make the ancestry appear slightly absurd.

In *LHD*, a story in an old book (in the early version a "yellow manuscript") which Mary finds in the thatch makes her long for Edain's world, and Edain subsequently turns up as a fairy princess. When asked by the priest what she is reading, Mary answers:

> How a Princess Edain,
> A daughter of a King of Ireland, heard
> A voice singing on a May Eve like this,
> And followed, half awake and half asleep,
> Until she came into the Land of Faery,
> . . .
> And she is still there, busied with a dance
> Deep in the dewy shadow of a wood,
> (Or where stars walk upon a mountain-top.)

VPl, p. 184

In the early version, Maire, according to the stage directions, *"sits on the settle reading a yellow manuscript"* (*VPl*, p. 181, under line), and Yeats actually refers to the binding of the manuscript (in the later version to a book) by making Maurteen say that his "grandfather wrote it,/And killed a heifer for the binding of it" (*VPl*, p. 183). This quite obvious allusion to Irish manuscript tradition—manuscripts like *The Yellow Book of Lecan* (14th century) and *Lebor na hUidre* or *The Book of the Dun Cow*—was retained also in later versions of the play, and certainly shows how Yeats was trying to connect oral and literary traditions and thus create a link in his play between the legendary past and the present time. To the young woman in the play it seems as though Princess Edain has stepped right out of the book, and has become the fairy child of modern folk belief. Edain represents one of the fairy dancers and there is, moreover, an implication that Mary believes that in joining these dancers she herself will become Edain. Mary sees and hears more than ordinary people; she is in league with unseen powers, with Edain and her invisible world. The concept of rebirth appealed strongly to Yeats, and in Mary, so close to the fairy dancers, he drew a character who was on the verge of entering into the Otherworld.

In the Irish legend itself, rebirth seems to be a natural and unquestioned procedure, but in Yeats's play, rebirth or reincarnation is a mystery, a secret source of joy. Edain's dancers have the last say. Their triumphant song ends the play. The last lines, spoken by a reed of Coolaney and carried by the wind

> (. . .
> 'When the wind has laughed and murmured and sung,
> The lonely of heart is withered away')

VPl, p. 210

link up with the Brahmaistic concept of the consumed heart.[60] Only by renouncing her love and all desire to remain in the world can the young woman find the Land of Heart's Desire, i.e. be reborn. It is obvious that in his portrayal of the Edain figure Yeats did not follow the Irish tale beyond a certain point. She appears in Yeats's play as a visionary figure embodying the poet's dream of paradise and his longing for the impossible.

However, nowhere in the three plays dealt with in this study is the visionary experience as strong as in *SW*. The Edain figure plays an all-important role, and Yeats experimented with different ideas at different times. He often mentions his interest in the Edain story. The editors of *Druid Craft* have drawn attention to a never-published prologue for the 1905 version of the dramatic poem. A Black Jester (probably the Jester of Aengus, an idea which Fiona MacLeod may have suggested to Yeats) is arguing with the Stage Manager (who is not on the stage) and refers to Aengus and Edaine (*Druid Craft*, p. 303):

No. I won't listen any more. . . . These two are Aengus & Edaine. They are spirits & whenever I am in love it is not I that am in love but Aengus who is always looking for Edaine through somebody's eyes. You will find all about them in the old Irish books. She was the wife of Midher another spirit in the hill but he grew jealous of her & he put her out of doors, & Aengus hid her in a tower of glass. That is why I carry the two of them in a glass bottle. (holds bottle in front of me) O Aengus! O Edaine! be kind to me when I am in love & to everybody in this audience when they are in love & make us all believe that it is not you but us ourselves that love. These others—the black dog, the red dog & the white dog.—I am always afraid of them. . . .

The rest of the Prologue explains the effect on the Jester of the different-coloured dogs, and also refers to other symbols, such as the King, the Queen, the flowers and the sea-birds, the eagle, and the "jewsharp". It need not surprise us that Yeats discarded this Prologue, which nevertheless throws some light on his symbolism. Apart from the Black Jester's

---

[60] F. F. Farag, "Oriental and Celtic Elements in the Poetry of W. B. Yeats", *Centenary Essays*, pp. 33–53; hereafter Farag.

speech being slightly naive, the Prologue must also have proved to be superfluous when Yeats was discarding needless symbols. Yeats kept one interesting feature in this dialogue, an idea he had had previously that the god was looking out of the lover's eyes, as though he had taken possession of the person in love. The Jester's invocation of Aengus and Edaine, two perfect lovers, also reminds one of Donne's poem "Canonization", in which Donne uses the conceit of ideal lovers becoming saints through their love, saints worthy of being prayed to by other lovers, who should take their pattern from them. Undoubtedly the Forgael-Dectora relationship is conditioned by Yeats's preoccupation with the ideal love of Aengus and Edain. He was also well aware of his deviations from the old legendary tale. Here we might draw attention to the two poems prefaced to the 1906 version of *The Shadowy Waters,* a long one beginning "I walked among the seven woods of Coole"—actually used as a Prologue in the 1905 London performance—dedicated to Lady Gregory, and another shorter poem entitled "The Harp of Aengus":

> *Edain came out of Midhir's hill, and lay*
> *Beside young Aengus in his tower of glass,*
> *Where time is drowned in odour-laden winds*
> *And Druid moons, and murmuring of boughs,*
> *And sleepy boughs, and boughs where apples made*
> *Of opal and ruby and pale chrysolite*
> *Awake unsleeping fires; and wove seven strings,*
> *Sweet with all music, out of his long hair,*
> *Because her hands had been made wild by love.*
> *When Midhir's wife had changed her to a fly,*
> *He made a harp with Druid apple-wood*
> *That she among her winds might know he wept;*
> *And from that hour he has watched over none*
> *But faithful lovers.*
>
> *Collected Poems,* p. 471

In the 1900 version this poem is used as a speech by Forgael to Dectora (*VP*, pp. 762–763), but when revising the dramatic poem Yeats finds these lines about Edain and Aengus more suitable as an introductory poem which is meant to set the tone of the dramatic poem as a whole and to make the reader or listener prepared for a love story of an unusual kind. He is conscious that he is making his own addition to the Edain story when he makes Edain weave seven harp-strings out of Aengus's long hair. Her hands weave her own love into the strings of the harp which Aengus has made of "Druid apple-wood". In a note to his lyrical-narrative poem *Baile and Aillinn* (1901), another love story based on Celtic myth, he explains his personal use of the Aengus myth in *SW:*

Midhir was a king of the Sidhe, or people of faery, and Etain his wife when driven away by a jealous woman, took refuge once upon a time with Aengus in a house of glass, and there I have imagined her weaving harp-strings out of Aengus' hair. I have brought the harp-strings into 'The Shadowy Waters', where I interpret the myth in my own way.

VP, p. 188, under line

In a letter of July 15 [1905], written to Florence Farr after the 1905 London performance, Yeats states that he is "getting rid of needless symbols" and "making the groundwork simple and intelligible";[61] in another letter probably written some time in July 1905, he states (Wade, *Letters,* p. 454):

> I am making Forgael's part perfectly clear and straightforward. The play is now upon one single idea. ... There are no symbols except Aengus and Aedane[62] and the birds—and I have into the bargain heightened all the moments of dramatic crisis—sharpened every knife edge. ... I am going to make some fine sleep verses for Forgael when he enchants Dectora and I have done a good bit where he sees her shadow and finds that she is a mortal.

It is of course an exaggeration on Yeats's part to say that Aengus and Edain (Aedane) and the birds are the only symbols, but it shows how great an importance he attached to these two legendary figures and their messengers, the birds. Of course, the harp is equally, if not more, important. In 1911 Yeats explained that his use of the Edain legend in *SW* was based on "poor translations of various Aengus stories", and yet he maintained that the plot was based on no definite story, but to a great extent on visionary experiences:

> I took the Aengus and Edain of *The Shadowy Waters* from poor translations of the various Aengus stories, which, new translated by Lady Gregory, make up so much of what is most beautiful in both her books.[63] They had, however, so completely become a part of my own thought that in 1897, when I was still working on an early version of *The Shadowy Waters,* I saw one night with my bodily eyes, as it seemed, two beautiful persons, who would, I believe, have answered to their names.[64] The plot of the play itself has, however, no definite old story for its foundation but was woven to a very great extent out of certain visionary experiences.[65]

---

[61] Wade, *Letters,* p. 453.

[62] Another of Yeats's spellings of "Edain". It may be noted that Lady Wilde in her *Ancient Legends, Mystic Charms, and Superstitions of Ireland* (London, 1888) has recorded a fairy tale entitled "Edain the Queen", pp. 94−96.

[63] *Cuchulain of Muirthemne* and *Gods and Fighting Men.*

[64] Yeats seems to refer to this in "A Voice" (1902), one of his stories in *The Celtic Twilight,* concerned with a vision of Aengus and Edain.

[65] *Collected Works,* II, p. 254. For further information about editions, texts, translations, and critical analyses of the Étain story, see e.g. R. Thurneysen, *Die irische Helden- und Königsage* (1921), and R. I. Best's two works *Bibliography of Irish Philology* (Dublin: Dublin

A prose poem relating to the legend had, however, aroused his special interest (*WR*, pp. 85—86):

The old Gaelic literature is full of the appeals of the Tribes of the goddess Danu to mortals whom they would bring into their country; but the song of Midher to the beautiful Etain, the wife of the king who was called Echaid the ploughman, is the type of all.

'O beautiful woman, come with me to the marvellous land where one listens to a sweet music, where one has spring flowers in one's hair, where the body is like snow from head to foot, where no one is sad or silent, where teeth are white and eyebrows are black... cheeks red like foxglove in flower. ... Ireland is beautiful, but not so beautiful as the Great Plain I call you to. The beer of Ireland is heady, but the beer of the Great Plain is much more heady. How marvellous is the country I am speaking of! Youth does not grow old there. Streams with warm flood flow there; sometimes mead, sometimes wine. Men are charming and without a blot there, and love is not forbidden there. O woman, when you come into my powerful country you will wear a crown of gold upon your head. I will give you the flesh of swine, and you will have beer and milk to drink, O beautiful woman. O beautiful woman, come with me![66] (Ellipsis points are Yeats's.)

It is worth noting that the appeal in this poem is made not by a beautiful woman to a brave and handsome young man as in the voyages and the dreams, but by a god to a beautiful woman who was once his wife. He entreats her to return to his land where she once lived with him. We may recall that the title of the tale contains the word "wooing" and that Étain is wooed several times. Undoubtedly Yeats drew upon this poem for the final development of the Forgael-Dectora relationship.[67] True, at the beginning

Institute for Advanced Studies, 1913), p. 84; hereafter Best 1; *Bibliography of Irish Philology 1913—1941* (Dublin: Dublin Institute for Advanced Studies, 1942), p. 71; hereafter Best 2. Early works most certainly studied by Yeats are Alfred Nutt's essays "Upon the Irish Vision of the Happy Otherworld" in *Bran* I, and "The Celtic Doctrine of Rebirth", in *Bran* II; John Rhŷs, *Celtic Heathendom* (London, 1886), and *Studies in the Arthurian Legend* (Oxford, 1891), pp. 25—28. The earliest translation of the Étain saga into English—but only the second part—was made by d'Eduard Müller, "Two Irish Tales. II. Scéla Ailill 7 Étaine", *RC*, 3 (1876—78), 351—360. Before this there were also translations into German. For some of Yeats's trancelike visions, see e.g. "Invoking the Irish Fairies", Frayne, I, pp. 245—247.

[66] For the original and a trans. of a different version of this poem, see O'Curry, *Manners and Customs*, III, p. 191. Also Arbois de Jubainville, *The Irish Mythological Cycle . . .*, trans. Richard Best (Dublin, 1903), pp. 179—180. The French original appeared in 1884. (In *WR* Yeats follows the Old Irish spelling of "Etain" with a "t".) In *The International Popular Tale and Early Welsh Tradition* (Cardiff: Univ. of Wales Press, 1961), p. 113, Kenneth Jackson points out that "the well-known theme of the man who dreams of an unknown girl, falls in love with this dream girl, and has a search made till he finds her" occurs in *The Dream of Macsen*, and is a motif well known not only in Welsh and Irish but also in Greek and Sanskrit literature.

[67] For a treatment of the Forgael-Dectora relationship as expressing ideal love, see P. Hühn, *Das Verhältnis von Mann und Frau im Werk von William Butler Yeats*, Studien zur Englischen Literatur, 5, ed. J. Kleinstück (Bonn: Bouvier, 1971), pp. 155—160; hereafter Hühn.

of the play, Forgael is enticed to the Otherworld by a visionary woman, as is Bran, but when the two ships meet on the shadowy waters, the situation is changed.[68] However, Dectora proves simply to be an ordinary mortal woman, who is not aware of having made an appeal to Forgael. Yet he is convinced that she must be the immortal woman whom he has known in a former life and seen in a dream, and he is determined not to let her go, but bring her with him to the land of the Ever-living, the land of his longing. Like Midhir—or according to another tradition Aengus—for both wooed Edain, he starts wooing Queen Dectora. The three magic strains of his harp, the strain of slumber, the strain of lament and the strain of laughter, cast their enchantment on Dectora, who forgets her murdered husband.[69] Consequently she is made to think that she is keening a man who is still alive and bursts out laughing with the words:

> Why, it's a wonder out of reckoning
> That I should keen him from the full of the moon
> To the horn, and he be hale and hearty.

VPl, p. 333

As Nathan points out (p. 60), the early version contains many allusions to Edain and Aengus, yet their names have disappeared from the final version, although their presence is strongly felt. In this play Yeats exploited the concept of the Happy Otherworld adapting it to his own symbolic pattern while at the same time casting in dramatic form his own emotional conflicts. The Otherworld is closely associated with the concept of rebirth. In the early version the rebirth pattern is closely linked with the figures of Edain and Aengus. Forgael and Dectora look at one another through the eyes of Aengus and Edain, that is with the same passionate love as those ideal lovers had once experienced.

In the 1906 version there is also an interesting use of a vision of two sea fairies seen by two of the sailors, that is, a vision of "a beautiful young man and girl" rising up out of the ocean "in a white breaking wave" (*Collected Poems*, p. 474). They take these two beautiful beings to be

---

[68] The idea that Forgael's dream and voyage are inspired by Irish legendary voyages and dreams, as well as by other Irish tales, need not exclude other interpretations. L. E. Nathan, who deals only with the 1900 version, i.e., the dramatic poem, asserts that "The actual subject and plot show marked resemblances to Shelley's *Revolt of Islam*". For this Interpretation of *SW*, see *The Tragic Drama of William Butler Yeats* (1965), Ch. II.

[69] In the saga entitled *Aislinge Óenguso, The Dream of Óengus*, Aengus falls sick for love of a woman who appears to him in a dream. See, e.g. d'Eduard Müller, "Two Irish Tales. I. Aislinge Oengusso", *RC*, 3 (1876–78), 342–350. Also Francis Shaw, ed., *The Dream of Óengus: Aislinge Óenguso* (Dublin: Browne & Nolan, 1934).

> Aengus and Edain, the wandering
> lovers,
> To whom all lovers pray.
>
> *Collected Poems*, p. 475

When seeing the vision, one of the sailors holds out his hand "To grasp the woman"; yet, being "but a shadow", she "slipped from" him (*Collected Poems*, p. 475). Like Aengus himself, who stretched out his hand for his dream woman to embrace her, but was unable to make her stay, the sailor is mocked when reaching out for the visionary woman he sees at sea. Yeats's symbolical use of a sea vision can be traced to the tradition of "The *Merrow*" which he writes about in *Irish Fairy and Folk Tales* (p. 65), but both the man and the woman are beautiful and have assumed the shape of the two ideal lovers. Edain and Aengus, who seem to have none of the characteristics attributed to sea fairies in *Irish Fairy and Folk Tales*.[70] They do, however, inspire a certain kind of fear, for the second sailor is afraid of "that wild Aengus", who, as his mother had told him when he was a boy, had abducted Edain

> . . . from a king's house,
> And hid her among fruits of jewel-stone
> And in a tower of glass, and from that day
> Has hated every man that's not in love,
> And has been dangerous to him.
>
> *Collected Poems*, p. 475

Yeats's version of the legend makes Aengus and Midir rivals for Edain. Aengus is pictured as a fearful love god, dangerous not only to the person he loves but also to those who are not in love. Furthermore, the sailor maintains that Forgael is caught in Aengus's net and just about to be dragged across the ocean by him. What Forgael himself pictures as a beautiful rebirth in the world beyond the sea, the sailor sees as a threat.

In choosing to make use of the saga which deals with the rivalry of the two gods Midir and Aengus—preserved in somewhat contradictory traditions—Yeats intentionally stressed the role of Aengus. In making the two

---

[70] In *Irish Fairy and Folk Tales*, p. 65, Yeats states that if the fishermen see the *Merrows*, "it always means coming gales". He also uses the phrase "male *Merrows*" adding that he never heard the masculine for *Merrow*. One wonders if, at the time, he had not read Matthew Arnold's poem "The Forsaken Merman" (based on a Danish tale). Yeats depicts the male water faries, or sea fairies, as "having green teeth, green hair, pig's eyes and red noses", whereas their women are said to be beautiful, "for all their fish tails and the little duck-like scales between their fingers". They have magic red caps "usually covered with feathers" and if robbed of them they cannot go back to the water once they have left it. Sometimes they appear as hornless cows walking about on the beach.

lovers Edain and Aengus appear in a sea vision, he grafted the old legend on to sea lore—an interesting innovation on his part. In a note to *WR* (pp. 87—88), he also relates a story which could underlie the sailor's vision in the sea:

The Tribes of the goddess Danu can take all shapes . . . A woman of Burren, in Galway, says, 'There are more of them [faeries] in the sea than on the land, and they sometimes try to come over the side of the boat in the form of fishes, for they can take their choice shape.' At other times they are beautiful women; and another Galway woman says, 'Surely those things are in the sea as well as on land. My father was out fishing one night off Tyrone.[71] And something came beside the boat that had eyes shining like candles. And then a wave came in, and a storm rose all in a minute, and whatever was in the wave, the weight of it had like to sink the boat. And then they saw that it was a woman in the sea that had the shining eyes. . . .'

Yeats must have heard many similar stories when he and Lady Gregory collected folklore in the Kiltartan district, Co. Galway. The beautiful figure of Étain and her love for Aengus fascinated Yeats excessively. His imagination was nourished by her beauty as well as by her association with the fairies and the Otherworld, by her many rebirths.[72].

Concluding Remarks

In the previous pages the relationship between traditional stories or tales and Yeats's three early plays, *CC, LHD,* and *SW,* has been traced. Only *CC* is directly based on one specific tale whereas the other two are based, partly on visions Yeats himself had, partly on a variety of tales, *LHD* being woven round one of the commonest themes in Irish folklore, the abduction of a human being into fairyland, and *SW* dramatizing a voyage to the Land of the Ever-living, a theme found in Irish *immrama* and *aislingi* (Voyages and Visions). A story recognizable in a submerged form in all three plays is *The Wooing of Étain.* Yeats himself stated that *SW* was based on visions he himself had, but these visions could of course have had their origin in folk tales and stories Yeats heard and read as a boy, or later. In 1903, he

---

[71] This somewhat surprising reference to fishing "off Tyrone" requires an explanation since the present Co. Tyrone has no coast line. The old woman consequently seems to have preserved a very old tradition which must refer to *Tír Eoghain* (the territory occupied by the *Cenél Eoghain,* the O'Neills), which about the year 1000 included not only the present Co. Tyrone but also the present Co. Derry with its coast line from Coleraine to Derry City (and in the 13th century including also Co. Armagh). I owe thanks to Dr. Terence Rafferty, Dublin, for this information explaining the phrase "off Tyrone".

[72] Étain's beauty became proverbial: " 'Every lovely form must be tested by Etain, every beauty by the standard of Etain.' " *Ancient Irish Tales,* p. 83.

declared in a dedication to Lady Gregory found in the first and second volumes *(Where There Is Nothing,* and *The Hour-Glass)* of his *Plays for an Irish Theatre:*

When I was a boy I used to wander about at Rosses Point and Ballisodare listening to old songs and stories. I wrote down what I heard and made poems out of the stories or put them into the little chapters of the first edition of 'The Celtic Twilight', and that is how I began to write in the Irish way.

VPl, p. 232

Yeats also put these songs and stories into his plays. In the plays dealt with in this study, he was not as concerned with what he called "the countenance of country-life" as when he was writing for example *Cathleen Ni Houlihan,* which he himself called "the first play of our Irish School of folk-drama" *(VPL,* p. 233). One of his early all-absorbing interests was the Otherworld and the fascination it held for certain select human beings. The greatest difference between the tales and Yeats's early plays is that the central characters, Mary in *LHD* or Forgael in *SW,* think of themselves, not as victims of the Otherworld, although others may do so, but as specially selected human beings whose destiny is the Otherworld. Countess Cathleen, who goes to Paradise, looks upon the Otherworld beings as her helpers, but she rejects their world, as she rejects Aleel's love. Mary, Forgael, and Cathleen have followed "the call of the heart, the heart seeking its own dream" *(VPl,* p. 235).

The three plays chosen for treatment in this study could be called quest dramas in which the major characters, although so different, emerge as romantic quest figures in search of an ideal world. In the next chapter our attention will be turned to the use Yeats made of popular beliefs which he found in both oral and printed sources, mostly in Irish, but also to some extent in Scottish and Welsh tradition.

Chapter II

The Function of Popular Belief in the Three Plays

The Irish-Celtic Otherworld

In his early work Yeats is constantly turning his imagination to the Otherworld,[1] and the idea of the closeness of that world to the real one fascinated him. In one of his *Celtic Twilight* stories he states: "In Ireland this world and the world we go to after death are not far apart" (*Mythologies*, p. 98). The veil between the two worlds is extremely thin, and it would seem as if there was a continuous struggle going on between the visible world and the invisible one. In Irish sagas, people can walk in and out of the two worlds, but there is not always a return to the real world for those who visit the Otherworld. Nera, in *Nera's Adventures,* goes back to his old world in order to tell his story and warn Queen Maeve of the impending invasion of her country by the fairy tribes, but he returns to his fairy bride.[2] Bran also returns to tell about the beautiful Land of the Young that he has visited, and so does Oisin, who is, however, doomed as soon as his foot touches the ground.

The Elysium of Irish saga tradition may to some extent differ from that of modern Irish folk imagination, but basically it is a land of youth and beauty, love and wisdom. It is located, sometimes all about us, sometimes in, under, or beyond the sea, in lakes or under lakes, or sometimes, as in the voyage literature, in far-off islands in the Western sea. Most often, however, it is said to be located in hills or mounds, i.e. *sidi (siodhe)*. P. W. Joyce states that "In Colgan's time [17th century] the fairy superstition had descended to the common people", and he also writes: "It was believed that these supernatural beings [the fairies] dwelt in habitations in the interior of pleasant hills, which were called by the name of *sidh* or *sith*

---

[1] Appearing not only in Celtic but also in other civilizations. See e.g. *Bran* I and *Bran* II, and Arbois de Jubainville, *The Irish Mythological Cycle,* works which refer chiefly to Celtic and Greek parallels.

[2] See *RC,* 10 (Paris, 1889), 214–227, esp. 219.

[shee]."[3] Joyce translates Father John Colgan's definition of the fairies: "Fantastical spirits are by the Irish called men of the *sidh,* because they are seen as it were to come out of beautiful hills to infest men; . . . and these habitations, and sometimes the hills themselves, are called by the Irish *sidhe* or *siodha.*"[4] The invisible people inhabiting these hills or mounds were called in Irish *aes sidhe* or *daoine sidhe,* the people of the hills or mounds, or *sluagh sidhe,* the host of the hills; a number of other appellations, such as *daoine maithe,* the Good People, are also given to the *Sidhe,* anglicized Shee, "a spirit folk", who, as Gerard Murphy states in his *Saga and Myth in Ancient Ireland,* are depicted as "living close to human beings, but normally concealed from them."[5] Eventually the name of their favourite dwelling-place came to denote the fairies themselves. Their land of youth and beauty was called by a variety of names, e.g. *Tír na nÓg,* the Land of the Young; *Tír inna mBeó,* the Land of the Living; *Tír na mBuadha,* the Land of Virtues; *Mag Mell,* the Plain of Delight; or, as Yeats calls it, "The Great Plain" (see his note on *Baile and Aillinn, VP,* p. 79); *Tír fo Thuinn,* the Country under the Waves; *Tír Tairngire,* the Land of Promise, a term certainly derived from the Old Testament, or as Yeats calls it, *The Land of Heart's Desire,* a very suitable title for this early play of his.[6] The inhabitants of the Happy Otherworld are believed to be exceedingly beautiful, ever young, and above all free from decay and death. Yeats himself refers to them as "the immortals" or "the Ever-living". In *The Voyage of Bran* their country is depicted as a land "Without grief, without sorrow, without death, / Without any sickness, without debility."[7] Whether the fairy realm be inside hills, under water, or in a far-off island of the sea, or perhaps even all about us, the world to which mortals are enticed is nearly always a happy one.

The Countess Cathleen—Three Otherworlds

Even though in his early work Yeats is preoccupied with the Irish-Celtic

[3] Joyce, *Irish Names of Places,* I, p. 179.

[4] Ibid. Father John Colgan (dead in 1658 at Louvain) was responsible for the title of the famous work *The Annals of the Four Masters.* See Douglas Hyde, *A Literary History of Ireland* (London: Fisher Unwin, 1901), pp. 576–577.

[5] *Irish Life and Culture,* 10 (Dublin: Published for The Cultural Relations Committee of Ireland by Colm O Lochlainn, 1955), p. 14.

[6] For some of these terms see e.g. "Lageniensis" (the pen name of Canon John O'Hanlon, 1821–1905), *Poetical Works* (Dublin, 1893), pp. 240n, 241n, *et passim.* See also Yeats, *Irish Fairy and Folk Tales,* pp. 214, 348.

[7] *Bran* I, pp. 6–7. Cf. also G. van Hamel, ed., *Immrama,* Mediaeval and Modern Irish Series, 10 (Dublin: Stationery Office, 1941), p. 10, stanza 10.

Otherworld, his picture of it varies. In *CC* there are actually three Otherworlds, one represented by the Irish love god Aengus, another by spirits and angels, and a third evil one by Satan and his two demons. In *LHD* the Otherworld is closely associated with fairy belief, and in *SW,* Yeats uses the idea of a world in the Western Sea, in some far-off island like Atlantis or Hy-Brasail, as the Land of the Ever-Living.

What makes the Otherworld picture of *CC* so complex, however, is the strange mixture of pagan, Christian, and Oriental elements found in the play. Aleel, in the early version Kevin, a romantic poet and visionary, considers himself to be Cathleen's specific helper. The love scene, written into Act III of the 1899 version of the play, shows Yeats's predilection for fire symbolism and dreams in his presentation of the Otherworld love god Aengus, who does not, however, appear as a character in the play. He comes to Aleel in a dream and inspires him with visionary power and Aleel's sleep changes to symbolical fire in which "Aengus of the birds" appears:

> I lay in the dusk
> Upon the grassy margin of a lake
> Among the hills, where none of mortal creatures
> But the swan comes—my sleep became a fire.
> One walked in the fire with birds about his head.

Poems, 1901, p. 53

Yeats uses the Celtic god of love and beauty, not as a kind of supernatural machinery, but rather as a symbol of love and fiery passion. However, Aleel fails in his attempt to persuade Cathleen to withdraw to the hills in order to escape the evil of the times. Cathleen's Eden, her "floor of peace" (*VPl,* pp. 167, 169), one of Yeats's poetic names for the Otherworld, is a blend of an Irish *Mag Mell,* or Plain of Delight, and the Christian Paradise. She has often heard of Aengus, the god with "birds about his head"— according to one tradition he himself had turned his own kisses to birds flying about his head.[8] To Aleel, Aengus is "angelical" but to Cathleen he is

> . . . of the old gods,
> Who wander about the world to waken the heart—

Poems, 1901, p. 55

[8] See Standish James O'Grady, *Story of Ireland* (London, 1894), p. 14. Cf. Yeats's own commentary quoted by Jeffares, *Commentary Poems,* p. 530. O'Grady mentions three kisses, Yeats four.

Cathleen is not prepared to bid a final farewell to Aleel:

> I kiss your brow,
> But will not say farewell. I am often weary,
> And I would hear the harp-string.

Poems, 1901, p. 57

Yeats expanded this scene in the 1912 version of the play by adding a few lines to Cathleen's speech, lines full of vague allusions to myths and tales:

> I kiss your forehead.
> And yet I send you from me. Do not speak;
> There have been women that bid men to rob
> Crowns from the Country-under-Wave or apples
> Upon a dragon-guarded hill, and all
> That they might sift men's hearts and wills,
> And trembled as they did it, as I tremble
> That lay a hard task on you, that you go,
> And silently, and do not turn your head;
> Goodbye; but do not turn your head and look;
> Above all else I would not have you look.
> *(Aleel goes)*

Poems, 1912, p. 60

By alluding in a somewhat loose way to myths and tales of miraculous tasks, Yeats created a mood of mystery. At the end of her speech Cathleen refers to Aleel's leaving her as "a hard task". She does not ask him to "rob crowns" in a land under the sea or in underground wells—a possible allusion to Nera's adventures in the Otherworld where he saw a "blinded man" carrying a "lamed man" to a well. Their task was to keep watch over a wonderful golden crown.[9] There is also in Cathleen's spech an allusion to the Greek mythological tale telling the story of how the Earth Goddess Ge gave apples to Hera when she married Zeus. These apples were guarded by the Dragon Ladon and nymphs called the Hesperides, a myth that has spread to many folk tales.[10] In hinting at miraculous tasks demanded of men by women, Cathleen compares Aleel's having to leave her to a severe task which, to be successful, must be done "silently" and without his turning

---

[9] In his play *The Cat and the Moon* (1917) Yeats uses another form of the tradition, according to which a blind man and a lame man visit the well in order to be cured. The play was first printed in the *Criterion* in 1924 (see Wade, pp. 145−146). Cf. *Ancient Irish Tales*, pp. 248−253.

[10] Yeats may also have read "Legendary Lore: The Story of Conn-Eda or, the Golden Apples of Loch Erne", in *The Cambrian Journal*, Part VI, June 1855 (London; Tenby, 1855), 101−115. In a year Conn-Eda, son of King Conn and Queen Eda, has to find a black steed, a hound of supernatural power, and three golden apples. A druid and a bird help him to achieve this.

to look back at her. It could be that in this way Yeats wanted to associate the harper and poet Aleel, not only with the Old Testament story about Lot and his wife, but also especially with the Greek poet and lyre player Orpheus, who lost Eurydice for ever to the realm of Hades by turning to look back at his beloved wife at the moment when they had almost reached earth again. It is, however, not clear whether it is for his own sake or for Cathleen's that Aleel is asked not to look back. Perhaps Cathleen's injunction on Aleel to go "silently" and without turning his head is meant as a magical prescription for Aleel, the frustrated lover. In folklore certain cures are believed to be more powerful if done in silence or while not looking back, etc. After her farewell speech to Aleel, Cathleen retreats to her chapel to pray, and this is the time that the Demon-Merchants choose to rob her treasury.

The demons are representatives of Hell, and in a fight for Cathleen's soul they clash with angels in the air. There is a certain similarity between this struggle and "a battle over the dying" mentioned by Yeats in one of his notes to *WR,* "a battle the Sidhe are said to fight when a person is being taken away by them", one of the three battles of the Sidhe, the other two being "a battle they are said to fight in November for the harvest" and the battle between "the Tribes of the goddess Danu . . . with the Fomor at Moy Tura, or the Towery Plain" (p. 100). In the same note Yeats also records that he has "heard of the battle over the dying both in County Galway and in the Isles of Arann . . ." (p. 100).[11] In *CC,* just as in many Irish tales, a magic storm rises up suddenly, and the storm carries Cathleen's soul heavenwards, or as Yeats puts it, takes it to "the floor of peace", or "the floors of peace", the latter form being used in the 1892 version of the play (*VPl,* pp. 167, 169). In the first version Yeats uses the idea of stormy weather spoken of by the peasants in Sc. V to forebode Kathleen's impending death. Dawn is breaking, and Neal, an old peasant, says:

> I sleep alone in the room under this.
> Last night was cold and windy, I had stuffed
> My muffler underneath the door, and pushed
> My great cloak up the chimney, yet the wind
> Sang through the keyhole.

VPl, p. 154

---

[11] Cf. Joyce, *Irish Names of Places,* I, p. 173, refers to *The Battle of Ventry (Cath Finntrágha),* a Fenian tale which may have contributed to the popular belief in the battles of the fairies. See e.g. Myles Dillon, *Early Irish Literature* (1948), p. 42.

The other peasant has heard a noise and a screech of owls:

> I'm coming to the noise. I lay awake
> Thinking I should catch cold and surely die,
> And wondering if I could close up the keyhole
> With an old piece of cloth shaped like a tongue
> That hangs over a tear here in my coat,
> When right above there came a screech of birds,
> A sound of voices and a noise of blows,
> It surely came from here, and yet all's empty.
>
> *VPl*, p. 156

The noise of the wind and the screeching of the owls symbolize the evil world of the demons, who earlier in the play have themselves appeared as grey owls. Yeats knew that he was using a well-known popular belief, one found for example in Shakespeare's *Macbeth* and used by many Romantic writers, for example Poe and Coleridge. But he stresses in a highly significant way the interdependence of wind and bird. In the first version of his play Yeats also manages to convey a realistic picture of the situation in the room where the peasants have been sleeping. We learn from their talk that they have been trying to keep the draft and the whistling wind out with their worn clothes, their only means of protection against the inclement weather. They are frightened, not only because of the noise of the storm and the screech of the owls, but also because they can see no sign of any birds.

In the 1895 and later versions, the "black storm" arouses an even greater fear in them and one of them says:

> And while we bore her hither cloudy gusts
> Blackened the world and shook us on our feet.
> Draw the great bolt, for no man has beheld
> So black, bitter, blinding, and sudden a storm.
>
> *VPl*, p. 159

Cathleen herself asks them to hold her, "for the storm / Is dragging me away", she exclaims.[12] Aleel fears that the bitter storm might drag her to Hell instead of to Heaven, as is apparent from his vision of Hell, beginning while the storm is raging.[13] Cathleen, however, sees the storm as a deliverer, a means of bringing her in touch with the unseen world, and "the

---

[12] *VPl*, pp. 159, 161.

[13] Cf. William Wilde in *Irish Popular Superstitions* (Dublin, 1852; rpt. IUP, 1972; rpt. Dublin: Irish Academic Press, 1979), p. 121, records that people would say about a man dying suddenly: "isn't it well known he got a *blast?*" Hereafter *Irish Popular Superstitions*.

dancers of the woods". Her farewell speech to Oona and Aleel, which begins

> Bend down your faces, Oona and Aleel;
> I gaze upon them as the swallow gazes
> Upon the nest under the eave, before
> She wander the loud waters[14]

VPl, p. 163

ends with her dying words:

> The storm is in my hair and I must go.

VPl, p. 163

The lonely swallow's flight across "the loud waters", an image of beauty and isolation, and of man's loneliness when confronted with death, symbolizes Cathleen and her last voyage, but it is also a foreshadowing of the heavenly grace awaiting her. Aleel, however, does not willingly accept Cathleen's death, and in a fit of violent despair he smashes the looking-glass which Oona puts in front of the dead Cathleen's mouth. Cathleen's words "The storm is in my hair and I must go", indicate that at the moment of her death she does not fear the sudden wild storm, the whirlwind, for it brings her helpers, the fairy host, or the "dancers of the woods", the hidden people of the raths and forts (*VPl*, p. 163). Yeats, and not only the early Yeats, attributed supernatural events to the wind, particularly a blast of wind rising up suddenly. In Irish popular belief the whirlwind is still often associated with fairy troops, but also with demons of the air, and in *CC* Yeats used this double notion very effectively to bring out a double point of view. A quotation from Yeats's own notes relating to his poem "The Hosting of the Sidhe" shows that he believed the Sidhe (or Shee) to mean not only fairies but also wind:

The powerful and wealthy called the gods of ancient Ireland the Tuatha De Danaan, or the Tribes of the goddess Danu, but the poor called them, and still sometimes call them, the Sidhe, from Aes Sidhe or Sluagh Sidhe, the people of the Faery Hills, as these words are usually explained. Sidhe is also Gaelic for wind,[15] and certainly

---

[14] In earlier versions these lines were italicized. James Joyce actually quotes these lines in *A Portrait of the Artist as a Young Man*. Text, Criticism and Notes, ed. Chester G. Anderson (New York: Viking Press, 1964; rpt. 1968), p. 225. Joyce uses Cathleen's farewell lines to symbolize Stephen's impending exile. See the present writer's "Allusions to Yeats in *Stephen Hero* and *A Portrait of the Artist as a Young Man*", *Nordic Rejoycings 1982* (James Joyce Society of Sweden and Finland, 1982), pp. 9–25, esp. p. 18.

[15] Yeats here declares that *sidhe* also means "wind". There is an Old Ir. word *side, sithe,* later *sith,* meaning a blast or gust of wind. P. S. Dinneen in *Foclóir Gaedhilge agus Béarla* (Dublin: Irish Texts Society, 1927; rpt. 1947), p. 1014, records the word *séideán* with the

54

the Sidhe have much to do with the wind. They journey in whirling winds, the winds that were called the dance of the daughters of Herodias in the Middle Ages . . . When the country people see the leaves whirling on the road they bless themselves, because they believe the Sidhe to be passing by.

WR, pp. 65–66

"Lageniensis" records a similar tradition:

It is believed, that the Fairies move from one rath to another, when those eddying winds converge, and which raise spiral columns of dust, straws, or decaying vegetable matter. Such appearances are denominated *Shee-geehy* or "Fairy blasts" by the peasantry; and, to propitiate the invisible elves, it is customary to exclaim, "God speed ye, gentlemen!" . . . it is always deemed prudent to avoid the direct course, in which the *Slua-shee* or "Fairy host" advances.[16]

Yeats in a note to his poem "The Host of the Air" stresses the dual character of the wind and also suggests that the idea of the host of the air, the air demons, being evil "came in with Christianity":

Some writers distinguish between the Sluagh Gaoith, the host of the air, and Sluagh Sidhe, the host of the Sidhe, and describe the host of the air as of a peculiar malignancy. Dr. Joyce says, 'of all the different kinds of goblins . . . air demons were most dreaded by the people. They lived among clouds, and mists, and rocks, and hated the human race with the utmost malignity.' A very old Arann charm, which contains the words 'Send God, by his strength, between us and the host of the Sidhe, between us and the host of the air', seems also to distinguish among them. I am inclined, however, to think that the distinction came in with Christianity and its belief about the prince of the air, for the host of the Sidhe, as I have already explained, are closely associated with the wind.

WR, pp. 78–79

This statement could be compared to Dr. Wilde's in *Irish Popular Superstitions* (pp. 120–126) where also, as in Yeats, two different traditions are recorded. Yeats, moreover, does not only record two distinct traditions, but he often makes subtle use of both in his poems and plays. His early notes often throw light on the origin of his folklore material and show that sometimes he took it from printed sources, sometimes straight from oral tradition and very often compared and linked the two in his own work. In *CC* he makes one character represent one tradition, and another character a different one, thus managing to voice two distinct points of view, on one hand the fear felt by the peasants and Aleel, at the sudden

---

meaning "blast", "whirlwind", "fairy wind", etc., and p. 1027, *sidhe gaoithe*, "a sudden blast of wind, a whirlwind". In *Irish Names of Places*, I, p. 181, Joyce writes: "It is doubtful whether the word [*sidhe, siodha*] is cognate with the Lat. *sedes*, or from a Celtic root, *side*, a blast of wind."

[16] *Poetical Works*, p. 151, n. 3.

black and bitter storm in which evil powers might spirit Cathleen away to
their realm, and on the other the confidence felt by Cathleen that invisible
dancers are her helpers, who at the moment of death remind her of the time
when she

> . . . was but a child and therefore happy,
> Therefore happy, even like those that dance.
> The storm is in my hair and I must go. [*She dies.*]
>
> VPl, p. 163

This is the final version, however. It may be of some interest to see how
Yeats deals with the death scene in the first version of the play. In Sc IV
the Countess can be seen signing the document and telling the peasants to
take the money and come with her:

> Take up the money, and now come with me.
> When we are far from this polluted place
> I will give each one of you what he needs.
>
> *VPl*, p. 150

These are her last words. In the following scene (Sc. V) she is, as the stage
directions inform us, dead: "*A row of spirits carrying the lifeless body of
the Countess Kathleen descend slowly from the oratory*" (*VPl*, pp. 160,
162). The Spirits sing a song ending with the words, "*And her guides are
angels seven,/ While young stars about her dance*",[17] and appear to Oona
in a vision which makes her anticipate her own death. They also reveal to
Oona that they are angelic spirits, and that they have saved her mistress
from the demon-owls who "Came sweeping hither, murmuring against
God" (*VPl*, p. 166). The seven spirits carry the soul of the Countess to
"The floors of peace" while another seven are taking care of her body.[18]
One of them says that people must look for their Countess in the flying
dawn:

> And when men gaze upon the flying dawn,
> We bid them dream of her.
>
> *VPl*, p. 166

The flying dawn here may be said to symbolize Cathleen's new immaterial
world as well as man's dreams and his delight in natural beauty, and the

[17] *VPl*, p. 164. Cf. poem "The Countess Cathleen in Paradise", *Collected Poems*, p. 48, and
VP, pp. 124–125.

[18] The motif of the soul being carried to heaven by spirits or angels is of course a religious
one, but not as common in early Irish literature as it may be in folklore. T. P. Cross's *Motif-
Index of Early Irish Literature* (Bloomington Indiana: Indiana Univ. Publications, 1952),
enumerates only about nine instances (No. E 754.2.2).

lines also contribute to the general tone of romantic melancholy pervading the play. It might be added that the Spirits here serve as a kind of supernatural machinery which Yeats found troublesome on the stage and, indeed, he removed from the play in later versions.

In Scene III of the first version there is a clear indication that the storm is in fact associated with sinister powers, for when Kathleen is speaking to the Merchants and asks them if they have heard about the soul-selling demons, one of them answers her:

> There are some men who hold they have
> wolves' heads,
> And say their limbs, dried by the infinite flame,
> Have all the speed of storms; . . .

VPl, p. 106

Yeats here associates the storm, or rather its speed, with the wolf. It should also be pointed out that in some of the early versions, some rather sinister spirits appear, such as "sowlths" and "thivishes". They are referred to as "mere shapes of the storm" blown there by "unnatural gusts of icecold air", or said to be "one with all the beings of decay", "vague forms" representing "Ill longings, madness, lightning, famine and drouth". The stage directions also describe them as follows: "[*The darkness fills with vague forms, some animal shapes, some human, some mere nebulous lights.*][19] The sowlths and tevishes or thivishes based on popular belief about lost souls are conjured up by the Merchants in an abortive attempt to capture Cathleen's soul. These hellish beings are defined by the Merchants as "lost souls of men, who died/ In drunken sleep, and by each other's hands. . . ./" and as beings "Who mourn among the scenery of [their] sins/ Turning to animal and reptile forms. . . ." (*VPl*, p. 105 under line). As they come, even the grass and leaves are frightened, and "A crying as of storm-distempered reeds" (p. 107, under line) is heard. All of them, except two recently dead peasants' souls, are too weak to help the Merchants carry the bags of gold, and even these two do this unwillingly, for they know that the Countess "Has endless pity even for lost souls"; their recollection of her beautiful face brings great misery to them and their hearts are burnt by "heaven's many-angled star reversed", and so turned into a "sign of evil" (p. 107, under line). Getting no real help from these poor lost souls, the Merchants bid them disappear. In the first version

---

[19] *VPl*, p. 107, under line. In a note Yeats explains "sowlth" as "A formless, luminous apparition . . ." or "A. . . phantom for which Father O'Hanlon was, I think my authority" (*VPl*, p. 1287). "Thivish" is in fact an anglicized form of Ir. *taidhbhse*, "appearance", "ghost".

another popular belief associated with the fairies is made use of. One of the young peasants tells Oona that he has seen Kevin in the wood listening to the hammering of the fairies:

> Sometimes he laid his head upon the ground.
> They say he hears the sheogues down below
> Nailing four boards.

VPl, pp. 156, 158

In other words he has heard the fairy joiner making a coffin, another omen foretelling the death of the Countess. Oona retorts that love has made Kevin crazy, "And loneliness and famine dwell with him" (*VPl*, p. 158).

The introduction of these different kinds of sinister spirits weighs the early versions down, but shows how deeply involved Yeats was at that time with popular belief of a darker kind than the ordinary happy fairies. On the whole it might be said that, in spite of its religious message, *The Countess Cathleen* is a rather sinister play. Yet it is a fascinating one which like a magic flower reveals its beauty in manyfold ways.

In 1913, all sinister spirits were removed. In an early review of *The Countess Kathleen and Various Legends and Lyrics* in the *Illustrated London News,* 10 September 1892, the poet Sir William Watson (1858–1935) criticized Yeats rather severely (*Yeats:* CH, pp. 76–77) because of his having had recourse in his play to

all manner of supernatural and elemental agencies, spirits and fairies, and what not, together with *sowlths* and *tevishes*. . . . There are also a great many *sheogues,* and we do not feel in the least called upon to know what a *sheogue* is like—. . . How many legs has it?[20] . . . The fact is—to drop into seriousness for a moment, with many apologies—the supernatural in poetry has no excuse for itself except where, as in 'The Ancient Mariner', for instance, it bites its way into the reader's consciousness and compels imaginative belief by the sheer despotism of imperious genius. All Mr. Yeats's grotesque machinery of sowlths and tevishes and sheogues, leaves us without a shudder; his fantasies are stage-properties of the most unillusive kind.

William Watson, then, finds Yeats's symbolism of this kind rather crude and also dislikes the idea of merchants appearing as demons. It is possible that Yeats took account of some of this criticism when revising the play. However, in the *Saturday Review* for 6 May 1899, Arthur Symons enthusiastically pointed out how good an acting play *CC* was (see *Yeats:* CH, p. 8). Symons, like Katharine Tynan before him, realized "that Yeats was

---

[20] Dr. Wilde records that Darby Doolin, an old Connaughtman stated that e.g. "the *sheogue* and the *thivish* are every year becoming scarcer" (*Irish Popular Superstitions,* p. 14). Cf. also *Bran* II, pp. 211–215.

making a significant contribution to poetic drama" (ibid., p. 8). The well-known editor and poet Ernest Percival Rhys (1859–1946) wrote of the 1895 version that Yeats had "cast the story in dramatic form; and although one may not feel altogether certain of its technical qualities as an acting play, it reads dramatically, as well as being imaginative and profound to a degree" (ibid., p. 94). Rhys, somewhat surprisingly, quotes the opening scene in Shemus Rua's kitchen as an excellent example of the charm of the play. The contemporary reviews throw interesting light on the different versions of the play and its stage history.

The Land of Heart's Desire—A Fairy Otherworld

That *LHD* deals with the fairy realm is obvious. It may undoubtedly be said that in this play, Yeats comes very close to Irish folk imagination. Mary, the newly-married bride both dreads and longs for the Otherworld, whose siren voices she is unable to withstand. As in *CC* the wind symbolizes the fairy world and its inhabitants, and in the wind and its sounds Mary hears the voice of the fairies, or the Shee, who live in the Land of the Young. In her loneliness, she is constantly thinking and talking of the fairies, and especially Bridget, her mother-in-law, and also her husband Shawn represent a point of view different to hers. They think of the fairies with dread and are sure that they are evil spirits as the priest claims. Bridget warns Mary:

> You know well
> How calling the Good People by that name,
> Or talking of them over-much at all,
> May bring all kinds of evil on the house.

VPl, pp. 191–192

Mary, however, leaves this warning unheeded and appeals directly to the fairies:

> Come, faeries, take me out of this dull house!
> Let me have all the freedom I have lost;
> Work when I will and idle when I will!
> Faeries, come take me out of this dull world,
> For I would ride with you upon the wind,
> (Run on the top of the dishevelled tide,)
> And dance upon the mountains like a flame.

VPl, p. 192

Mary has a passionate longing to be free as the wind, to be one with the fairy host, to be a dancing flame. However, both Mary and her mother-in-law believe in the fairies, but the elderly woman is full of superstitious fear.

According to her, Mary is bringing ill luck on herself and her family whereas Mary herself is above all striving to achieve greater freedom. She considers the world of the fairies to be free from dullness and bitterness. The antagonism between her and Bridget, who is always nagging at her to do her work, is largely responsible for Mary's desperate reaction, and for her denial of her home:

> What do I care if I have given this house,
> Where I must hear all day a bitter tongue,
> Into the power of the faeries!

VPl, p. 191

That a fundamental social problem is pointed to in this play is obvious: the situation arising when a young newly-married couple moves into the same house as the old farmer and his wife. In making Bridget blame Mary for calling "the Good People" fairies and talking of them too much, Yeats relied on a firmly established belief among Irish countrypeople that for fear of annoying the fairies one should either avoid speaking of them altogether or refer to them in terms like "the Good People", "the Gentry", or simply "they" or "them". The very same idea is recorded by Yeats in *Irish Fairy and Folk Tales* (p. 1):

Beings so quickly offended that you must not speak much about them at all, and never call them anything but the "gentry," or else *daoine maithe,* which in English means good people, yet so easily pleased, they will do their best to keep misfortune away from you, if you leave a little milk for them on the window-sill over night.

Yeats also registers various theories about the origin of the fairies. Are they "fallen angels", as the Irish peasant believes;[21] are they "gods of the earth", as stated in *The Book of Armagh,* or are they "the pagan gods of Ireland", as stated by the antiquarian? In Dr. William Wilde's *Irish Popular Superstitions,* particularly his "Fairy Archeology" (Ch. IV) are found the very same ideas, some of which Yeats developed in his play and in his *Irish Fairy and Folk Tales.* Wilde writes (p. 125):

It would be a difficult task to reduce to precise terms all the popular ideas on Irish pantheology, and as they can only be gleaned and sifted from the tale, the rite, or legend, they are best expressed by the same means. The general belief, however, is, that the "good people" or the "wee folk", as they are termed in Ulster, are fallen angels, and that their present habitations in the air, in the water, on dry land, or under ground, were determined by the position which they took up when first cast from heaven's battlements. These are almost the very words used by the

---

[21] Cf. Reidar Th. Christiansen, "Some Notes of the Fairies and the Fairy Faith", *Béaloideas,* 39–41, 1971–1973 (1975), 95–111, esp. 96–97.

peasantry when you can get one of them to discourse upon this forbidden subject. They believe that God will admit the fairies into his palace on the day of judgment, and were it not for this that they would strike or enchant men and cattle much more frequently. They sometimes annoy the departed souls of men who are "putting their pains of purgatory *over them*" on the earth. The idea of their being *fallen angels,* came in with Christianity. In the "Book of Armagh" they are called *"the gods of the earth"*; and in the "Book of Lismore" they are described as the spirits or rather the immortal bodies and souls of the Tuatha De Dananns.

Wilde continues (p. 125): "The popular impression is, that the great majority of them are old, ugly, and decrepit, but have a power of taking on many forms, and that they generally assume a very diminutive size." This contradicts the probably older notion that they are ever young and beautiful and often of the same size as human beings. Wilde adds, "It is also believed that they can at will personify or take on the shape of men or animals when they reveal themselves to human beings."

Yeats records not only all the explanations of the origin of the Irish fairies given by Wilde, but also adds (*Irish Fairy and Folk Tales,* pp. 1—2):

Many poets, and all mystic and occult writers, in all ages and countries, have declared that behind the visible are chains on chains of conscious beings, who are not of heaven but of the earth, who have no inherent form but change according to their whim, or the mind that sees them. . . . In dreams we go among them, and play with them, and combat with them. They are, perhaps human souls in the crucible— these creatures of whim.

The suggestion that the fairies are "perhaps human souls in the crucible" seems to foreshadow Yeats's later belief in the "plastic power of the soul", a concept which he adopted from the Cambridge Neo-Platonist Henry More (1614—1687)[22] and later integrated into his own philosophy of life in *A Vision.* The "chains on chains of conscious beings" which Yeats speaks of are found symbolically woven into the texture of both *LHD* and *SW.* Mary's soul is in contact with this invisible world of fairies or spirits, whose song strikes a familiar note in her soul. There seems to her to be but a short step between her world and that of the fairies. Nevertheless she is frightened to hear the voice persistently singing in the wind, and, in a vain attempt to escape the powers she herself has summoned, she appeals pathetically to her husband Shawn:

> O, cling close to me,
> Because I have said wicked things to-night.
>
> *VPl,* p. 194

[22] See the present writer's *The Interpretation of the Cuchulain Legend in the Works of W. B. Yeats* (Uppsala: Almqvist & Wiksell, 1950), p. 149.

Her melancholy cry comes too late, however. She is already beyond human help. Not only has she denied her home in favour of fairyland, she has given gifts to the "unappeasable host" on May Eve,[23] that is milk to a Faery Child (in the early version "a woman cloaked in green") and a sod of turf from the fire to "a little queer old man", a forerunner sent by the Faery Child, who finally entices her away. Her own actions have attracted the invisible beings, the unseen powers, and her mother-in-law scolds her:

> You've given milk and fire
> Upon the unluckiest night of the year and brought,
> For all you know, evil upon the house.

VPl, p. 191

Here Yeats puts a strongly established superstitious belief into his play, and it is typical that it is Bridget, the elderly woman, who expresses this popular belief, which Dr. Wilde (p. 55) recorded in this way:

On no account would either fire or water—but, above all things, a coal of fire, even the kindling of a pipe—be given [to fairies], for love or money, out of a house during the entire of May Day. The piece of lighted turf used to kindle another fire is styled the *seed* of the fire; and this people endeavoured to procure from the bonfire of the previous night, and to keep it alive in the ashes to light the fire on May morning; but a large fire should not be "made down" early on May morning, as it is believed that witches and fairies, whom they desire to propitiate, have great horror to the first smoke.

The danger associated with "giving away" fire or anything at all on May Day is also stressed in another passage (p. 56):

Not only is it considered unlucky to permit fire to be removed from the house until after the meridian at least, but many people would not give away, even in charity, a drop of milk, or a bit of bread or butter, on May Day, or lend churn, churndash . . .

As Wilde says further, anyone asking for such things would be taken "for a witch" (p. 56). One might easily understand that these and many other superstitions governed the life of the peasantry very strongly and made them take precautions against the invisible powers. In Yeats's play Bridget is the person most strongly influenced by the beliefs of generations of country people. When referring to May Eve as "the unluckiest night of the year", she could, however, be said to be exaggerating, for in Ireland, in oral as well as in literary tradition, November Eve or Hallow E'en is considered to be the most dangerous of all nights, for then the door of Faeryland swings open (as for example in *Nera's Adventures*), and, as

---

[23] Cf. Yeats's poem "The Unappeasable Host", *Collected Poems,* p. 65.

recorded by Yeats (*Irish Fairy and Folk Tales,* p. 2), it is then that the fairies

are at their gloomiest, for, according to the old Gaelic reckoning, this is the first night of winter. This night they dance with the ghosts, and the *pooka* is abroad, and witches make their spells, and girls set a table with food in the name of the devil, that the fetch of their future lover may come through the window and eat of the food.

To Mary, who is newly married, May Eve, is, however, charged with singular danger. There are certain precautions which can be taken in order to protect oneself from the influence of fairies and sprites, and in these precautions lie what may be said to be the greatest difference between the early and the final versions of *LHD,* i.e. the use made by Yeats in the early version of primroses, in the final one of the quicken or rowan bough. Both were used in Ireland as a kind of magic protection against the power of the fairies, but in Yeats's play they have the opposite effect of attracting the fairies.

The stage directions of the early version include *"a great bowl of primroses on the sill of the window"* (*VPl,* p. 181, under line). In this first primrose scene, Maurteen Bruin is anxious that his daughter-in-law should throw primroses outside the door for good luck:

> Maire, have you the primroses to fling
> Before the door to make a golden path
> For them to bring good luck into the house.
> Remember they may steal new-married brides
> Upon May Eve.
>
> *VPl,* pp. 185–186, under line

Maurteen clearly believes that a newly-married bride may protect herself from being kidnapped by the fairies by strewing primroses before the entrance to the house. It is quite likely that Yeats picked up this idea when collecting folklore in the West of Ireland, and again he could have found support for it in Wilde's *Irish Popular Superstitions* (p. 61). Although primroses are not mentioned, white and yellow flowers, especially the marsh-marigolds *(Caltha Palustris),* are said to be favoured:

The custom which has remained longest and most perfect amongst us is the floral decoration of the doors and windows, chiefly with May flowers, then found in full blow in deep meadows and moist places. This gay plant, the marsh-marigold (Ca[l]tha Palustris), called in Irish the shrub of Beltine, *Bearnan Bealtaine,* or the *Lus-ubrich Bealtaine,* always forms the chief ornament of the garlands and other floral decorations, and is generally strewn plentifully before the doors and on the threshold; but when such can be procured, wild flowers, white or yellow (butter or milk colour), and those that grow in meadows and pastures, are ever preferred to garden flowers, to place in the cottage windows, scatter round the doors, or adorn the May bush and May pole.

The strewing of primroses before the door in Yeats's play also consolidates the idea that the fairies are closely associated with the wind, for as soon as Maire strews the primroses outside, they are blown away by what Maurteen takes for a puff of wind, but which Maire looks upon as the invisible beings, the fairy host. She actually sees a child dressed in green and with hair "of red gold" (*VPl*, p. 187, under line) taking the primroses up and playing with them. Maurteen Bruin unexpectedly declares that on May Eve the Good People have power to "work all their will with primroses", and

> Change them to golden money, or little flames
> To burn up those who do them any wrong.
>
> *VPl*, p. 186, under line

As in other passages in the play Yeats uses fire symbolism. The Faery Child symbolizing nature has the power to change her tokens, the primroses, into flames. As soon as she touches them, they become enchanted, almost sacred, like Nature herself. However, Maire, who is herself of the element of fire, is not burned by the magic flames into which the primroses are transformed. On the contrary she herself becomes one of the flames. The Faery Child casts an enchantment on everybody in the house. All except Shawn give her gifts, thus falling under her power. In the second primrose scene which follows after the giving of gifts and the removal of the crucifix by the priest, the following stage directions are given:

[They all except Maire Bruin gather about the priest for protection. Maire Bruin stays on the settle as if in a trance (. . .) of terror. The Child takes primroses from the great bowl and begins to strew them between herself and the priest and about Maire Bruin. During the following dialogue Shawn Bruin goes more than once to the brink of the primroses, but shrinks back to the others timidly.]

> *VPl*, pp. 203–204, under line

Instead of acting as a protection, the primroses turn into a means by which the Faery Child can exercise her power over Maire. While strewing the primroses, the Faery Child, whose power now exceeds the Priest's, says:

> No one whose heart is heavy with human tears,
> Can cross these little cressets of the wood.
>
> *VPl*, p. 204, under line

These words are charged with incantatory force, and the Faery Child's strewing the floor with primroses may perhaps be compared to the strewing of primroses on graves, a custom upheld at one time both in England

and Ireland, as pointed out by Hilderic Friend.[24] The strewing of primroses around Maire is an act by which the Faery Child singles out Maire, the flame-like, newly-married bride for another existence. The phrase "newly-married bride" repeated several times by the Faery, takes on a new dimension of meaning:

You shall go with me, newly-married bride

VPl, p. 205

and   Stay and come with me, newly-married bride

VPl, p. 205

and   But I can lead you, newly-married bride

VPl, p. 206

The primroses, changed to flames by Maire's kisses, point the way to her new life in the Otherworld. Her love for Shawn, for his face and voice, is sinking away. To use Yeats's own words in *The Tables of the Law and The Adoration of the Magi*, she is "trembling between the excitement of the spirit and the excitement of the flesh".[25] All except Maire shrink back when trying to draw close to the magic flames which symbolize the supernatural dancers. However, Maire is of the same element and joins the flames. Her words "Then take my soul" are like the last prayer of a dying person and imply that she is indeed dying. Maire is in fact about to join the supernatural dancers she herself has invited to the house. She leaves Shawn and his world: cleansed by fire, she is free from "the heavy body of clay" and lets "clinging mortal hope" fall (*VPl*, p. 207, under line). She is on the point of gazing "upon a merrier multitude", the land of such Celtic deities as "White-armed Nuala, Aengus of the Birds,/ Fiachra of the hurtling foam", and such fairy rulers as "the ruler of the Western Host,/ Finvara" and "Ardroe the Wise" (*VPl*, p. 205), the latter "a Ballyshannon faery ruler", (as Yeats stated in a note, *VPl*, p. 1285), not retained in the later version.

The threefold combination of flower-fire-dance is a significant pattern in the early version of *LHD*. The primrose symbol—discarded and never again used by Yeats—is undoubtedly akin to his "Alchemical Rose", a mystical flower also associated with supernatural fire and supernatural dancing as for example in *The Tables of the Law*, in which the spirits of the Order of the Alchemical Rose appear as "faint figures robed in purple,[26]

---

[24] *Flowers and Flower Lore*, 2 vol. (London, 1883), II, p. 573.

[25] (London: Elkin Mathews, 1905),p. 12.

[26] According to Cabbalistic belief, purple is a protective colour assumed by spirits visiting the lower regions. See, e.g. Denis Saurat, *Victor Hugo et les dieux du peuple* (Paris, n.d. [1948]), p. 264.

and lifting faint torches with arms that gleamed like silver'' (pp. 35–36). Owen Aherne, like Maire in *LHD* is drawn, as if by an unseen power, to the supernatural dancers, immortal torch-bearing figures embodying ''divine ecstasy'' and ''divine intellect'', two concepts used by Yeats in *The Tables of the Law and the Adoration of the Magi* (pp. 34–35).[27]

In later versions of *LHD* we find Yeats discarding not only the primrose symbol but also that of the climbing red nasturtium, a plant to which Maire compares herself, at the same time as speaking of her husband as ''the great door-post of the house'' (*VPl*, p. 192, under line). Yeats here seems to allude symbolically to the Victorian idea of the subservient woman clinging to her protective husband. He must have found both the primrose and the nasturtium unsuitable symbols to use about a woman who does not really correspond to the picture of a woman as a weak and clinging person. Instead Yeats introduced another image more forceful and also perhaps closer to the living tradition of Ireland. In the early version of *CC* he had already used a superstitious belief about the quicken bough. Shemus Rua is warned by his wife not to ''burn the blessed quicken wood'' (*VPl*, p. 20), for it was considered very unlucky to burn the wood of certain trees, e.g. the quicken tree. In his wish to throw it on the fire, Shemus Rua has, moreover, deprived the bough of its protective power and his calling out to the evil powers to come into the cottage—the sin of despair—lays his house open to the powers of evil. Maire/Mary commits a similar mortal sin in *LHD,* in whose later version the quicken bough figures in as prominent a role as the primroses in the earlier.

Yeats drew on an ancient popular belief still alive in his own time (and even today) that certain bushes, trees and plants were thought of as lucky or unlucky. The quicken (i.e. the mountain-ash or rowan tree), the hazel, and the hawthorn are those most often associated with fairy belief. ''The Fairy Palace of the Quicken Tree'', one of the romances of the Fenian cycle of tales, shows how deeply rooted is the belief in the mystic virtues of the quicken tree.[28] In *The Celtic Twilight* there are several references to hawthorn bushes underneath which souls are forced to do penance, and it is a wide-spread popular belief that the fairies dance underneath a lonely hawtorn tree. Quicken wood is thought to be a powerful protection against demons and evil fairies. Note also that in *The Dominion of Dreams* Fiona

---

[27] See also Robert O'Driscoll, ed. ''The Tables of the Law'', *Yeats Studies: an international journal,* 1, ed. R. O'Driscoll and L. Reynolds (Shannon Ireland: IUP; Toronto UP, 1971), 88–118.

[28] See e.g. P. W. Joyce, *Old Celtic Romances* (Dublin 1871; rpt. Dublin: Talbot Press, 1961), pp. 123–153; hereafter *Old Celtic Romances*.

MacLeod states that "The quicken (rowan, mountain-ash and other names) is a sacred tree with the Celtic peoples, and its branches can either avert or compel supernatural influences."[29] Wilde records a similar belief in *Irish Popular Superstitions* (p. 58): "But the great means of averting the threatened danger resides in the employment of the mountain-ash, or rowan-tree (the *cran-keeran*) . . ." Many more examples of this old custom could be afforded, and it is well known that magic power was ascribed to the quicken bough not only in Ireland and Scotland and other Celtic districts but also in Germany, Scandinavia, and elsewhere.[30] The custom of hanging branches of quicken wood on the door-post on May Eve and at other festivals so as to keep evil spirits out was apparently still observed in various parts of Ireland when Yeats was growing up.[31] Maurteen, Mary's father-in-law, who is not as critical as his wife, refers to the protective power of the quicken bough in the following passage:

> And maybe it is natural upon May Eve
> To dream of the Good People. But tell me, girl,
> If you've the branch of blessed quicken wood
> That women hang upon the post of the door
> That they may send good luck into the house?
> Remember they may steal new-married brides
> After the fall of twilight on May Eve,
> Or what old women mutter at the fire
> Is but a pack of lies.

VPl, pp. 185–186

Yeats here makes women the tradition bearers, whereas in the early version, when using primroses as a magic protection against evil powers, he does not explicitly refer to any tradition bearers. Otherwise this scene is similar to the corresponding primrose scene, for the quicken bough is snatched away by the Faery Child, as were the primroses in the earlier version (although the quicken bough is not transformed into magic flames). The stage direction for the scene concerned reads:

---

[29] *The Dominion of Dreams* and *Under the Dark Star* (London: Heinemann, 1895; first publ. in the Uniform Ed. in 1910), p. 94 n 2; hereafter *Dreams*.

[30] See Hilderic Friend, *Flowers and Flower-Lore*, 2 vol. (London, 1883), I, pp. 243–263. Cf. also Peter Alderson Smith, " 'Grown to Heaven Like a Tree': The Scenery of *The Countess Cathleen*", in *Éire: Ireland* (Fall 1979) (St. Paul, Minnesota: IACI, 1979), 65–82, esp. 76.

[31] In *Irish Popular Superstitions*, p. 40, Wilde refers to a work by W. G. Stewart, *The Popular Superstitions and Festive Amusements of the Higlanders of Scotland* (1823), which gives an account of how crosses of "the blessed rowan-tree are" . . . "inserted in the different door-lintels in the town . . ." as a protection against witches. Wilde also records (p. 69) that "Rods of mountain-ash are placed, at May Eve, in the four corners of the cornfields, which are also sprinkled with Easter holy water."

[Mary Brown has taken a bough of quicken wood from a seat and hung it on a nail in the door-post. A girl child strangely dressed, perhaps in faery green, comes out of the wood and takes it away.

VPl, p. 186

Mary knows that the disappearance of the quicken bough is caused by the activity of the fairies:

> They have taken away the blessed quicken wood,
> They will not bring good luck into the house;

VPl, p. 187

The taking away of the quicken bough fatally affects Mary's relationship with her husband. Later in the play when she is frightened because she has called out to the fairies to come into the house, she identifies herself with "the branch of blessed quicken wood" and her husband with "the great door-post":

> O, you are the great door-post of this house,
> And I the branch of blessed quicken wood,
> And if I could I'd hang upon the post
> Till I had brought good luck into the house.

VPl, pp. 192–193

This is a crucial passage in which Mary acknowledges her utter powerlessness. Her words also depict the unsatisfactory relationship between husband and wife, which is disturbed by the relationship between Mary and the elemental powers. As pointed out by Peter Hühn in *Das Verhältnis von Mann und Frau im Werk von William Butler Yeats* (although he has not dealt with *The Land of Heart's Desire*), there is in Yeats's work a conflict between the ideal image which man creates of woman and the real image she presents to him.[32] In other words if a woman does not correspond to this ideal picture, a complete union between the two will prove impossible except in another dimension of time (or beyond time and space, as is the case for example in *SW* where the lovers are ideally united in the land of sunset, that is in death).

It might be said that Mary is torn between the call of the elemental powers and her duty to her husband, whom she really loves, but not strongly enough to resist the call of the alien powers invading the house. Moreover, the daily nagging of her mother-in-law has also turned her mind towards the Otherworld. Yeats used magic and folk belief in this depiction of the relationship between Mary and her husband, and the result is a tantalizing drama going on in the heart and mind of a young woman unable

---

[32] See Hühn, pp. 84–130.

to live up to her husband's expectations. He may be the door-post of the house, but she is no climbing flower, no nasturtium that clings to him. Instead she is a quicken bough hanging on a nail in the door-post. The image of the quicken bough serves a double purpose, as a magic branch hung up to avert evil spirits and as a metaphor for a young woman. Yet, the blessed quicken bough cannot help Mary against the elemental beings she herself has called into the house. Instead, it attracts them and is snatched away by them, for Mary herself has summoned the unseen powers. Therefore Mary is unable to hold on to her husband and feels that she herself will be taken away. In her relationship with her husband Mary seems to be a mere ornament hanging on the door-post ready for the elemental powers to take away, and when she hears the voice of the Faery Child in the wind, nothing can detain her. On May Eve she is drawn to the world of her dreams, to her heart's desire. Her joining the immortal dancers is a symbolical way of depicting her death. Whereas her husband is a tragic figure, Mary can hardly be said to be such, for the Otherworld is a place of many delights, whereas her home is a place of drudgery and misery. Undoubtedly Yeats used popular belief very effectively in order to heighten the conflict between the visible world and the invisible one. The Faery Child symbolizes the ideal world of love and beauty. Since Mary's husband has no part in such a world, he and Mary are drawn apart never to be reunited.

In summing up what has been said about *LHD* in the previous pages, it may be stressed that in the play the Otherworld seems to be all around Maire/Mary, who hears the alluring voice in the wind. When finally drawn away from this world to the other, she dies, and her soul is conveyed to the fairy realm in the shape of a white bird, about which more will be said later in this chapter. It will, however, be seen that the picture of the Otherworld emerging from *SW* is quite a different one.

The Shadowy Waters—An Otherworld Vision in the Western Sea

As the title of *SW* implies, we are taken to dark waters, and the happy land which Forgael is in search of, is to be found in the west, the land of the sunset. The Otherworld is definitely placed at sea, and the voyage undertaken by Forgael is a quest for this land and the immortal love to be enjoyed there. As already mentioned, one of the sources of the play is undoubtedly "Hy-Brasail—the Isle of the Blest", a poem by Gerald Griffin included in *Irish Fairy and Folk Tales* (pp. 226—227).[33] This is the island

[33] Cf. Introduction to the present work.

which sailors and others have seen at a distance, yet anyone trying to reach it has failed. In Gerald Griffin's poem we learn that "A peasant who heard of the wonderful tale" set out from the isle of Ara in search of Hy-Brasail. He never returned to Ara but "died on the waters, away, far away!" as the poem ends. This peasant started looking for an Eden he had heard about in a tale, whereas Forgael had seen his Otherworld in a dream. Giraldus Cambrensis also records a story about an isle which appears enticingly on the horizon: "Among the other islands is one newly formed, which they call the Phantom Isle . . . When, however, they came so near to it that they thought they should go on shore, the island sank in the water and entirely vanished from sight." It was only when they fired "an arrow, barbed with red-hot steel, against the island" that they could land on it. This story entitled "The Phantom Isle", included in *Irish Fairy and Folk Tales* (p. 228), is told as an example of "the many proofs that fire is the greatest of enemies to every sort of phantom."

In a description of the Land of the Young in *Irish Fairy and Folk Tales,* Yeats records various beliefs about this imaginary country and also refers to "the bard, Oisen, who wandered away on a white horse, moving on the surface of the foam with his fairy Niamh, lived there three hundred years, and then returned looking for his comrades. . . . He described his sojourn in the Land of Youth to Patrick before he died" (p. 214). The vision of distant shadowy waters is an important symbol for immortal love and beauty in *The Wanderings of Oisin* as well as in *SW*. Like Oisin, Forgael is a voyager, but instead of travelling on a white fairy horse he travels on a magic ship. The natural elements, the sea and the storm, are important symbols and, as in *CC* and *LHD,* stormy weather plays a highly significant role. Dectora's ship, blown by the wind towards Forgael's, emerges from a mist—just as the mighty Túatha Dé Danann, who were expert magicians, were believed to have come to Ireland "in clouds of mist".[34] The attention of the sailors is drawn to the strange ship because of its sweet smell of spices:

First Sailor. Look there! there in the mist! A ship of spices!
Second We would not have noticed her but for
Sailor. the sweet smell through the air. Ambergris and
sandalwood, and all the herbs the witches bring
from the sunrise.
First Sailor. No; but opoponax and cinnamon.

VPl, p. 323

---

[34] See *Ancient Irish Tales,* p. 28.

Forgael is convinced that the strange ship has been blown by magic storms from the Otherworld, bringing an Otherworld woman to him, for, referring to his dream, he exclaims:

> The Ever-living have
> kept my bargain; they have paid you on the nail.
>
> *VPl*, p. 323

There is also in this play clear evidence of the association of the storm with the Ever-living. When Forgael asks Dectora why she, who should be immortal, casts a shadow, she answers, referring to her husband:

> Would that the storm that overthrew my ships,
> And drowned the treasures of nine conquered nations,
> And blew me hither to my lasting sorrow,
> Had drowned me also. But, being yet alive,
> I ask a fitting punishment for all
> That raised their hand against him.
>
> *VPl*, p. 326

A little later when she proudly declares that, being a queen, she can leave Forgael at her will, Forgael answers her with confidence:

> . . .
> But if I were to put you on that ship,
> With sailors that were sworn to do your will,
> And you had spread a sail for home, a wind
> Would rise of a sudden, or a wave so huge
> It had washed among the stars and put them out,
> And beat the bulwark of your ship on mine,
> Until you stood before me on the deck—
> As now.
>
> *VPl*, p. 327

The magic of the whirlwind is stressed. The combination of a strong sense of doom and the rising of a sudden strong wind that would blow Dectora, should she try to escape, on a high wave back to Forgael seems to her such an impossible suggestion that she questions Forgael's sanity:

> Has wandering in these desolate seas
> And listening to the cry of wind and wave
> Driven you mad?
>
> *VPl*, p. 327

Forgael assures her that he is not insane, but that both he and she are "taken in the net" of the Ever-living:

> It was their hands that plucked the winds awake
> And blew you hither; and their mouths have
>   promised

71

I shall have love in their immortal fashion.

VPl, pp. 327–328

The Otherworld vision is concerned primarily with love, desire and hope for immortality. Forgael sees the wind as the performer of the will of the Ever-living. Let us turn again to a note in *WR* (p. 86), in which Yeats declares that in his poem "The Cradle Song" he uses the wind

as a symbol of vague desires and hopes, not merely because the Sidhe are in the wind, or because the wind bloweth as it listeth, but because wind and spirit and vague desire have been associated everywhere. A highland scholar tells me that his country people use the wind in their talk and in their proverbs as I use it in my poem.

In *SW* there is a similar symbolic use of the combination of wind, spirit, desire and hope, but "the vague desires and hopes" are changed into a strong desire to experience love in "immortal fashion". The wind and the huge wave are thought of as being sent by the Ever-living to whose world Forgael's ship is drifting.[35] Dectora is as magically bound to the supernatural powers of the elements as Forgael himself, although at first she fails to realize this. She will be drawn to Forgael's watery realm without the chance of ever going back.

In this play, as in *CC* and *LHD,* Yeats depicts the visible world as being in constant conflict with the invisible or ideal world to which certain selected people, sometimes men, sometimes women, are fatally drawn. This is an important feature of the relationship between men and women in the plays, for the ideal world often disturbs an ordinary human relationship. In *CC* the unhappy love of the poet Kevin/Aleel for the Countess forms a subplot and a minor motif—Cathleen, however, obeys the call of her soul. Her death separates her from the poet, who is driven almost crazy by his love for her. In *LHD,* Maire/Mary and her husband are likewise separated by forces outside their control. In both plays the major female character dies a death which is a tragedy for the people around them, but not for themselves. Particularly the man who loves can be looked upon as a tragic figure. In this respect *SW* marks a new departure, for in this play, Forgael, the lover in quest of immortal love, is endowed with magic power and can determine his fate according to his own wish although he says he is

---

[35] Probably Yeats has *Tonn Cliodhna,* Cliodhna's Wave, in mind. See e.g. *Gods and Fighting Men,* Ch. XII; Cliodhna, daughter of Manannan's chief druid, was killed by a huge wave the day before she was to have gone away with Ciabhán, the King of Ulster's son. The wave was called after her and the beach where she was swept away called *Tonn Cliodhna.* This is one of the stories told in the *Dinnshenchas* ("History of Places").

caught in the nets of the gods: he has a ship and a magic harp—the harp of Aengus which has the same qualities as the harp of the Dagda, and with it he can influence the woman he loves. His harp plays the three strains of sorrow, laughter and sleep,[36] and it has also once belonged to the White Fool, the Fairy Fool, a figure who can turn foam into birds (*VP*, p. 761).

In a letter to AE dated August 27 [1899] Yeats states that he "may be getting the whole story of the relation of man and woman in symbol—all that makes the subject of *The Shadowy Waters*". He is anxious for Russell to "call up the white fool", and to "make a sketch of him, for Dalua seems to be becoming important among us. Aengus is the most curious of all the gods. . . . He has some part perhaps in all enthusiasm. I think his white fool is going to give me a couple of lines in *The Shadowy Waters*."[37]

The White Fool or Fairy Fool mentioned in this letter haunted Yeats's imagination for many years, and he associated him with the Otherworld and particularly with the love god Aengus. Insanity plays a great part in Yeats's early poems and plays. In his long poem "Baile and Aillinn" (1902), the love god appears as a wild, strange-looking man, very like a madman. "Baile and Aillinn" is based on a tale of two lovers, whose marriage was prevented by a wild, strange-looking man who told Baile the false story that Aillinn had died "of the heart-break" because the men of Leinster had prevented her from going to her tryst with Baile at Dundealgan. At this news Baile died of sorrow on Baile's Strand. When the same supernatural being told Aillinn that Baile was dead, she died in the same way, and from her grave grew an apple-tree and from Baile's a yew-tree, and, according to one version, the tops of these trees joined. Yeats states that he chiefly followed Lady Gregory's version of the story as told in *Cuchulain of Muirthemne* (pp. 305–306), but he had probably also read it elsewhere.[38] In any case he deviated from Lady Gregory's version, for in it

---

[36] Notice that Fiona Macleod, in an essay preceding the poems included in the collection *Foam of the Past*—dedicated to Yeats and publ. between 1896–1910, rpt 1910, 1923, some of them written as early as 1893—states that in the story *Táin Bó Fráich (The Spoil of the Cows of Froech)*, the hero has three harpers, "Tear-bringer, Smile-bringer, and Sleep-bringer", and that their names derive from *Uaithne*, the self-playing harp of the Dagda. Forgael, combining these three moods, is almost like an Otherworld god himself. For various editions of *Táin Bó Fráich*, see Best I, p. 97.

[37] Wade, *Letters*, p. 324.

[38] E.g. "Scél Baili Binnbérlaig" ("The Story of Baile Sweet-Spoken"), ed. and trans. Eugene O'Curry, in *RC*, 13 (1892), 220–225. When the two lovers die, they live on as trees (growing from their graves) for seven years; Aillinn's apple-tree has a top resembling her head, and Baile's yew-tree a top resembling his head. At the end of seven years they are cut down and turned into two tablets telling their story. The two tablets finally join and twine together and are kept like precious jewels for a long time.

the wild, strange-looking man appears in his own right, without revealing that, in spite of his comic and tramplike appearance, he is the love god Aengus, something that shows in his eyes:

> They found an old man running there:
> He had ragged long grass-coloured hair;
> He had knees that stuck out of his hose;
> He had puddle-water in his shoes;
> He had half a cloak to keep him dry,
> Although he had a squirrel's eye.

VP, p. 190

With his predilection for swans, Yeats in this poem depicts the two faithful lovers as transformed into two swans linked by a gold chain, a detail which in Celtic sagas indicates that they are human beings transformed into birds. Aengus then appears to the swan lovers in his own shape. He is playing on his harp which has harp-strings woven by Edain, the god Midhir's wife, out of Aengus's long hair. Edain was passionately in love with Aengus, and Midhir lost his wife not only to King Eochaidh but also to the love god, although he won her back in due time. When Aengus assumed his own shape, the swan lovers recognized him:

> They knew him: his changed body was
> Tall, proud and ruddy, and light wings
> Were hovering over the harp-strings
> That Edain, Midhir's wife, had wove
> In the hid place, being crazed by love.

VP, p. 195

The Fool of Aengus, who in "Baile and Aillinn" turns up in the shape of a wild, strange-looking man, in early versions of *SW* appears as the White Fool of the Wood, who is, however, a messenger of Aengus, not a personification as in "Baile and Aillinn". Wade in *Letters* (p. 324n) points out specifically that the first published version of *SW* introduces "the fool of the wood" (another phrase for the White Fool) in the very first lines where we learn that Kevin's

> face has never gladdened since he came
> Out of that island where the fool of the wood
> Played on his harp.

VP, p. 747

These lines are spoken by the Helmsman, a character removed in later versions. Wade also refers to an essay "The Queen and the Fool" included in *The Celtic Twilight* (1902). According to Wade, Yeats had AE in mind when writing his story about "a truly great seer, who saw a white fool in a

74

visionary garden.''[39] This is certainly so, but there is also another source for this important symbol. In the letter to AE just quoted, Yeats mentions "Dalua", a figure used with great force and variety by Fiona MacLeod (William Sharp, 1855−1905) in his work. The opening story of *The Dominion of Dreams* entitled "Dalua" relates for example how Dan Macara became insane after being touched by "the Amadan-Dhu, the Dark Witless one, or Fairy Fool", or Dalua, as Fiona MacLeod calls him.[40] The story ends:

> He was ever witless, and loved wandering among the hills. No child feared him. He had a lost love in his face. At night, on the sighing moors, or on the glen-road, his eyes were like stars in a pool, but with a light more tender.
>
> *Dreams*, p. 11

In another story entitled "The Birds of Emar" (*Dreams*, pp. 217−234), Dalua, who loves Emar, manages to separate the two lovers Emar and Manànn (i.e. Manannan) by turning Emar into a white flower and himself "into the green stalk with grey silky petals which enclosed and upheld her" (*Dreams*, p. 231). Like the strange-looking man in Yeats's poem, the White Fool here separates two lovers from one another. Manànn's son Ailill was, however, able to throw a spell on Dalua, which broke the enchantment inflicted on Emar. This story explains how Dalua, when forced by Ailill to follow the White Hound to "the edge of the world", became insane and how the White Hound that he pursued also got "the touch of Dalua" and died, for that touch "gives madness or death" (*Dreams*, p. 234).

Another story "The Amadan" (included in *Under the Dark Star*) relates how Alasdair the Proud, cursed by the evil music of Gloom Achanna, became insane but was cured by a saintly man, Allan Dall (Blind Allan). After that Alasdair no longer hears the mad laughter of Dalua.[41]

In his two-act play *The Immortal Hour*, first published in the *Fortnightly Review*, Fiona MacLeod also makes Dalua play the role of an invisible shadow laughing and whispering, unseen but heard by the lovers and finally appearing as Death to King Eochaidh after his loss of Etain to the god Midhir. In a note preceding *The Immortal Hour* there is an interesting passage giving MacLeod's own view on Dalua:

> Of Dalua I can say but a word here. He is the Amadan-Dhu, or Dark Fool, the Faery Fool, whose touch is madness or death for any mortal: whose falling shadow even causes bewilderment and forgetfulness. The Fool is at once an elder and

---

[39] Quoted by Wade, *Letters*, p. 324n. Also *Mythologies*, p. 115.

[40] *Dreams*, pp. 3−11. The story begins with a poem "I have heard you calling, Dalua, Dalua!"

[41] Ibid., pp. 414−424.

dreadful god, a mysterious and potent spirit, avoided even of the proud immortal folk themselves: and an abstraction, "the shadow of pale hopes, forgotten dreams, and madness of men's minds." He is, too, to my imagining, madness incorporate as a living force. In several of my writings this dark presence intervenes as a shadow . . . sometimes without being named, or as an elemental force, as in the evil music of Gloom Achanna in the tale called "The Dan-nan-Ron," sometimes as a spirit of evil, as in "Dalua," the opening tale in *The Dominion of Dreams*.[42]

Undoubtedly Yeats and MacLeod must have learned a good deal from one another, as letters and review articles show.[43] Yeats was certainly impressed by MacLeod's Dalua, or the Dark Fool, based on Scottish, especially Hebridean, folk belief. Yeats changes Dalua from a Dark Fool into a White Fool of the Wood, the Fairy Fool of Irish folk belief. White is a colour often associated with fairies and spirits in Ireland and elsewhere, and those who were taken by the fairies but returned were said to be "touched", that is insane.[44] Both MacLeod's Dark Fool, who had become insane while following a White Hound,[45] and Yeats's White Fool produce insanity in mortals. MacLeod and Yeats were both interested in similar symbols which they found in Celtic folklore and they both felt attracted to one another's work.[46]

In *SW* the harp remained a symbol of primary importance throughout all the revisions,[47] and the hound image also for many years remained a

---

[42] *Poems and Dramas* (Uniform ed. 1910; London: Heinemann, 1923), pp. 312–313. See "Bibliographical Note" by Elizabeth A. Sharp, pp. 447–449.

[43] Yeats had written about Fiona MacLeod in "Le Mouvement Celtique", an article published in *L'Irlande Libre* (April 1898). A review article by Fiona MacLeod, "The Later Poetry of Mr. W. B. Yeats", dealing with *SW* and *WR,* appeared in the *North American Review* (July–December [October] 1902); cf. *Yeats:* CH, pp. 117–123.

[44] See Yeats's story "The Queen and the Fool", *The Celtic Twilight,* in *Mythologies,* pp. 112–116, which tells a story concerning the "*Amadán-na Breena,* a fool of the forth" (p. 112), or "the white fool" (p. 115). Douglas Hyde in *Legends of Saints and Sinners* (London, Dublin, Belfast, n.d.) also mentions the dangerous "amadán na bruidhne" . . . "the 'fool of the palace' ", p. xi. Hyde explains the word *amadán* used in this context as "a folk perversion or a diminutive of *amait*" used "in the sense of witch", male or female (pp. x–xi).

[45] See p. 79 below.

[46] In a letter to Yeats dated "Midlothian, Scotland, 2 June, 1898", Fiona MacLeod writes: "As you know, there is no living writer with whom I find myself so absolutely in rapport as with you." He praises both *SW* and *WR,* and also reveals his interest in Yeats's folklore articles. See Richard J. Finneran, George Mills Harper and William M. Murphy, ed., *Letters to W. B. Yeats,* 2 vol. (London: Macmillan, 1977), I, pp. 38–39. Yeats, on his part, wrote to MacLeod in January 1897 from Paris (not knowing that Fiona MacLeod was William Sharp's pen name) that "Mr. Sharp heard some of it [*SW*] in London in its first very monotonous form" (Wade, *Letters,* p. 280).

[47] In *The Wanderings of Oisin,* Oisin played on a silver harp and sang songs "of human joy" which made the people of the Otherworld weep; one boy even threw the harp "down in a leaf-hid, hollow place" (*VP,* p. 17).

symbol of great importance, as is shown by numerous MSS versions as well as the early printed versions. Since in the 1896–99 MSS of *SW* Yeats introduced not only the hound but also three more of the symbols he had already used repeatedly in *The Wanderings of Oisin,* that is "a hornless deer" (pursued by "a phantom hound/All pearly white save one red ear") and two figures on horses following rapidly in their steps, a beautiful young man in pursuit of a young maiden with a golden apple in her hand, we shall now have a look at Yeats's perennial use of these symbols. The hound and the deer are not isolated animal images in Yeats's work, as we also meet e.g. the boar, the horse, and of course birds of various kinds, particularly eagles, owls and swans, and imaginary animals like the unicorn and the centaur, as well as dog-headed and eagle-headed monsters. Often Yeats alludes to the use such symbols have in Celtic saga and mythology. As Anne Ross states, "the stag, the bull, the horse, the ram, boar, dog and serpent play, in conjunction with birds, an impressive part in the religious symbolism of the Celtic world."[48] All these, and of course the wise salmon from whom Finn, according to tradition derived his wisdom, turn up in the Fenian tales and ballads, but of all the supernatural animals associated with Finn, two especially are of importance here, the hound (with red ears) and the hornless deer. And these two images as well as the young man on a white horse pursuing a young woman with a golden apple in her hand haunted Yeats not only in the eighties when he was writing *The Wanderings of Oisin* but also in the 90s when he was rewriting this long poem, and was also at work on *SW*. Transformations of human beings into animals are all-important in the Fenian tales. Tuirenn, Finn's maternal aunt, was transformed into a hound by a jealous fairy druid. While in this shape, she gave birth to Bran and Sceólan, who, although their mother was given back her human shape in the end, had to remain in their hound shape for ever, and were Finn's favourites. Lomair was one of their three whelps, in other words Bran and Sceólan were Finn's "hound-cousins", and Lomair his "hound-nephew". One of Finn's wives was the beautiful fairy woman Saeve (Sadhbh or Saba), whom a druid of the Fairy People had transformed into a fawn, and who escaped being killed by Finn on one of his hunting-expeditions, thanks to her beautiful eyes. In the night-time she came as a ravishing woman to him and told him that since she had been able to reach his dún without being killed, she had been allowed to resume

---

[48] *Pagan Celtic Britain* (London: Routledge & Kegan Paul, 1967), p. 351.

her human shape. Finn and she were married, but one day when Finn had gone out to fight the Lochlanners, the Druid came and transformed Saeve into a fawn a second time. After seven years Finn found a naked boy under a tree. This was his son by Saeve and he called him Oisín, which means "little deer".

When Yeats turned to the story of "Ossian in the Land of Youth" he sometimes in his own poem followed his original very closely, as is shown by two passages taken from *The Wanderings of Oisin* and two from a prose tale included in *Old Celtic Romances*. Yeats writes:

> . . .
> We galloped; now a hornless deer
> Passed by us, chased by a phantom hound
> All pearly white, save one red ear;
> And now a lady rode like the wind
> With an apple of gold in her tossing hand;
> And a beautiful young man followed behind
> With quenchless gaze and fluttering hair.
>
> *VP,* pp. 11–12

> Now, man of croziers, shadows called our names
> And then away, away, like whirling flames;
> And now fled by, mist-covered, without sound,
> The youth and lady and the deer and hound;
> 'Gaze no more on the phantoms', Niamh said,
> And kissed my eyes . . .
>
> *VP, p. 29*

The prose tale runs as follows (pp. 262, 264):

A hornless fawn once crossed our course, bounding nimbly along from the crest of one wave to the crest of another; and close after, in full chase, a white hound with red ears. We saw also a lovely young maiden on a brown steed, with a golden apple in her hand; and as she passed swiftly by, a young warrior on a white steed plunged after her, wearing a long, flowing mantle of yellow silk, and holding a gold-hilted sword in his hand.

I knew naught of these things, and, marvelling much, I asked the princess what they meant.

"Heed not what you see here, Oisin," she said, for all these wonders are as nothing compared with what you shall see in Tír na nÓg."

As in Yeats's poem the passage is repeated in a shorter form a little further on in the narrative:

We saw again the fawn chased by the white hound with red ears; and the maiden with the golden apple passed swiftly by, followed by the young warrior in yellow silk on his white steed.

Consequently it is obvious that Yeats did not invent the combination of the four images he used so effectively, the white hound with a red ear, [49] a hornless deer, a young woman with a golden apple in her hand pursued by a young man on a swift-riding horse, although he changed the details and also invested his symbols with meanings other than those found in the source. He also used the same device of repetition as in his original. We need be in no doubt about his source, for as is well known he himself stated that *The Wanderings of Oisin* "is founded upon the Middle Irish dialogues of Saint Patrick (. . .) and Oisin and a certain Gaelic poem of the last century . . ." (*VP*, p. 793).[50] In fact, as is the case with the Étain story, he used many versions also of Oisin's visit to the Otherworld, not only the long poem *Acallamh na Senórach (The Colloquy of the Old Men)*[51] and the lay of "Oisin in Tír na nÓg" but also as has been shown above the prose translation of the tale. The manner in which Yeats introduced his symbols is allusive and moreover leaves no doubt but that the white hound with one red ear is a spectral hound chasing another spectre, a hornless deer. What marks them out as magic or supernatural animals is the special characteristic which distinguishes them from ordinary animals of their species; the hound's red ear shows that he is from the Otherworld and since antlers are the most characteristic feature of most kinds of deer, the lack of horns or antlers implies that the pursued deer is also an Otherworld creature. They are in their turn pursued by other phantoms, a young man "With quenchless gaze and fluttering hair" in pursuit of a young woman with a golden apple in her hand, like an Otherworld poet in wild pursuit of his muse. The "fluttering hair" may perhaps allude to the floating hair of the poet in Coleridge's "Kubla Khan". The speed with which they fly past Oisin and Niamh certainly emphasizes their symbolic meaning and, as the editors of *Druid Craft* stress (pp. 143—144), they could be "shadows of desire",[52] but they also seem to be warnings sent to Ossian by other Fenians who had

[49] Cf. MacLeod's "white hound" mentioned above. In *The King of the Great Clock Tower* (1934—35) the symbols hound, stag and a wild man in pursuit of a woman clasping an apple occur in an allusive and realistic manner.

[50] "Laoidh Oisín ar Thír na nÓg", "The Lay of Oisin on Tír na nÓg", ed. with trans. and notes by Bryan O'Looney, *Transactions of the Ossianic Society,* 4 (Dublin, 1859); Michael Comyn, "Tír na nÓg, The Land of Youth, an Ossianic Poem", metrically translated by a member of the Ossianic Society (Dublin, Tralee, 1863).

[51] *Ancient Irish Tales,* pp. 457—468. The trans. used by the editors is Standish Hayes O'Grady's in *Silva Gadelica,* 2 vol. (London, 1892), II, pp. 101—265; 557—565. See also Whitley Stokes, ed., *Acallamh na Senórach* in *Irische Texte,* vierte Serie, 1 Heft (Leipzig, 1900); contains trans. of parts omitted in *Silva Gadelica,* ed. S. H. O'Grady.

[52] In this they follow Yeats's own interpretation given in a note to a poem entitled "Mongan Laments the Change That has Come Upon Him and His Beloved," first printed in *The Dome,* June 1897, under the title "The Desire of Man and of Woman" (see note, *WR*, pp. 92—93).

already been lured away to the Otherworld, for Niamh does not want Oisin to pay any heed to these passing figures. The first time she says, 'Vex them no longer' (*VP*, p. 12), and the second time she warns Oisin not to gaze any more "on the phantoms" (*VP*, p. 29). Yeats also made a revealing statement in a long note in *WR* (pp. 91–92) showing the author's wish to produce a certain single effect of mysterious otherwordliness:

My deer and hound are properly related to the deer and hound that flicker in and out of the various tellings of the Arthurian legends, leading different knights upon adventures, and to the hounds and to the hornless deer at the beginning of, I think, all tellings of Oisin's journey to the country of the young. The hound is certainly related to the Hounds of Annwvyn or of Hades, who are white, and have red ears, and were heard, and are, perhaps, still heard by Welsh peasants following some flying thing in the night winds; and is probably related to the hounds that Irish country people believe will awake and seize the souls of the dead if you lament them too loudly or too soon, and to the hound the son of Setanta [Cuchulain] killed,on what was certainly, in the first form of the tale, a visit to the Celtic Hades. An old woman told a friend and myself that she saw what she thought were white birds, flying over an enchanted place, but found, when she got near, that they had dog's heads; and I do not doubt that my hound and these dog-headed birds are of the same family.

These symbols were not just of fleeting interest to Yeats, for he returned to them again and again although they certainly were not always invested with the same meaning. Several years after he wrote *The Wanderings of Oisin,* he returned to the animal images used in this poem and in *SW*. In his Introduction to *The Resurrection* (1927) he wrote about these images in a way that reveals that the Oisin legend seems to have helped him for some time to rid his imagination of images of public disaster and ruin in which he had taken satisfaction:

I took satisfaction in certain public disasters, felt a sort of ecstasy at the contemplation of ruin, and then I came upon the story of Oisin in Tir-nan-Oge and reshaped it into my *Wanderings of Oisin*. He rides across the sea with a spirit, he passes phantoms, a boy following a girl, a hound chasing a hare,[53] emblematical of eternal pursuit, he comes to an island of choral dancing, leaves that after many years, passes the phantoms once again, comes to an island of endless battle for an object never achieved, leaves that after many years, passes the phantoms once again, comes to an island of sleep, leaves that and comes to Ireland, to S. Patrick and old age. .... I remember rejecting, because it spoilt the simplicity, an elaborate metaphor of a breaking wave intended to prove that all life rose and fell as in my poem.
. . .   *VPl,* p. 932

It is apparent that in the manuscripts of *SW* the hound is a much more

---

[53] Yeats's memory failed him when he wrote "hare" instead of "hound".

sinister image than in *The Wanderings of Oisin*—hell hounds are chasing
the soul of Forgael, in fact the hounds accompany the "Seabars" to whom
Forgael, who practises druidic rites, is forced to make human sacrifices.
Yeats turned the "Seabhra" or "Seabar"—a kind of fairy—into a horribly
bloodthirsty, eagle-headed monster whose phantom companions are
hounds of hell deriving perhaps more from Welsh than from Irish popular
beliefs. In *Irish Fairy Tales* (1892) there is, however, a story, P.W. Joyce's
"Fergus O'Mara and the Air-Demons" (pp. 112–122), which relates how
demon hounds led Fergus O'Mara astray during a hunt and kept him away
from mass and out in the open a whole night when a terrible thunderstorm
was raging. "A great black ragged cloud. . . . full of frightful faces" (p.
119) came towards him, but a child of his who had died some time before
came "floating in the air between him and the demons" (p. 119) and helped
him to escape the demons and finally reach home.

However, in John Rhŷs's *Celtic Folklore: Welsh and Manx*, 2 vol. (1901)
there is a story (recorded by Owen Edwards) which might well have been
Yeats's source of inspiration. It was first published in *Cymru* for 1897 and
is quoted by Rhŷs (I, pp. 215–216):

'Ages ago as a man who had been engaged on business, not the most creditable in
the world, was returning in the depth of night across Cefn Creini, and thinking in a
downcast frame of mind over what he had been doing, he heard in the distance a
low and fear-inspiring bark; then another bark, and another, and then half a dozen
and more. Ere long he became aware that he was being pursued by dogs, and that
they were *Cwn Annwn*. He beheld them coming: he tried to flee, but he felt quite
powerless and could not escape. Nearer and nearer they came, and he saw the
shepherd with them: his face was black and he had horns on his head. They had
come round him and stood in a semicircle ready to rush upon him, when he had a
remarkable deliverance: he remembered that he had in his pocket a small cross,
which he showed them. They fled in the greatest terror in all directions . . .'

Rhŷs adds, "It would be right probably to identify them [*Cwn Annwn*] in
the first instance with the pack with which Arawn, king of Annwn, is found
hunting by Pwyll, king of Dyfed, when the latter happens to meet him in
Glyn Cuch in his own realm" (Ibid., p. 216). In other words, the hounds
found in *Pwyll Pendeuic Dyuet* (one of the stories in the *Mabinogion*) are
the ancestors of hounds turning up in later Welsh folk stories. Also in the
Black Book of Carmarthen, another Welsh literary source, there are what
could be called spectral hounds (belonging to a Welsh folklore figure,
Gwyn ap Nudd, a king of the Otherworld in the *Mabinogion*) "led by
Dormarth, a hound with a red snout". In later stories such as the one by
Owen Edwards, the devil is the leader or huntsman of the hell hounds,
whose barking is believed to forebode death and who chase through the air

for the souls of the departed, particularly those who have led a sinful and wicked life (see Rhŷs, I, p. 216).[54]

The first time a sinister hound appears in *SW* is in MS HLIII where there are several beginnings, one in which Forgael, after lighting "the holy lamp", drinking "the druid wine" and eating "the druid apple", fails to experience his former kind of "ecstasy" "& visions of delight", but is weighed down by "omens of the darkness" (*Druid Craft*, p. 124):

> hound with one red ear pursued & [=a] pearl
> white doe over the waves. A youth
> with pale face & bright eyes pursued
> a maide[n] who bore an apple of
> gold. The[y] rode upon horses that
> were swifter than the wind . . .

Druid Craft, p. 125

Or to quote another passage with the same images:

> . . .
> And power to break down gods deamons & men
> A pearl pale hound with one red ear pursued
> A whimpering doe . . .
>
> . . .
> And a youth followed at a headlong speed
> . . .
> A maid who held an apple in her right hand
> . . .

Druid Craft, pp. 127−128[55]

In the version of *SW* which Yeats sent to Leonard Smithers for publication late in 1896, the four images of hound, deer, young man and young woman,[56] symbolize both desire and doom, in other words combine the themes of passion and eternal pursuit leading to death.

However, one need hardly be surprised that Lady Gregory did not know what to make of the early MSS versions of *SW,* in which appear not only

---

[54] Cf. Richard Hunt, *Popular Romances of the West of England* (London, 1896), records two stories about "Wish hounds" or spectral hounds being omens of death (pp. 145−146), and another story about "The Devil and his Dandy-Dogs" (pp. 223−224), which concern the Cornish correspondence to *Cwn Annwyn*. One might also recall that Milton in *Paradise Lost* uses "Hell-hounds" (Bk. II)—perhaps thinking of Cerberus. The belief that Satan can appear as a black dog is a common one in the folklore of many countries.

[55] Cf. also *Druid Craft*, pp. 129, 130, 164, 174. In NLH, an almost complete draft of *SW*, a new element enters into the hound image, the whip (see p. 186). The idea of disobedient hounds and an idle whip was also introduced in NLK, a typed pre-1899 version of the play (*Druid Craft*, p. 215).

[56] Introduced also in the 1899 MS version of the play (*Druid Craft*, p. 215).

the lascivious Orchil and the evil-eyed Balor (as in *CC*) but also the frightening death god Tethra and his eagle-headed, long-taloned Fomors and Seabars. George Moore thoroughly disliked the Fomors and Seabars and persuaded Yeats to drop them. George Russell's recommendations also had a salutory effect on the play (see *Druid Craft*, pp. 268–271). But the hounds were retained both in a version of 1899 in which for the first time the stage directions describe three rows of hounds depicted on the sail (*Druid Craft*, p. 281), and in the first printed version (1900), in whose stage directions Forgael, sleeping on skins still strikes one as a pirate-magician rather than a mysterious seeker:

The deck of a galley. The steering-oar, which comes through the bulwark, is to the left hand. One looks along the deck toward the high forecastle, which is partly hidden by a great square sail. The sail is drawn in toward the stern at the left side, and is high enough above the deck at the right side to show a little of the deck beyond and of the forecastle. Three rows of hounds, the first dark, the second red, and the third white with red ears, make a conventional pattern upon the sail. The sea is hidden in mist, and there is no light except where the moon makes a brightness in the mist.

Forgael *is sleeping upon skins a few yards forward of the steering-oar. He has a silver lily embroidered over his breast. A small harp lies beside him.* Aibric *and two sailors stand about the steering-oar. One of the sailors is steering.*[57]

VP, pp. 746–747

The red hound appearing in the text may perhaps be said to have some kinship with the spectral hell hounds found in the MSS versions, but as a symbol he is not very well integrated with the new mysterious message of the play. The Helmsman states somewhat surprisingly at the beginning that "The red hound/ Was Forgael's courage that the music killed" (*VP*, p. 747), and one of the sailors asks how long it was since "something that was bearded like a goat/ Walked on the waters and bid Forgael seek/ His heart's desire where the world dwindles out" (*VP*, p. 747). Dectora also refers to the red hound:

The red hound is fled.
Why did you say that I have followed him
For these nine years? O arrow upon arrow!
My eyes are troubled by the silver arrows;
Ah, they have pierced his heart! (*She wakes.*) . . .

VP, p. 761

---

[57] For details of dates of publication see Ch. I, n. 44 above.

And Forgael walks over to Dectora and says:

> A hound that had lain in the red
>   rushes
> Breathed out a druid vapour, and crumbled away
> The grass and the blue shadow on the stream
> And the pale blossom . . .

VP, p. 761

This is a troublesome kind of demon hound which the winds and the waters, that is the elemental powers, have "overturned" (*VP*, p. 762). Whereas the red hound "is fled", "The pale hound and the deer wander for ever/Among the winds and waters" (*VP*, p. 764), that is the pursuit they symbolize is going on eternally—and, in a Pre-Raphaelite manner, "the unappeasable gods/ Cover their faces with their hair and weep" (*VP*, p. 764). The White Fool is said to have made all these messengers so as to lure lovers to "the holy woods" (*VP*, p. 764). The numerous symbols and allusions of the early version of *SW* certainly drown the chief message of the play, Forgael's quest for the love of an immortal woman. This is a defect which is probably due to Yeats's failure to base his symbolism more firmly on well-known Irish folk belief. The dark hounds, living in the woods with "golden-armed Iolan and the queen" (*VP*, p. 766), once let loose so that Mananan could sack a land under the waves and take "a thousand women" (*VP*, p. 766), convey such vague allusions to Irish tales that they create confusion in the reader's mind, although one's curiosity is aroused. Since a variety of difficulties caused by the vague symbolism of the hounds has been dealt with in *Druid Craft* (pp. 292–294), and to some extent also by critics such as S. Bushrui, R. Ellmann, and F. H. C. Wilson, I have not found it necessary to repeat these ideas here, and agree that "the message on the sail [i.e. the rows of different-coloured hounds] has only the most tenuous overt relation with the dialogue" (*Druid Craft*, p. 294). Moreover, if, as Yeats himself suggested in a programme note to the play, "the dark hounds, red hounds, and light hounds correspond to the *Tamas, Rajas* and *Sattva* qualities of the Vedanta philosophy, or to the three colours of the Alchemists" (*Druid Craft*, p. 294),[58] this idea does not seem to me to be very well integrated with the concept of the "ultimate Nirvana" that the two protagonists of the play, Dectora and Forgael, may perhaps in the light of the Vedanta philosophy be said to reach, at the end of their journey, when drifting on to the land of sunset, or the Otherworld of the Ever-living.

[58] *Inis Fail*, No. 11 (mí lúnasa [August] 1905), n. p. Cf. *Druid Craft*, p. 294n, and Ellmann, Ident., pp. 81–82.

Furthermore, it may be stated that the hound as a pursuer is a much more successful image in *The Wanderings of Oisin* than in *SW*, perhaps because Oisin and Niamh are travelling across the ocean on a white fairy horse and see the phantoms passing swiftly by as they are moving along towards their various islands. In *SW*, on the other hand, Forgael and Dectora are on board a ship which moves slowly, and most of the time not at all. The play itself progresses slowly and there is never any real conflict between the Ever-living and the hounds, even though the red hound disappears in a druidic mist causing everything growing around him to wither up.

Bird Lore and Associated Beliefs in the Three Plays

Along with the hounds, "a bewildering variety of symbolic birds are gathered together in the published versions of 1900"—white birds, gray birds, the "bird among the leaves", a kingfisher, owls, a raven, eagles, all with different meanings (cf. *Druid Craft*, pp. 294–295).

In "The Winged Image" (in *In . . . Luminous Wind*),[59] G. B. Saul points out that "Yeats's concern with birds was . . . an abiding source of reference contributing most pervasively to background, atmosphere, and casual imagery" in his work (p. 255). One can only agree with Saul that when reading Yeats one soon becomes conscious "of a horizon veritably dense with birds" (p. 255), although some of them have symbolically but vague value. This is true of some of the birds appearing in the early version of *SW*, for they all seem to be vague messengers of the Ever-living eager to deliver some message to the soul of Forgael to help him in his search for ideal love. But in the Acting Version, ash-grey seabirds have, as will be demonstrated below, become the prime messengers of the gods, but also some kind of moral guides. Hitherto in this chapter bird lore has been but slightly touched on, but in the following pages it will be our major concern.

Bird lore plays a significant part in all three plays, as it does in so many of Yeats's works.[60] To a large extent Yeats based his bird symbolism not only on his own subjective observation of birds' habits but also on beliefs embraced for generations by Irish country-people. He found evidence both in contemporary oral lore and in beliefs already incorporated into literary material.

[59] (Dublin: Liam Miller, 1961), pp. 245–256.
[60] For various interpretations of Yeats's bird symbolism, see e.g. Donald A. Stauffer, Giorgio Melchiori, F. A. C. Wilson, G. B. Saul, Richard Ellmann, A. Norman Jeffares, and others.

Closely connected with bird lore both in Irish popular belief and in Yeats's poetry are transformation motifs which also find their place in the three plays under examination. The transformation of soul into bird is characteristic of *LHD*. In oral as well as in literary tradition the soul is often said to leave the body in the shape of a white bird, and sometimes, as for example in Lady Wilde's story "The Priest's Soul" (used by Yeats in his play *The Hour-Glass*), in the shape of a butterfly.[61] In Yeats's last play, the hero's soul takes "a soft feathery shape".[62] Turning first to *LHD*, we might recall that the Faery Child, after repeatedly addressing Maire/Mary as "newly-married bride" further entices her by calling her "white bird":

"White bird, white bird, come with me, little bird". (*VPl*, p. 208). This summons is repeated again, three times (*VPl*, p. 209) as in a fairy tale:

> Come, come with me, little bird.
> . . .
> Come, little bird with crest of gold.
> . . .
> Come, little bird with silver feet!

It is particularly noticeable that the white bird is to have "silver feet" and a "crest of gold", details which distinguish it from ordinary white birds and mark it out as a magic or supernatural bird, with perhaps solar and lunar connotations. We might compare this bird to the white hound with one red ear and the deer without horns, whose unusual features also denote that they are supernatural. Note also the golden bird "set upon a golden bough" in "Sailing to Byzantium" (*Collected Poems*, pp. 217–218), a form the poet would like his soul to assume after death—i.e. a perfect artefact.

The mysterious transformation of Mary's soul into a bird takes place gradually, to the sound of the Faery Child's voice and to the accompaniment of "songs and dancing" (*VPl*, p. 209). Mary is magnetically drawn to the Otherworld, the invisible world of the fairies and at the moment of death her soul assumes the shape of a white bird "with crest of gold" and "silver feet".

White is a colour which is often associated with fairies, and in a poem "The White Birds" Yeats, addressing Maud Gonne, says: "I would that

---

[61] *Irish Fairy and Folk Tales*, pp. 230–235. See also "The Soul Cages", a similar story in Crofton Croker, *Irish Fairy Legends and Traditions of the South of Ireland* ([London], 1898; first printed in 1825), pp. 194–215.

[62] W. B. Yeats, *Collected Plays*, p. 209. Cf. also the present writer's *The Interpretation of the Cuchulain Legend in the Works of W. B. Yeats*, pp. 55f.

we were, my beloved, white birds on the foam of the sea!" In a note after the poem in its first printing in the *National Observer* (7 May 1892) Yeats states: "(*The birds of fairyland are said to be white as snow. The Danaan Islands are the Islands of the fairies)*". The poem itself was inspired by a conversation at Howth with Maud Gonne, in which she "had said that if she was to have the choice of being any bird, she would choose to be a seagull above all", and Yeats sent her the poem three days afterwards (Jeffares and Knowland, *Commentary Plays*, pp. 25–26).

Not only white but also other colours are characteristic of fairyland—in some versions the Faery Child itself is dressed in a green jacket and has a red cap, or as stated in one stage direction *"dressed in pale green and with red gold hair"* (*VPl*, p. 195). Pale green and red gold are also colours often associated with the Otherworld. Mary's being transformed into a white bird also stresses her purity.

The birdlike quality of the Faery Child is noticed, ironically enough by Father Hart, who is struck by her dazzling youth and her frail birdlike appearance, something that deceives him into taking down the crucifix and removing it to another room. Just before doing so, he says:

> Because you are so young and like a bird
> That must take fright at every stir of the leaves,
> I will go take it down.
>
> *VPl*, p. 199

At this moment when the Faery begins to dance and Mary hears "Other small steps beating upon the floor" (*VPl*, p. 201), Maurteen is tempted to give the Child some ribbons for her wild hair. Only when Father Hart asks her how old she is, does she reveal her true origin:

> When winter sleep is abroad my hair grows thin,
> My feet unsteady. When the leaves awaken
> My mother carries me in her golden arms.
> I'll soon put on my womanhood and marry
> The spirits of wood and water, but who can tell
> When I was born for the first time? I think
> I am much older than the eagle-cock
> (That blinks and blinks on Ballygawley Hill,)
> And he is the oldest thing under the moon.
>
> *VPl*, p. 203

The Faery Child stresses her extreme old age and claims to be even older than the oldest thing in the world, the eagle-cock on Ballygawley Hill (either in Co. Sligo, Co. Tyrone or Co. Donegal), an eagle which also occurs in a poem quoted by Red Hanrahan in the story "Red Hanrahan's

Curse'' (*Mythologies,* p. 243).[63] Nobody knows when the Faery was "born for the first time", which suggests that she has been reborn several times. By associating the Faery Child with a wise traditional old eagle, Yeats also stresses her dangerous qualities and probably also the unpurged state of her soul. Only too late does Father Hart realize that the Child, taken by everybody to be a poor child in need of food and protection, is a creature of the fairy realm, to him a spirit of evil. Towards the end of the play the priest remarks in dejection:

> Thus do the spirits of evil snatch their prey
> Almost out of the very hand of God;
> And day by day their power is more and more,
> And men and women leave old paths, for pride
> Comes knocking with thin knuckles on the heart.

VPl, p. 210

The priest's point of view is the direct opposite to that of the Faery Child, who sings "Of a land where even the old are fair", the land Mary has visualized in her dreams and to which she is brought in the shape of a small "white bird with silver feet" and "a crest of gold". On the other hand, to Bridget, her mother-in-law, Mary's dead body represents an object of terror, the dead image of a changeling. Bridget warns Mary's husband not to touch the body:

> Come from that image; body and soul are gone.
> You have thrown your arms about a drift of leaves,
> Or bole of an ash-tree changed into her image.

VPl, pp. 209—210

Here popular belief is again used to express a definite point of view, the opinion of the elderly Bridget that Mary's body is not real, but a mere heap of leaves or a tree-trunk that has assumed the shape of a dead body. In his *Irish Fairy Tales* (pp. 224—225), Yeats refers to the fairies stealing children, men and women, and leaving a changeling instead:

These Sheoques are on the whole good; but one most malicious habit have they—a habit worthy of a witch. They steal children and leave a withered fairy, a thousand or maybe two thousand years old, instead. . . . At times full-grown men and women have been taken.

---

[63] In this context one might draw attention to Eleanor Hull's translation of the poem of the Hawk of Achill into English in her article "The Hawk of Achill or the Legend of the Oldest Animals", in *Folk-Lore,* 43 (London, 1932), 376—409, esp. 389—402. The poem is in the form of a conversation between Fintan and the Hawk, who both tell their strange adventures. They have both lived before the Flood, and the mysterious old bird is one of the oldest animals in the world. "The eagle-cock on Ballygawley Hill" and the wise salmon are both variants of the oldest animal in the world.

Yeats also relates a Donegal tale entitled "Jamie Freel and the Young Lady", which records a changeling tradition (*Irish Fairy and Folk Tales,* p. 57):

The [faery] troop dismounted near a window, and Jamie saw a beautiful face, on a pillow in a splendid bed. He saw a young lady lifted and carried away, while the stick which was dropped in her place on the bed took her exact form.

This is a transformation similar to the one Bridget imagines that Mary's body has undergone. To her the Faery Child is one of the shape-changers who has taken not only Mary's soul but also her body and left nothing but a dead image behind. In depicting Mary's death, Yeats combined two beliefs, one that the soul is transformed into a bird, another that the dead body is not a real corpse but an image of a changeling which, when touched, might become a tree-trunk or a heap of dead leaves.

However different they may appear, the Faery Child with her magic dance and her birdlike quality anticipates a figure in Yeats's later drama, the Hawk-Guardian of the well in one of the Noh plays, *At the Hawk's Well,* who is a kind of deity, partly a woman, partly a hawk. The young Cuchulain is being deceived by her just as the Old Man has been for years while waiting for the water of life to burst forth. The changeling motif used in a limited way in *LHD* becomes much more prominent in another of the Noh plays, *The Only Jealousy of Emer,* in which Cuchulain's body is washed up by the sea as a "senseless image". Emer, his wife, is afraid to kiss this image of her husband and says to Eithne Inguba, Cuchulain's mistress:

It may be
An image has been put into his place,
A sea-borne log bewitched into his likeness.
Collected Plays, pp. 284−285

This is an example of the same superstitious belief of an image taking the place of a person's body as voiced by Bridget in *LHD.* In *the Only Jealousy of Emer* it is a matter of having to reclaim Cuchulain from the power of the Otherworld, and Emer, who tries to kill her Otherworld rival, the Woman of the Sidhe, with a knife, is told by the Figure of Cuchulain that her only chance of saving her husband is by renouncing her love for ever. She accepts this condition, and when Eithne Inguba kisses the image, Cuchulain himself wakes up and takes his mistress in his arms. Emer's sacrificial love has saved Cuchulain from the Otherworld. There is no such solution in *LHD,* in which the Otherworld is a land of wonder to which Mary goes willingly, whereas in the later play it is revealed as a highly sinister place from which Cuchulain is, however, rescued.

If in *LHD* the white bird symbolizes Maire's (Mary's) life in the Other-world, two more sinister birds play a conspicuous role in *CC*. Birds can be demons in disguise, a popular belief symbolically used by Yeats in this play. Yeats makes the two soul-bartering demons assume, now the shape of horned owls, now the shape of Oriental merchants. The arrival of the demons is foreboded at the beginning of the play by the appearance of two ghosts, and the dark realm of the demons is making its presence felt at the very outset.

The exposition of the play is worked out as a conversation between Teigue and his mother Mary Rua, a conversation in which the characters talk past one another and leave questions unanswered. Yeats retained this opening with some revisions made in later versions. He apparently wished to strike an immediate note of vague fear of some impending unknown terror revealing itself in the intuitive reactions of the domestic animals, a dog and a grey hen. In the 1892 version Mary is worried and Teig is so nervous that he spills some water. The version begins as follows:

> *Mary.* You are all thumbs.
> *Teig.*   How yon dog bays,
> And how the grey hen flutters in the coop.
> Strange things are going up and down the land
> These famine times. By Tubber-vanach cross roads,
> A woman met a man with ears spread out,
> And they moved up and down like wings of bats.
> *Mary.* Shemus stays late.
> *Teig.*   By Carric-orus churchyard,
> A herdsman met with one who had no mouth,
> Nor ears nor eyes—his face a wall of flesh.
> He saw him plainly by the moonlight.
>
> *VPl*, pp. 6, 8

In the final version the conversation runs as follows:

> *Mary.* What can have made the grey hen flutter so? [*Teigue, a boy of fourteen, is coming in with turf, which he lays beside the hearth.*]
> *Teigue.* They say that now the land is famine-struck
> The graves are walking.
> *Mary.*   What can the hen have heard?
> *Teigue.* And that is not the worst; at Tubber-vanach
> A woman met a man with ears spread out,
> And they moved up and down like a bat's wing.
> *Mary.* What can have kept your father all this while?
> *Teigue.* Two nights ago, at Carrick-orus churchyard,
> A herdsman met a man who had no mouth,
> Nor eyes, nor ears; his face a wall of flesh;
> He saw him plainly by the light of the moon.
>
> *VPl*, pp. 5, 7

In the first version both the dog and the grey hen sense something strange and frightening and also show their fear. In the final version the barking dog has been eliminated but the grey hen's fluttering, which is a cause of worry to Mary Rua, has been retained. In both versions Teig(ue) tells his mother of strange ghosts seen by people, one at Tubber-vanach cross roads, another at Carrick-orus churchyard, the churchyard and the cross roads being notorious for ghostly appearances. One of the ghosts with his ears like bats' wings clearly associates with a belief that bats are not only evil-omened but also—if not incarnating—at least representing evil spirits, demons and witches. The ghost with a face without mouth, eyes and ears is a Swedenborgian figure which has struck terror into Teig(ue)'s simple heart. Teig(ue)'s mother is worried about her husband, and in the first version she prays to the Virgin that he may be saved from "the wolves" and "the demons of the woods" (*VPl*, p. 8) when suddenly Shemus *"comes in with a dead wolf on his shoulder"* (*VPl*, p. 10). Shemus has natural explanations both for the dog's fierce barking and the grey hen's fluttering; the dog had caught the scent of the wolf and the dog's barking had frightened the hen. The day before, Shemus had brought home a carrion crow for food, another sinister element to be eliminated in the later versions. In the final version of the play, Shemus simply tells his wife that there is no food to be had except what is in the house, that is some mouldy flour and the hen, and that he himself has been sitting all day among the beggars holding out "a hollow hand among the others" (*VPl*, p. 11).

In both versions Yeats prepares the reader for the fatal results of the disastrous famine. The final version, stripped of dog and wolf, shows even more clearly the state of despair into which Shemus has been thrown. Whereas his wife and son, both superstitious in different ways, are frightened by the unknown evil powers, Shemus himself fears one thing only— the famine and its effects. The ghostly omens mentioned above may be seen as a lead-in to the fatal appearance of the two horned owls, the representatives of the hellish realm struggling for the souls of men.

Teig(ue) is the first to discover two grey horned owls hiding in the bush outside the cottage. In the first version he sees them after his father's return, in the final version before, and he says to his mother:

> In the bush beyond,[64]
> There are two birds—if you can call them birds—
> I could not see them rightly for the leaves—
> But they've the shape and colour of horned owls,
> And I'm half certain they've a human face.
>
> *VPl*, pp. 7, 9

[64] Hiberno-English usage of "beyond" in the sense of "over there".

In a note to the 1892 version of the play Yeats remarked that the horned owl is associated in popular belief with evil fairies, and it is quite obvious that to Teigue the horned owls represent an evil power which is moreover about to invade his mind.[65] "What is the good of praying? father says", (*VPl*, p. 9), he exclaims. Whereas in *LHD* Bridget blames Mary for bringing misfortune on them all by talking too much about the fairies and by giving gifts to them on May Eve, in *CC* Mary Rua maintains that her son will bring misfortune on the family as a result of his blasphemies:

> You'll bring misfortune with your blasphemies
> Upon your father, or yourself, or me.

VPl, p. 9

There are numerous examples in Yeats's early plays of how people bring ill luck on themselves by angering the unseen powers. There are, as has been shown earlier in this chapter, various ways in which demons, fairies, evil spirits and influences may be either averted or attracted. Mary Rua intuitively shuns evil, and fears those who cast no shadow. She tries to bring her husband and her son back to the path of righteousness, but in the end her hunger forces her to "eat dock and grass, and dandelion" (*VPl*, p. 49), as the demons foretold. In spite of, or perhaps because of, her faith in God and her rejection of the demons she dies of starvation. Mary's sufferings resemble William Carleton's description in *The Black Prophet* of the miseries of the poor during the famine of 1817 when

miserable women might be seen early in the morning, and, in fact, during all hours of the day, gathering weeds of various descriptions, in order to sustain life; and happy were they who could procure a few handfuls of young nettles, chickenweed, sorrell, *presgagh,* buglass, or seaweed, to bring home as food, either for themselves or their unfortunate children.[66]

Before settling outside Shemus Rua's cottage, the demon-owls have been busy working magic in another part of the forest and have led Countess Cathleen and her foster-mother Oona astray with their hootings. Aleel, a poet "Wandering and singing like a wave of the sea" (*VPl*, p. 17), has joined them but he is unable to guide them back to Cathleen's castle. The hooting of the owls takes them to the hunger-struck cottage which they visit for a short while. Before leaving, Aleel warns the cottagers against the grey horned owls he has heard:

---

[65] *The Countess Kathleen and Various Legends and Lyrics* (London, 1892), p. 8. Notice also that in *Vivian Grey* (1881), B. Disraeli makes "the great horned owl" or "the Stut Ozel" act as the precurser of the Wild Hunter. See the Earl of Beaconsfield, *Vivian Grey*, Hughenden Ed. of *Novels and Tales*, I, p. 267.

[66] *The Black Prophet* (1847; rpt. Shannon Ireland: IUP, 1972), pp. 225–227.

92

Shut to the door before the night has fallen,
For who can say what walks, or in what shape
Some devilish creature flies in the air; but now
Two grey horned owls hooted above our heads.

VPl, p.25

Aleel, the poet, has the same presentiment of evil as Teigue, the boy. Aleel's words convince Teigue that the birds observed by him are evil:

He's seen the horned owls too,
There's no good luck in owls, but it may be
That the ill luck's to fall upon his head.

VPl, p. 25

The superstitious Teigue is comforted by the thought that the misfortune may befall Aleel and not him and his parents.

Old Shemus Rua, despairing of finding any food for his family, falls easy prey to the demons. He kills his own belief in God and the good powers when he crushes the shrine of the Virgin underfoot and exclaims:

The Mother of God has dropped asleep . . .

VPl, p. 31, under line

words which help to bring the demons into the house. In the early version when Mary says that she fears "the wood things", Shemus challengingly answers her:

Famine fear
Addles your mind. I'll chew the lean dog-wolf
With no less mirth if, chaired beside the hearth,
Rubbing its hands before the bogwood flame,
Be Pooka,[67] Sowlth, or demon of the pit.

VPl, p. 20

---

[67] The Pooka, Irish *Púca*, is a kind of fairy or goblin, but originally a designation for the Devil. (Cf. Old Swedish and Swedish dialects "Puke", the Devil. The arms of the Puke family had the horn of a monster in the shield. See Elof Hellquist, *Svensk etymologisk ordbok*, 2 vol. 3rd ed. [Lund: Gleerups, 1948], II, pp. 795, 955). The Pooka is "an odd mixture of merriment and malignity", like Puck. He can assume many shapes, e.g. that of a horse, a bull, an eagle etc., and his name forms part of many Irish placenames, e.g. Pollaphuca, Co. Wicklow, "a wild chasm where the Liffey falls over a ledge of rocks into a deep pool, to which the name properly belongs, signifying the pool or hole of the Pooka" (Joyce, *Irish Names of Places*, I, pp. 188–189). In *Irish Fairy and Folk Tales* Yeats explains the Pooka as "essentially an animal spirit" (p. 100). His name is listed under "Phooka *(pooka)*, the", in Katharine Briggs, *A Dictionary of Fairies* (London: Allen Lane, 1976), pp. 326–327.

"Phuka" ("Phooca") is an aspirated form appearing in the genitive in compound place names, e.g. Pollaphuca and is not as a rule used as a basic form in Ireland (although Lady Wilde uses it).

A footstep is heard outside, there is a knock at the door and the two merchants are outside waiting to come in. When Mary is forced to cook the wolf for them, the water will not boil without one of the merchants whispering to it, and Mary refuses to cook for them.

In the later version Shemus even more openly challenges the evil powers when ordering the door to be left invitingly open for the spirits of the wood to come in:

> Whatever you are that walk the woods at night,
> So be it that you have not shouldered up
> Out of a grave—for I'll have nothing human—
> And have free hands, a friendly trick of speech,
> I welcome you. Come, sit beside the fire.
> What matter if your head's below your arms[68]
> Or you've a horse's tail to whip your flank,
> Feathers instead of hair, that's all but nothing.
> Come, share what bread and meat is in the house,
> And stretch your heels and warm them in the ashes.

VPl, p. 31

Shemus does not even wish to protect himself against evil. In his despair he has not only summoned the demons as his allies, he has also cursed the rich, including Cathleen, who wants to help him; moreover, he has cursed the beggars for taking his food—according to an old Irish tradition an unjustified curse will revert and strike the curser instead of the person cursed; he has even struck his wife for trying to forbid him to "Call devils from the wood" (*VPl,* p. 29). He has denied man, he has denied God. In welcoming evil spirits he himself has brought about an occasion for the demons to enter. Outside they are owls, but before entering the cottage, they assume the shape of Oriental merchants, who take money out of richly embroidered purses. They soon make sure of the souls of Teigue and Shemus, but have no power over Mary. Seeing that they cast no shadow, she immediately associates them with the two grey horned owls she has seen outside and refuses to cook the last fowl for them:

> I will not cook for you, because I know
> In what unlucky shape you sat but now
> Outside this door.

VPl, p. 39

[68] The headless phantoms or ghosts, so-called "Dullahans" or "Dullaghans", are described by Yeats in *Irish Fairy and Folk Tales,* p. 116. See also "Lageniensis", *Poetical Works* (Dublin, 1893), pp. 219−221, and Joyce, *Irish Names of Places,* I, p. 193, where it is stated that a dullaghan "can take off and put on his head at will."

94

Mary is the direct opposite to Shemus; she would die rather than yield herself up to evil. After agreeing to sell their souls, Shemus and Teigue are forced by the demon-merchants to cry out at the cross-roads that "two gentlemen" will buy men's souls for "sweet yellow money":

> 'There's money for a soul, sweet yellow money.
> There's money for men's souls, good money, money.'
>
> *VPl*, p. 73

Mary's curse has been of no immediate avail, but anticipates the final destruction of the demons:

> Destroyers of souls, God will destroy you quickly.
> You shall at last dry like dry leaves and hang
> Nailed like dead vermin to the doors of God.
>
> *VPl*, pp. 47, 49

The fact that they can assume two different shapes helps the demons in their dealings with and plottings against Cathleen, but in neither shape can they hide their predatory nature. As owls they are frightening because they have human faces and human voices, as Oriental merchants because their eyes shine dangerously "like the eyes of birds of prey" (*VPl*, p. 77), and "their claws clutch in their leathern gloves" (*VPl*, p. 151).

In their owl shape they can easily gain access to Cathleen's treasury and carry out the robbery almost in the eye of the porter. Not until the deed is done, does the porter understand what has happened:

> Demons were here. I sat beside the door
> In my stone niche, and two owls passed me by,
> Whispering with human voices.
>
> *VPl*, p. 123

In their merchant shape the demons can converse with Cathleen after the robbery, and persuade her that her ships are becalmed at sea and that the man she has sent for food is lying ill in the Bog of Allen. Yet their eyes and voices intuitively fill her with fear:

> There is a something, Merchant, in your voice
> That makes me fear. When you were telling how
> A man may lose his soul and lose his God
> Your eyes were lighted up, and when you told
> How my poor money serves the people, both—
> Merchants, forgive me—seemed to smile.
>
> *VPl*, pp. 117, 119

She soon realizes what has happened and retires to her oratory for prayer and meditation, which is her special way of protection against evil.

The demons rejoice at having been able to deceive Cathleen, but at the

95

same time they are afraid, for on their nightly flight as horned owls they have realized that they are working against time. They have but three days in which to achieve their task:

First Merchant.   When the night fell and I had shaped myself
                    Into the image of the man-headed owl,
                    I hurried to the cliffs of Donegal,
                    And saw with all their canvas full of wind
                    And rushing through the parti-coloured sea
                    Those ships that bring the woman grain and meal.
                    They're but three days from us.[69]
Second Merchant.   When the dew rose
                    I hurried in like feathers to the east,
                    And saw nine hundred oxen driven through Meath
                    With goads of iron. They're but three days from us.

                                                              VPl, p. 131

Yeats was particularly fascinated by stories about man-headed birds and animals. Here in the above passage the demons have changed themselves into man-headed owls, who on their flights to Donegal in the North, and to Meath in the East have seen that shiploads of corn and flower as well as 900 oxen are sure to reach Cathleen within three days. They are both equally frightened that her soul will escape them. The one person they are afraid of is Aleel. His only protection against the demons is his love, and his world and theirs are in sharp contrast to one another. Also the peasants are afraid of Aleel. He is ready to give the demons his soul in exchange for Cathleen's, but is told that his soul is not his to give since it belongs to Cathleen. Her unselfishness leads to her being exploited by the demons, yet even after she has signed the document they are afraid of losing her soul. They would be prepared to sit for years above her tower as horned owls—waiting for her precious soul to depart; but once she has signed her soul away, she has but a few minutes to live. Exulting, the two demons rush out, in the shape of owls, eager to meet the other hellish creatures, as is obvious from the farewell words of one of them to his comrade:

                    Leap feathered on the air
          And meet them with her soul caught in your claws.[70]

                                                              VPl, p. 155

Their hope of catching Cathleen's soul in their claws is frustrated and they vanish for ever. Their power is broken. Our final attention is centred not on

---

[69] In the early version the Demons have five days at their disposal (*VPl*, p. 124).

[70] In the early version, Sc. IV ends with the First Merchant's words: ''Now leap we feathered on the air'' (*VPl*, p. 152).

96

the two demons, but on Cathleen's fate, her death and redemption. She has rejected Aleel's world, and she has escaped the demons. In spite of the pagan and Oriental elements in the play, the ending is basically Christian. Cathleen's soul-struggle is ultimately seen as a struggle between good and evil, and the aim of the demons is defeated through Cathleen's self-sacrifice. It could be said that Yeats here has applied not only Christian belief in miracles but also up to a point accepted the Christian explanation of Cathleen's final apotheosis, which also includes the defeat of the demonic power. In old age Yeats expressed this in his poem "The Circus Animals' Desertion":

> And then a counter-truth filled out its play,
> *The Countess Cathleen* was the name I gave it;
> She, pity-crazed, had given her soul away,
> But masterful Heaven had intervened to save it.
> I thought my dear must her own soul destroy,
> So did fanaticism and hate enslave it,
> And this brought forth a dream and soon enough
> This dream itself had all my thought and love.
>
> *Collected Poems*, pp. 391–392

In *LHD*, bird lore is closely linked up with the fairies and the Happy Otherworld, whereas in *CC* it is associated with demonic powers. In *SW* bird lore is conspicuously connected with "the world we go to after death", an Otherworld in which lovers can find beauty, eternal life and ideal love. In the Acting Version of *SW*, Forgael's chief guides are grey sea-birds with human voices. One of the sailors has seen such birds—the souls of the dead floating on the waves but suddenly flying up as grey man-headed birds with human voices:

> I was sleeping up there by the bulwark,
> and when I woke in the sound of the harp a change
> came over my eyes, and I could see very strange
> things. The dead were floating upon the sea yet, and
> it seemed as if the life that went out of every one
> of them had turned to the shape of a man-headed
> bird—grey they were, and they rose up of a sudden
> and called out with voices like our own, and flew
> away singing to the west. Words like this they were
> singing: 'Happiness beyond measure, happiness
> where the sun dies'.
>
> *VPl*, p. 319

Here in the words of the superstitious sailor recollecting a vision of his, the transformation theme of soul into bird is clearly stated. He took these birds to be souls of dead sailors floating on the waves—supernatural birds which again have characteristics distinguishing them from ordinary sea-birds. They are not white, they are grey, and above all they have men's heads and human voices. Another sailor has heard his mother mention such strange birds:

> My mother used to be talking of birds of the sort.
> They are sent by the lasting watchers to lead men
> away from this world and its women to some place
> of shining women that cast no shadow, having lived
> before the making of the earth. But I have no mind
> to go following him [Forgael] to that place.

VPl, p. 319

The colour of ash-grey or grey generally signifies death in Irish folk belief, which is probably why Yeats makes these supernatural messengers this colour.[71] The man-headed birds incarnate the souls of the dead. Forgael himself is well aware that they are messengers between this world and the world of the Ever-living, the invisible world to which Forgael is on his way:

> There! There! They
> come! Gull, gunnet, or diver,
> But with a man's head, or a fair woman's.
> They hover over the masthead awhile
> To wait their friends, but when their friends have
> come
> They will fly upon that secret way of theirs
> One—and one—a couple—five together.
> . . . .
> Ah! now they all look down—they'll speak of me
> What the Ever-living put into their minds,
> And of that shadowless unearthly woman
> At the world's end. I hear the message now,
> But it's all mystery.

VPl, pp. 324–325

As stated in Ch. I, in the early manuscripts "about half his characters have eagles' faces", as the startled Lady Gregory noted in her diary for

---

[71] However, in a later poem, "In Memory of Alfred Pollexfen", a white visionary sea-bird functions as the messenger of death. The lamenting cries of the banshee were heard by old women every time a Pollexfen died (*Collected Poems*, pp. 175–177). In *Reveries over Childhood and Youth* (London: Macmillan, 1916), p. 12, Yeats writes that once his "sister awoke dreaming that she held a wingless sea-bird in her arms", which proved to be an omen of the death of one her Pollexfen uncles "in his mad-house, for a sea-bird is the omen that announces the death or danger of a Pollexfen." Cf. Patricia Lysaght's article "*An Bhean Chaointe*: The Supernatural Woman in Irish Folklore", in *Éire: Ireland* (Winter 1979) (St. Paul Minnesota: IACI, 1979), 7–29.

1898,[72] but Yeats reversed this symbolism and endowed the birds with human faces and voices instead. The role of the sea-birds becomes more and more important in *SW*, and in the Acting Version they can be said to be a primary symbol. Every sound uttered by the birds is full of meaning. They circle around Forgael's ship; they tell the Ever-living about the expected arrival of Forgael and Dectora; they flutter anxiously about Forgael and seem to reproach him for using magic spells to enchant Dectora. Forgael, who "did not relish the idea of going alone to the world of the immortals", as Hone puts it,[73] wonders why they reproach him:

> What are the birds at there?
> Why are they all a-flutter of a sudden?
> What are you calling out above the mast?
> If railing and reproach and mockery
> Because I have awakened her to love
> By magic strings, I'll make this answer to it:
> Being driven on by voices and by dreams
> That were clear messages from the Ever-living,
> I have done right. What could I but obey?
> And yet you make a clamour of reproach.
>
> *VPl*, p. 333

In this passage Forgael does not only speak about the birds, he also addresses them directly, just as Maire in *LHD* addresses the invisible fairy dancers. But here Yeats introduces a moral message from the birds to Forgael: they disapprove of his having used magic to win Dectora's love. He, however, asserts his right to do as he pleases—"I have done right", he states. A similar assertion is made by King Conchubar in *Deirdre* when he proudly defends his behaviour and proclaims at the end of the play that he did right in choosing Deirdre as Queen:

> Howl, if you will; but I, being King, did right
> In choosing her most fitting to be Queen,
> And letting no boy lover take the sway.
>
> *VPl*, p. 388

Forgael, however, shamed by the clamouring voices of the birds, acknowledges his deceit, but only at the moment when Dectora, moved by the magic strings of the harp, has already forgotten her dead King and husband and is prepared to love Forgael.

---

[72] Lady Gregory, *Our Irish Theatre* (London and New York: G. P. Putnam's Sons, 1913), p. 3.

[73] *W. B. Yeats, 1865–1939* (New York: Macmillan, 1943), p. 175.

Dectora does not find the birds as unusual as Forgael does. To her they seem but ordinary sea-birds. In the Acting Version of 1907 she is very suspicious of them and feels that they are "shadows, illusions" sent to mock them (*VPl*, p. 337, under line). In the final version she asks, "What is there but the crying of the birds?" (*VPl*, p. 336), yet the birds make her tremble. However, Forgael claims that they are his supernatural pilots:

> They have been circling over our heads in the
>   air,
> But now that they have taken to the road
> We have to follow, for they are our pilots;
> They're crying out. Can you not hear their cry?—
> 'There is a country at the end of the world
> Where no child's born but to outlive the moon.'

VPl, p. 336

The last two lines echo William Morris's romances, but are also deeply rooted in the pattern of many fairy tales. Yeats was certainly right when he defined his play *SW* as a fairy tale. The mysterious ship with the two lovers Forgael and Dectora on board sets off in the same direction as the grey man-headed sea-birds, across the shadowy waters, in search of a beautiful dream, to the sound of harp music and the human voices of the birds. Dectora and Forgael are united in a mystical union, for the rope between the two ships is cut and the power of the "ancient worm" is broken (*VPl*, p. 338). Even though the two lovers reject the physical world, one has no feeling that this should be an expression of pessimism, as is the case in Villiers de l'Isle-Adam's *Axël*.[74] This is probably due to the picture of the world of the Ever-living as a land of ideal love and beauty.

Concluding Remarks

As stated at the beginning of this chapter, the Otherworld is found in different forms in the three early plays dealt with in this investigation. Forgael and Dectora are piloted to the Otherworld by supernatural sea-birds. Maire/Mary in *LHD* was irresistibly drawn to the world of the fairies

---

[74] See e.g. H. Goldgar, "*Axël* de Villiers de L'Isle Adam et *The Shadowy Waters* de W. B. Yeats", *Revue de Littérature Comparée*, 24 (24e Année), 1950, 563—574; Marie-Hélène Pauly, "W. B. Yeats et les Symbolistes Français", *Revue de Littérature Comparée*, 20 (20e Année), 1940—46, 13—33. See also *Druid Craft*, p. 297, and William Norman Guthrie, "Two Poets". I. W. B. Yeats." *Sewanee Review*, 9 (July 1901), 329—331. W. B. Yeats reviewed a performance of *Axël* in "A Symbolical Drama in Paris", The *Bookman* (London, April 1894); rpt. in Frayne, I, pp. 320—325. See also Yeats's Preface to H. P. R. Finsberg's trans. of *Axël* (London, 1925).

where she went in the shape of a supernatural bird. The Countess Cathleen, rejecting the world of love and dream symbolized by Aengus, the Celtic god of love and beauty, sacrificed her soul for her people and went to Heaven, in fact became Heaven, in spite of having sold her soul to the two Demons. Thus she escaped both the Hell of the Demons and the frightful Celtic Hell visualized by Aleel.

This investigation of the function of popular belief in the three plays has shown that such beliefs concern the invisible world, the Happy Otherworld, as well as the Christian Paradise, and the world of Evil, the world of demons and ghosts. Whether Yeats chose to represent folk belief by means of natural phenomena like the wind or the thunderstorm, or by flowers or trees, by birds of different kinds, natural as well as supernatural, by spectral hound and deer, or by musical instruments such as the Dagda's harp, these features nearly always have some association with the Otherworld, which is filled with enticing and dangerous beings, not only fairies of different kinds, who charm human beings with their singing and dancing, or enchanters like Forgael playing a magic harp, but also demons in search of human souls. The underground joiner's hammering for example, is as much a death omen as is the hooting of the horned owl. Also the water-spirits, symbolizing the ideal lovers Étain and Aengus, forebode death, as does the enchanter himself, Forgael with his magic harp, who has been given his power by the White Fool of Aengus, the Fairy Fool, coming out of enchanted woods or turning up in a green island in the sea. By making popular belief function symbolically Yeats enriched his plays and also added another dimension to the conflict he placed his characters in, critical moments in their lives when they have to make a fatal choice.

Chapter III

Impact of Folk Poetry and Music on the Songs in the Three Plays

The principal justification for this chapter is my contention that songs and music are such significant elements in the plays that they deserve our special attention. Yeats attached as much importance to song and music in his plays as did Shakespeare, and in the plays dealt with here, the protagonists are all musical. Kevin/Aleel is a bard and musician who carries his lute or harp with him, and composes music and songs which he himself sings. The Countess is likewise musical and finds comfort in his songs. Maire/Mary Bruin in *LHD* is enticed away by a musical voice heard in the wind and assuming the shape of a singing and dancing Faery Child. Forgael in *SW* has a magic harp which helps him to produce tears, laughter or sleep. The songs are not just ornamental but essential features in the structure of the plays whose moods, as will be seen, they strongly influence. It will be most suitable to deal with the songs play by play beginning with *CC* and going on in turn to *LHD* and *SW*. In the three plays selected, there are lyrics which can be sung, and it will be seen that Yeats drew on popular poetry (also ballads) as well as on other sources with folklore in them, such as novels and romances, when he composed the lyrics which he wrote into the plays at various times.

Yeats on Popular Poetry

What is also important for my investigation is Yeats's own conception of what constitutes "popular poetry", or folk poetry. Yeats began *Ideas of Good and Evil* with an article called "What is 'Popular Poetry'?"[1] in which he reveals not only his own impression of it but also some of his own "illusions" about such poetry. After, as he said, having been for a while "busy among the verses and stories that the people make for themselves",

---

[1] (1903; rpt. London and Stratford-upon-Avon: A. H. Bullen, 1914), pp. 1–11; hereafter *IGE*.

it did not take him long to realize that "what we call popular poetry never came from the people at all" (*IGE*, p. 4). He then tries to establish, in his own personal manner, indicative of his own poetic creativity, the interdependence between "the unwritten tradition", i.e. oral transmission, and "the written tradition". As examples he takes Scott's longer poems and the poetry of Longfellow, Burns, and a few lesser names. To such poetry he opposes for example Shelley's *Epipsychidion*. He also points out that Walt Whitman, when writing "in seeming defiance of tradition", nevertheless "needs tradition for protection" (p. 6). In other words, Yeats is firmly convinced that good poetry presupposes the written tradition, just as "the true poetry of the people" "presupposes the unwritten tradition" (p.7). Moreover, continuous interaction between the two is necessary. As fine examples of anonymous folk poetry Yeats quotes translations of two untitled love songs, one sung by an "Aran fisher-girl", another by a Scottish Gael, poems moreover, Yeats feels, with faint traces of "the worship of sun and moon" (*IGE*, pp. 7–8).[2] Here are the first, second and last stanzas of poem 1 ("Donal Óg"), and the second and third stanzas of poem 2:

1.   'It is late last night the dog was speaking
of you; the snipe was speaking of you in her
deep marsh. It is you are the lonely bird
throughout the woods; and that you may be
without a mate until you find me.
   'You promised me and you said a lie to
me, that you would be before me where the
sheep are flocked. I gave a whistle and three
hundred cries to you; and I found nothing
there but a bleating lamb.

  . . . .
  'You have taken the east from me, you
have taken the west from me, you have taken
what is before me and what is behind me;
you have taken the moon, you have taken
the sun from me, and my fear is great you
have taken God from me.'[3]

                                             IGE, p. 8

---

[2] Yeats gives no source.

[3] Another version of this song, "the well-known Irish folk-song, Domhnall Óg, in which a girl describes her unhappy love-affair" is quoted in Irish and English by Seán Ó Súilleabháin in "Irish Oral Tradition", *A View of the Irish Language,* ed. Brian Ó Cuiv (Dublin: Stationery Office, 1969), pp. 47–56. The third stanza is almost identical with the last stanza quoted by Yeats: "You have taken east from me, and west; / You have taken before from me, and behind; / You have taken moon and sun from me. / And great my fear that you have taken God from me." Cf. Michael Yeats, p. 156.

2. ....
     Thou art the joy of all joyous things,
     Thou art the light of the beam of the sun,
     Thou art the door of the chief of hospitality,
     Thou art the surpassing pilot star,
     Thou art the step of the deer of the hill,
     Thou art the step of the horse of the plain,
     Thou art the grace of the sun rising,
     Thou art the loveliness of all lovely desires.

     The lovely likeness of the Lord
     Is in thy pure face,
     The loveliest likeness that was upon earth.'

IGE, p. 9

These two songs, one on lost love that has robbed the person of every-thing, even of God, the other on the great love of a Scottish Gael for his bride, represented to Yeats true folk poetry. Although he himself hardly wrote any poetry like this, it inspired him to attempt something similar and he did want, as Michael Yeats stresses (p. 153), to write poetry for the people. In "What is 'Popular Poetry'?" Yeats tells us that he was so moved by the Irish poets who wrote in English that he praised them whether they deserved it or not, for "such romance clung about them, such a desire for Irish poetry was in all our minds, that I kept on saying, not only to others but to myself, that most of them wrote well, or all but well" (*IGE*, p. 1). He also thought that " 'If somebody could make a style which would not be an English style and yet would be musical and full of colour, many others would catch fire from him, and we would have a really great school of ballad poetry in Ireland. . . .' " (*IGE*, p. 1). Yeats also claims that it was beside the turf fires in Connaught that he came to understand what true folk poetry is, and this even made him at times try to get inspiration "by eating little and sleeping upon a board" (*IGE*, p. 3), in imitation of the ancient bards who found inspiration in darkness.

Like Michael Yeats (p. 156), Colin Meir in *The Ballads and Songs of William Butler Yeats* stresses the importance for Yeats of poets like J. J. Callanan, James Clarence Mangan, William Allingham, Sir Samuel Ferguson, and not least Douglas Hyde's translations of Gaelic poems into English.[4] Yeats himself also pointed to English and French poets as important for the creation of an Irish poetic style. For this purpose the Elizabethans were also as important to him as Shelley and Keats, Poe and Whitman. The poems in his plays were written to be sung or chanted in the specific

---

[4] (London and Basingstoke: Macmillan, 1974), Chs. I and II.

manner defined by Yeats, about which more will be said later in this chapter. At this time poetry and music were equally sacred to Yeats and he also stresses in his article "Magic" (*IGE*, p. 39) that poetry and music are in close communion with magic:

Have not poetry and music arisen, as it seems, out of the sounds the enchanters made to help their imagination to enchant, to charm, to bind with a spell themselves and the passers-by?

The Poet/Musician in *The Countess Cathleen*

Kevin/Aleel, the poet in the play, may be said to be such an enchanter, although not endowed with a magic harp like Forgael in *SW*. Before we turn to the songs themselves, let us look more closely at Kevin/Aleel, the alleged composer of the songs in *CC*. He is a character firmly rooted in song and music, but is also, as we have seen in Ch. I, a visionary. Can the poet in the play, Kevin/Aleel, and for example Red Hanrahan, be said to be modelled on Torlough O'Carolan (1670−1738), often referred to as the last bard,[5] and other Irish eighteenth- and nineteenth-century poets? We know that Yeats was particularly familiar with many Irish poets, especially Owen Rua O'Sullivan, Blind William Heffernan (the author of two versions of "Caitilín Ní Uallacháin"[6]), and the folk poet Anthony Raftery, about whom Yeats and Lady Gregory could still in their time collect folklore. Although not as learned as earlier bards, Owen O'Sullivan and William Heffernan were, as Douglas Hyde states in *Songs Ascribed to Raftery*, "learned men. Masters of the Irish language, old and new", with "a vocabulary of their own . . ."[7] In contrast to them, Raftery was a wandering folk poet, who could neither read nor write, "but spoke out the thing that was in his heart, simply and directly" (ibid, p. 45). Does Raftery's poetry qualify as folk poetry? Seán O'Súilleabháin states in *A View of the Irish Language* (p. 48) that "Irish folk-poetry, whatever its theme may be, is, for the most part anonymous, not made by highly educated poets, but by the common people themselves." However, Raftery's poems may be said to be good examples of folk poetry, for not only was Raftery a man of

[5] According to Donal O'Sullivan, in *Songs of the Irish* (Dublin: Browne & Nolan, 1960), p. 180, more than 200 of his airs have been preserved; hereafter Donal O'Sullivan.

[6] Donal O'Sullivan assigns this poem "to the period 1779−1782" and also states that the use of Caitilín Ní Uallacháin as a symbol for Ireland "did not occur until the close of the eighteenth century" (p. 142). He also states that there should be no "h" after "Ní" in front of "Uallacháin, but that he has retained it in his translation of "Cathleen Ni Houlihan".

[7] *Abhráin atá leagtha ar an Reachtúire: Songs Ascribed to Raftery. Being the Fifth Chapter of the Songs of Connacht* (Baile Átha Cliath: Gill agus a Mhac, 1903), p. 45.

105

the people, he was also often, as for example when composing his "Story of the Bush", a poem relating the history of Ireland, "only giving out the knowledge that existed among the people". "The people of the country obtained their knowledge of the history and antiquities of Ireland in those days from the mouth-instruction of the old folk . . .", Hyde also states (*Songs Ascribed to Raftery,* p. 19). Besides, Raftery's poems were of course not written down by the poet himself, but by others. Hyde's collection of Raftery's poems or "Songs" as he calls them is well worth reading for its intrinsic value, not just as a source book for Irish Renaissance writers, although as such it is invaluable.

That Yeats's imagination often turned to Raftery is hardly strange since both he, Hyde and Lady Gregory often met people who had known the poet in his old age or heard stories about him, for Raftery was one of those characters who like Swift attached himself to the folk imagination. To Yeats, anyhow, he was a folk poet, a folk musician, but also a romantic solitary figure, an itinerant bard and visionary, with the poetic gift of a prophet, quite in line with Romantic theories about the poet. Kevin/Aleel is a lonely figure like Raftery, a visionary, a poet and a musician, who is, however, not as close to the people as Raftery and whose entire life seems to consist in his love for the Countess Cathleen, a love which makes him singularly unhappy, almost unfit for life. He is the absolute contrast to the fiddler in "The Fiddler of Dooney" (1892), a happy representative of the folk. Parallels can be drawn between Aleel and such characters in Yeats's early poetry as Oisin and Goll,[8] yet the three are also markedly different. Oisin finds the Promised Land but loses it in the end, whereas Goll, a sad and melancholy king who, like Suibne Geilt, becomes mad in the battle, is cured by his magic harp, and may be said to anticipate Kevin/Aleel as well as Forgael, who are both harpers. The harp has very old ancestry in Ireland and harpers were highly esteemed—not only in the ancient literature but in real life.

In this context let me say a few words about the Statutes of Kilkenny enacted by Lionel, Duke of Clarence, in 1366. These Statutes were meant to bring about "a complete reduction of the whole island to English law and Norman lordship."[9] In Ireland "the English are forbidden by severe

---

[8] "King Goll, an Irish Legend", written as early as 1884, first appeared in the *Leisure Hour,* September 1887. Before being included in *Collected Poems,* it was considerably altered; see Norman A. Jeffares, *W. B. Yeats Man and Poet* (London, 1948), p. 39, where the early form of the poem is recorded.

[9] Edmund Curtis, *A History of Ireland* (1936; rpt. London: Univ. Paper Books, Methuen, 1961), p. 113. Referred to as Curtis in the text.

penalties to make fosterage, marriage or gossipred with the Irish or in law cases to use Brehon law . . . or to entertain Irish minstrels, poets or storytellers. . . . If they use the Irish speech they shall forfeit their lands to their lords until they undertake to use English. The Irish are excluded from cathedrals, abbeys, and benefices among the English. . . ." (Curtis, pp. 112–113). As Curtis points out, the Statutes of Kilkenny actually meant "the *Outlawry of the Irish race*" (p. 115). All association with the Irish was forbidden, even buying and selling, and Irish surnames were forbidden, etc. However, the Statutes were so severe that the task of enacting them was all but impossible. "What was to prevent the feudal English from intermarriage and fosterage with so attractive and proud a race as the Gaels?" Curtis asks (p. 116). Contrary to the Statutes, the Anglo-Norman lords learnt to speak Irish, not the English of Chaucer. Consequently in 1495, Poyning's Parliament, which again enacted the Statutes, had to disregard the "two acts which forbade the speaking of Irish and riding after the Irish fashion" (Curtis, p. 117). Yet, the Gaelic order was strongly threatened under Elizabeth I, was broken under Cromwell, and driven underground more and more during the time of William of Orange and the Penal Laws. Irish storytelling and harp-music were forbidden in Elizabeth's time, and bards and harpers were persecuted, as is shown, e.g. by an "Irish Privy Council Book of Queen Elizabeth . . ." (MS dated 1584), in which Sir John O'Reyley in Co. Cavan was forbidden to "keepe within his house, any Irishe Barde, Carroghe or Rymor, but to the uttermost of his power help to remove them from his countrie".[10] However, during the Middle Ages and down to the 17th century Irish music flourished. In his *Irish Bards,* Joseph Walker points out that John Major refers to the Irish as "the most eminent harpers" in the time of King James I of Scotland, and praises the king for touching "the harp more exquisitely than either the Highlanders or the Irish".[11] But under Queen Elizabeth I the harp "fell into disrepute". Consequently, when Irish harpers no longer wandered over

[10] Quoted in Hardiman, II, p. 160. The word "Carroghe" means a gambler, a card-player. I owe thanks to Ailbhe Ó Corráin, B.A., for this translation. In Patrick Dinneen, *Foclóir Gaedhilge agus Béarla: An Irish-English Dictionary* (Dublin: Publ. for the Irish Texts Society by the Educational Company of Ireland, 1927), p. 180, the word occurs as *cearrbhach* "a gambler". Apparently in Queen Elizabeth I's time, Irish harpers, rhymers and gamblers were equally badly thought of. It may be interesting to note that Yeats's Red Hanrahan has an almost magic knowledge of card-playing.

[11] Joseph Walker, *Historical Memoirs of the Irish Bards* (London, 1786), pp. 121–122. Cf. Pádraig A. Breatnach, "The Chief's Poet", *Proceedings of the Royal Irish Academy*, 83 C 3 (Dublin: Royal Irish Academy, 1983), 37–79, which stresses the close ties between the chief and his poet, whose prestige "was closely linked to that enjoyed by the patron who appointed him" (p. 78). We might also recall Giraldus Cambrensis' panegyric of Irish music.

Europe, French jongleurs and minstrels also gave up visiting Ireland,[12] and Irish music became part of the hidden Irish heritage.

Music cannot be killed. So in the eighteenth and nineteenth centuries, Irish harpers lived on as "itinerants, travelling Ireland on horseback and staying as honoured guests at the Big Houses" where they played at "weddings and funerals", and on other important occasions (Donal O'Sullivan, p. 180). Yeats's Red Hanrahan is such a poet and also a musician, although a fiddler, not a harper. Kevin/Aleel can also be seen as an example of the many itinerant poets and harpers who wandered around Ireland and perhaps as a dramatic embodiment of Yeats's own wish to revive ancient Irish music.

A model for Kevin/Aleel can also be sought elsewhere, i.e. in Irish Jacobite poetry, e.g. in allegorical poems written by poets like Owen Rua O'Sullivan. In such poems, which in the end became rather conventional-ized, the poet is introduced "as wandering in a wood or by the banks of a river, where he is astonished to perceive a beautiful lady approaching him." They converse, and the lady reveals that she "is Erin, who is flying from the insults of foreign suitors and in search of her real mate."[13] One can easily distinguish the political allegory behind such a poem, a suppressed Ireland looking for her liberator. Kevin/Aleel is also wandering in a wood and there he meets the beautiful Countess (likewise a symbol of her country and her people), whose suitor he becomes and to whom he plays on his stringed instrument, a lute or a harp. In Aleel we can, however, see a blend of the itinerant latter-day bard and the poet introduced in Jacobite poetry. A typical Jacobite poem is Owen Rua O'Sullivan's "Le h-ais na Suire" ("Beside the Suir").[14]

Compared with such a poet, Kevin of the 1892 version strikes one, however, as being a rather helpless figure, who is occasionally seized by fits of madness, but is yet quite harmless as indicated in Shemus Rua's condescending description of him:

> He is called Kevin,
> And has been crazy now these many days;
> But has no harm in him: his fits soon pass,
> And one can go and lead him like a child.

> VPl, p. 138

---

[12] Eugene O'Curry, *Manners and Customs,* I, p. dc viii.

[13] Douglas Hyde, *A Literary History of Ireland* (London: Fisher Unwin, 1901), pp. 596–597.

[14] Hardiman, II, pp. 94–101. Trans. of the Irish poem by the Rev. William Hamilton Drummond, a contemporary of Hardiman's.

108

Here he is more like a village fool than a poet. But he has eyes which strike fear even into the Demon-Merchants, and in the "large book of souls" he is described as

> A man of songs—
> Alone in the hushed passion of romance,
> His mind ran all on sheogues, and on tales
> Of Finian labours and the Red-branch kings,
> . . .

VPl, p. 134

Kevin is half crazed by love, wandering about in the wood carrying a harp with broken strings, a symbol of his broken heart. He becomes desperate when learning that Kathleen has decided to sell her soul, and her sad face makes him tear the strings of his harp as if in anticipation of her sad fate. Both he and she carry the theme of self-sacrifice:

> The face of Countess Kathleen dwells with me.
> The sadness of the world upon her brow—
> The crying of these strings grew burdensome,
> Therefore I tore them—see—now take my soul.

VPl, p. 136

In the final version Aleel's grief and despair are even more pronounced:

> The trouble that has come on Countess Cathleen,
> The sorrow that is in her wasted face,
> The burden in her eyes, have broke my wits,
> And yet I know I'd have you take my soul.

VPl, p. 141

Cathleen herself finds comfort in Aleel's music and song:

> Do not blame me,
> Good woman, for the tympan and the harp:
> I was bid fly the terror of the times
> And wrap me round with music and sweet song
> Or else pine . . . grave. . . .

VPl, p. 21, under line

In the final version this passage has been changed to:

> Ah, do not blame the finger on the string;
> The doctor bid me fly the unlucky times
> And find distraction for my thoughts, or else
> Pine to my grave.

VPl, p. 21

Aleel and Cathleen both like music, but Shemus Rua, who is far from being a romantic peasant figure, thoroughly dislikes music and displays great irritation when hearing Aleel playing on his "stringed instrument" outside the cottage:

> Who's passing there?
> And mocking us with music?

VPl, p. 13

The second time he hears Aleel playing, he mutters disapprovingly: "What, music, music!" (*VPl*, p. 21). His aversion to music presents a counter-truth to Aleel's love for it. Cathleen's music is an escape from wordly cares, at least temporarily. Aleel believes in the magic power of music and asks the musicians to play as if their music could master the world:

> . . . Tympan and harp awake!
> For though the world drift from us like a sigh,
> Music is master of all under the moon;
> And play 'The Wind that blows by Cummen Strand.'

VPl, pp. 21, 23, under line

The tune "The Wind that blows by Cummen Strand",[15] which Aleel asks the musicians to play, associates him with Kathleen Ni Houlihan and Red Hanrahan, for Cummen Strand also occurs in "Red Hanrahan's Song about Ireland", which begins "The old brown thorn-trees break in two high over Cummen Strand" (*VP*, pp. 206−208).[16]

Songs in *The Countess Cathleen*

Kevin/Aleel, the poet in the play, composes the songs, and in the final version he himself also sings the songs. In the first version, one song is

---

[15] I have not been able to identify this tune (if it is a tune and not just a poetic invention on Yeats's part). Cummen Strand is situated westward of Sligo town.

[16] This poem first appeared untitled in the story "Kathleen-Ny-Houlihan" (*National Observer*, 4 August 1894), then as "Kathleen the Daughter of Houlihan and Hanrahan the Red" in *The Secret Rose* (1897), and as "The Song of Red Hanrahan" in *In the Seven Woods*. Cummen Strand occurs in the first and third versions, but not in the second. Cf. Jeffares, *Commentary Poems*, p. 90, and Ole Munch-Pedersen, "Some Aspects of the Rewriting of W. B. Yeats's 'Red Hanrahan's Song About Ireland' ", *Orbis Litterarum*, 36 (1981), 155−172; hereafter Munch-Pedersen. This article investigates Yeats's use of place-names and coloured winds in the different versions of the poem. The different-coloured winds go back to *Saltair na Rann* ("Psalter of Quatrains"), ed. Wh. Stokes (Oxford, 1883), poem I, lines 53−80. They also occur in an entry in *Seanchas Mór* (the Great Brehon Law Book); quoted in Hyde's *Literary History of Ireland*, p. 416. See also W. Hancock et al., ed., *Ancient Laws of Ireland* (Dublin, 1865). One might also recall that Lionel Johnson, who wrote several poems concerned with Celtic themes, in a poem called "The Red Wind", included in *Yeats's Book of Irish Verse* ([1895]; 2nd ed. 1900), used the idea of coloured winds, but confined himself to the red wind.

sung by Oona, another by the seven Spirits. There is no trace of these two songs in the final version of the play. Here, for convenience sake, follows a list of the songs as they occur in the different versions:

1892 (V Scenes)
  Epigraph: "The sorrowful are dumb for thee" (taken from
        "Lament of Morian Shehone for Miss Mary Bourke")
  "Who will go drive with Fergus now...?" (Sc. II)
  "All the heavy days are over" (Sc. V)
1895 (3 Acts)
  Epigraph
  "Impetuous heart, be still, be still" (Act I)
  "Who will go drive with Fergus now...?" (Act II: Part II)
  (Notice that Aleel's vision (Act III) replaces the earlier vision of Oona.)
1899—1908) (4 Acts)
  Epigraph
  "Impetuous heart, be still, be still" (Act I)
  "Who will go drive with Fergus now...?" (Act II: Sc. II)
  (Aleel's vision is further revised; Act IV)
1912 (V Scenes)
  Epigraph
  "Impetuous heart, be still, be still" (Sc. I)
  "Lift up the white knee" (Sc. II)
  "Our hearts are sore" (Sc. IV)
  (Aleel's vision further revised; Sc. V)
1913—1934 (V Scenes)[17]
  Epigraph
  "Were I but crazy for love's sake" (Sc. I)
  "Lift up the white knee" (Sc. II)
  "Impetuous heart, be still, be still" (Sc. IV)
  (Aleel's vision further revised, Sc. V; notice also that Aleel turns up in all five scenes.)

Let us first have a closer look at the epigraph, "The sorrowful are dumb for thee", which sets the sad tone of the play. This elegiac half-line derives from a translation of an anonymous Irish keen or lament entitled "Lament of Morian Shehone for Miss Mary Bourke", which Yeats regarded as being worthy of inclusion in his own collection *A Book of Irish Verse* (pp. 242—245):[18]

[17] Cf. *VPl*, p. xv: Yeats "continued using the revision of 1912 in the 1914, 1916, 1917, 1919, and 1921 reprintings of *The Poetical Works of W. B. Yeats,* Vol. II, Dramatic Poems . . .", but "in the 1921 American *Selected Poems* the 1913 Tauchnitz version of the play", somewhat confusing for bibliographers and editors.

[18] *Selected from Modern Writers with an Introduction and Notes by W. B. Yeats* (London, 1895; rev. and enl. ed., London: Methuen, 1900), pp. 242—245. Yeats gives no source for this anonymous lament said to be translated from Irish. I have not seen a copy of the 1895 ed., which in 1983 was reported as mislaid in the British Library, and missing since 1974 in the National Library of Ireland.

111

'There's darkness in thy dwelling-place, and silence reigns
    above,
And Mary's voice is heard no more, like the soft
    voice of love.
Yes! thou art gone, my Mary dear! and Morian
    Shehone[19]
Is left to sing his song of woe, and wail for thee
    alone.
O! snow-white were thy virtues—the beautiful, the
    young,
The old with pleasure bent to hear the music of thy
    tongue:
The young with rapture gazed on thee, and their
    hearts in love were bound,
For thou wast brighter than the sun that sheds its
    light around.
My soul is dark, O Mary dear! thy sun of beauty's
    set;
The sorrowful are dumb for thee[20]—the grieved their
    tears forget,
And I am left to pour my woe above thy grave
    alone;
For dear wert thou to the fond heart of Morian
    Shehone.
Fast-flowing tears above the grave of the rich man
    are shed,
But they are dried when the cold stone shuts in his
    narrow bed;
Not so with my heart's faithful love—the dark grave
    cannot hide
From Morian's eyes thy form of grace, of loveliness,
    and pride.
Thou didst not fall like the sere leaf, when autumn's
    chill winds blow—
'T was a tempest and a storm-blast that has laid my
    Mary low.
Hadst thou not friends that loved thee well? hadst
    thou not garments rare?
Wast thou not happy, Mary? wast thou not young
    and fair?
Then why should the dread spoiler come, my heart's
    peace to destroy,
Or the grim tyrant tear from me my all of earthly
    joy?

---

[19] Yeats spells ''Morian Shehone'' in this poem, but in ''Irish National Literature, IV'', he
writes ''Moria Shehone'' (Frayne, I, p. 385).

[20] My emphasis.

O! am I left to pour my woes above thy grave alone?
Thou idol of the faithful heart of Morian Shehone!
Sweet were thy looks and sweet thy smiles, and kind
    wast thou to all;
The withering scowl of envy on thy fortunes dared
    not fall;
For thee thy friends lament and mourn, and never
    cease to weep—
O! that their lamentations could awake thee from
    thy sleep!
O! that thy peerless form again could meet my
    loving clasp!
O! that the cold damp hand of Death could loose
    his iron grasp!
Yet, when the valley's daughters meet beneath the
    tall elm tree,
And talk of Mary as a dream that never more
    shall be,
Then may thy spirit float around, like music in the
    air,
And pour upon their virgin souls a blessing and a
    prayer.
O! am I left to pour my wail above thy grave
    alone?
Then sinks in silence the lament of Morian Shehone![21]

This Irish dirge or lament relates how Mary Bourke has been killed by a storm and how Morian Shehone is alone, lost in grief, beside her grave. The catastrophe that struck Mary Bourke down "was a tempest and a storm-blast". "The sorrowful are dumb for thee—the grieved their tears forgot", is the mysterious message of the tenth line of the poem. The half-line "The sorrowful are dumb for thee" appealed so much to Yeats that he chose it as an opening epigraph to *CC*. It both sets the sad tone of the play and introduces the *Leitmotif* of the sorrow of love which is of such significance in the play. This epigraph was never changed throughout the many revisions, only slightly differently written, in the first version as *"The sorrowful are dumb for thee"*. / The Lament of Morian Shehone for Mary Bourke," and in the final version as " 'The sorrowful are dumb for thee'/ *Lament of Morian Shehone/* for Miss Mary Bourke". (In some versions "Morian" appears as "Morion".) It is perhaps worth noticing

[21] This poem is also included in Joseph Barry, *Songs of Ireland* (Dublin, 1845; 2nd ed. 1869), and in *The Universal Irish Song Book: A Complete Collection of the Songs and Ballads of Ireland* (New York: P. J. Kenedy, 1886), p. 220, but has only 24 lines as compared to the 36 lines recorded by Yeats.

that Yeats chose the most beautiful and mysterious line of the poem, one which high-lights the absolute silence of the mourners dumbfounded by their grief, in contrast to Morian Shehone who is weeping out his grief beside the grave. That Yeats had a great liking for this line is borne out by what he states in his fourth article on "Irish National Literature":[22] ". . . and even some few poems which, like 'The Lament of Moria[n] Shehone for Miss Mary Bourke' in 'The Book of Irish Verse', are precious because of a single line that is the signature of an ancient and Celtic emotion" (Frayne, I, p. 385). The intensity of the emotion is what Yeats singles out as especially "Celtic". It is also significant that in the lament, as in *CC*, the storm is an outstanding feature, a force which had killed Mary Bourke. The romantic combination of storm and grief is also found in Yeats's play.

The same lament from which the opening epigraph to *CC* derives, also occurs, although in a somewhat different version, in a romance written by Mrs. Frances Peck, but whether Yeats knew this or not is difficult to know.[23] The title of the first three-volume edition is *The Bard of the West; Commonly Called Eman Ac Knuck Or Ned of the Hills: An Irish Historical Romance, Founded on Facts of the Seventh Century.*[24] Mrs. Peck claims to have got some of her material from an old document in Irish script from her mother, a document which had been found "amongst the papers of the late Doctor Andrews, Provost of Trinity College", and Mrs. Peck's uncle, "Dr. Magee, late Archdeacon of Dublin" had the document translated. It has an interesting story, for it had been "found, by an Irish cottager, at Outerard, in Connemara . . . digging in his potatoegarden; and was concealed in a stone jar, buried several feet under ground. . . . in consequence of penal laws." It had even been taken to China by "a learned Clergyman" (see 1842 rev. ed., pp. 270–271). In this romance Mrs. Peck mixes Gothic,

[22] *Bookman,* London, October 1895; rpt. in Frayne, I, pp. 382–387.

[23] Mrs. Frances Peck, who also wrote under the pseudonym "Candida" (e.g. *Tales of the Barrack Room,* 1847), is listed neither in *The Dictionary of National Biography* (1908) nor in any of the dictionaries of authors, except for a short notice in J. Brown, *Ireland in Fiction* (new ed., Dublin and London: Maunsel and Company, 1919), p. 253. Brown lists *Edmund of Erin,* and *Tales for the British People.* Other works of hers are *Maid of Avon, The Welch Peasant Boy* (1808), *Young Roisinière, Vage.*

[24] (London and Dublin, 1818). There were several revised editions, e.g. in 1842, and 1869 (6th ed.). Mrs. Peck's relation, the Right Hon. Francis Andrews was Provost of Trinity College Dublin, 1758–1774, a period when "the prestige of the University was high, for there were a number of distinguished Fellows" (Constantia Maxwell, *History of Trinity College, Dublin, 1591–1929* [Dublin, 1946], pp. 115–122). For information about this source giving facts about Provost Andrews, I owe thanks to W. E. Mackey, Research Librarian, Trinity College Dublin.

grotesque, sublime and romantic Celtic and Oriental features into a rather bizarre novel on an Irish heroic figure called "Eman ac Knuck" (or *Eamonn an Chnuic*—Edmund of the Hill) and his love for Princess Eva. Mrs. Peck is aware of her numerous anachronisms and realizes that her character Eman ac Knuck did not live in the 7th century, as she states in the 1818 edition, but much later. She writes in the 1842 edition: "Mr. Edmund Ryan, a man of talent and enterprise, who, according to Mr. O'Halloran, commanded a company of free-booters after the battle of the Boyne",[25] became a leader of outlaws who carried on a guerilla campaign, were looked upon as robbers and bandits, and were called rapparees. Precise dates for Edmund Ryan are missing, but he was probably born in the 1670s and had a price on his head in 1702.[26] This man does not have anything in common with the character in Mrs. Peck's romance which is, however, of particular interest to us here because she makes use of "Morian Shehone's Lament for Mary Bourke", although the heroine of the romance is Princess Eva, not Mary Bourke. In the 1818 edition Eva's nurse is called Maga, but in the 1842 edition she is called Moreen Shehone. Eva died as "the benefactress of the people" like Cathleen in Yeats's play. While people were searching for her after she had been abducted by Fergus (referred to as the Ruthless Red), "a female form" rose on Tara Hill: "her flaxen hair flowed loosely over her shoulders, and, she was arrayed in a long, dark-blue Irish mantle." She was shrieking in grief like the Banshee, and, "rushing down the hill stood in an attitude of mute woe, near the remains of the princess. . . . It was *Moreen Shehone!* the affectionate nurse, and faithful follower of Eva" (1842 ed., p. 222). Then in a loud voice she recites "The Funeral Lament of Moreen Shehone over the Princess

[25] Sylvester O'Halloran, *Introduction to the History and Antiquities of Ireland* (1778), I, p. 382. O'Halloran just mentions "regiments of *Free Booters*", but Charlotte Brooke gives more information: "a very celebrated personage, of the name of Edmond Ryan, concerning whom many stories are still circulated, but no connected account has been obtained further than that he commanded a company of those unhappy free booters, called Rapparees, who after the defeat of the Boyne, were obliged to abandon their dwellings and possessions . . .", *Reliques of Ancient Irish Poetry* (Dublin, 1789), p. 205. See also pp. 206–213 and 309–310 for an elegy written by Edmond Ryan. In *Spoken English in Ireland 1600–1740*, p. 267, Alan Bliss explains the word *rapparee* as "a compromise between" Ir. *rópaire* ("snatcher, robber") and the loanword *rápaire* ("rapier").
[26] For an account of Eamonn an Chnuic, i.e. "Ryan of the Hill", see also Donal O'Sullivan, pp. 150–152. The song recorded by O'Sullivan was very popular in the 18th and 19th centuries. Yeats himself wrote a "Love Song. From the Gaelic" (based on Edward Walsh's prose translation of "Eamonn an Chnuic"), included in *Poems and Ballads of Young Ireland* (Dublin, 1888), p. 80. The poem begins: "My love, we will go, we will go, I and you." See Wade, *Letters*, p. 47, and Michael Yeats, p. 156. Cf. also Mary Helen Thuente, *W. B. Yeats and Irish Folklore*, Ch. 5, in which a number of rakes and rapparees are dealt with.

Eva''. The text of the poem recorded by Mrs. Peck is inferior to that from which Yeats drew his epigraph. The line corresponding to Yeats's epigraph runs: ''Sorrow for thee is dumb'', and continues ''save the wailings of Moreen Shehone''.

Yeats's epigraph ''The sorrowful are dumb for thee'', words which convey Morian's deep grief, is drawn from an elegy whose power and appeal lie in its combination of passionate grief and love. These feelings also permeate the songs of the play, which as will be seen, all deal with some form of love. Songs of a different character are ''All the heavy days are over'', turning up only in the first edition of 1892, and ''Our hearts are sore'' in the 1912 version.

The first song or lyric to be considered here is ''Who will go drive with Fergus now . . .?'',[27] which Oona refers to as ''the ballad young bard Kevin sang/ By the great door, the light about his head,/ When he bid you cast off this cloud of care'' (*VPl*, p. 44). This lyrical poem or song was composed by Kevin in order to make the Countess forget her wordly cares. Just as she has settled her head on old Oona's lap, to hear the song sung in Oona's thin voice, her gardener enters and tells her that on the previous night ''A crowd of ugly lean-faced rogues'' had stolen all the apples, trodden down the asparagus and strawberry beds and torn down the pear and plum trees and robbed them of all their fruit. A ''yellow vapour'' also affected his saplings, the gardener complains. This destruction of the Countess's garden is symbolical of the great affliction which has struck her country and her people. Faced with these difficulties Kathleen seeks comfort in Oona's song about Fergus:

> *Who will go drive with Fergus now,*
> *And pierce the deep wood's woven shade,*
> *And dance upon the level shore?*
> *Young man, lift up your russet brow,*
> *And lift your tender eyelids, maid,*
> *And brood on hopes and fears no more.*

VPl, pp. 52, 54

Again two worlds are opposed, the world of reality and the invisible world of Fergus, whose horn Kathleen can hear in her heart (*VPl*, p. 54). To old Oona the symbolic meaning expressed by the horn and the song is hidden, and at first the poem may appear somewhat enigmatic also to the reader. Does the poet invite us to share Fergus's company in the woods, or does he

---

[27] Entitled ''Who Goes with Fergus?'' unitalicized, unindented in *Collected Poems*, pp. 48–49; *VP*, pp. 125–126.

warn us? The second stanza certainly asks us to give up brooding on "Love's bitter mystery":

> *And no more turn aside and brood*
> *Upon Love's bitter mystery;*
> *For Fergus rules the brazen cars,*
> *And rules the shadows of the wood,*
> *And the white breast of the dim sea*
> *And all dishevelled wandering stars.*

VPl, pp. 54, 56

In order to grasp the hidden meaning of the poem, we must study the figure of Fergus. Yeats states in a note in *Poems* (1901) that Fergus "was the poet of the Red Branch cycle, as Oisin was of the Fenian. He was once King of all Ireland, and, as the legend is shaped by Ferguson, gave up his throne that he might live at peace hunting in the woods" (p. 301).

When Oona sings the song in her thin old voice, we should be able to hear also the imaginary music of the hunting-horn which Kathleen takes as a summons to her to join Fergus's realm, the Otherworld in which he drives his brazen chariot as ruler of the woods, the ocean and the sky. The Fergus of Yeats's lyric is very different from the ancient legendary King of Ulster—a heroic king who in order to be able to marry the beautiful Nessa pledged his kingship for a year to Conchubar (or Conor), Nessa's son by the druid Cathbad. Nessa agreed to marry Fergus but when the year was up, the Ulstermen refused to reinstate Fergus, and Conchubar remained High King of Ulster.[28]

Here we may also refer to another poem on Fergus, "Fergus and the Druid", a poem first published in the *National Observer* in 1892 and consisting of a colloquy between Fergus and a Druid. He has followed the Druid all day long among the rocks, has seen him changing "from shape to shape" (*Collected Poems*, p. 36)—"a raven", "a weasel", a "thin grey man"—and tells him that he himself has laid down his crown for "Young subtle Conchubar" and now wants to learn druidic wisdom (Ibid., p. 36). Fergus has gone through a long series of lives, in which he has appeared in many shapes, one of which is as king:

> I see my life go drifting like a river
> From change to change; I have been many things—
> A green drop in the surge, a gleam of light
> Upon a sword, a fir-tree on a hill,

---

[28] See Whitley Stokes's trans. of this ancient tale in *Ériu*, IV (1910), 18–33, esp. 25, and also Thomas Kinsella, trans. and ed., *The Tain: Translated from the Irish Epic Táin Bó Cuailnge* (London, New York: OUP, 1970), pp. 3–6.

An old slave grinding at a heavy quern,
A king sitting upon a chair of gold—
And all these things were wonderful and great;
But now I have grown nothing, knowing all.
Ah! Druid, Druid, how great webs of sorrow
Lay hidden in the small slate-coloured thing!

Collected Poems, p. 37

"The small slate-coloured thing" is "the little bag of dreams" given him by the Druid. Neither in his life as a wise man nor as a king will Fergus be free from sorrow. The poem is based on the idea of rebirth, including also metempsychosis, in which man undergoes a long series of rebirths, not only as a human being, but also in animal shape, or in some form in the vegetable world, or even as one of the four elements, in fact reminding us of Amergin's "Triumph Song" (cf. n. 34). The Druid can of course assume different shapes by means of his magic, but in Fergus's case, it would seem that his life in different shapes and forms is the result of a kind of rebirth pattern idiosyncratic to Yeats at this time, for no matter how many rebirths the soul is passing through, there is no release from sorrow. Both this poem and the song "Who goes with Fergus?" are permeated by a romantic sadness and melancholy which can almost be called *Weltschmerz.* Yeats stated himself that one of his chief sources of inspiration for this poem was Ferguson's poetry, especially the poem entitled "The Abdication of Fergus Mac Roy",[29] i.e. "the poet-king who loves hunting and the freedom of the great wood".[30] Ferguson's poem like Yeats's depicts a Fergus willingly giving up his crown in favour of his stepson Conor. Fergus recalls his former life as king when he had enjoyed the chase and the mead more than the judgement-seat. Bewitched by Nessa's beauty he lets her son, the fourteen-year-old Conor, sit beside him and judge in his place and in the end abdicates in his favour. In Ferguson's poem one is reminded of the situation from Tennyson's "Ulysses" of a dissatisfied king who hands over his crown and sceptre to a son (in Ferguson's poem to a stepson), who is better equipped to rule and judge:

So young Conor gained the crown;
So I laid the kingship down;
Laying with it as it went
All I knew of discontent.

Ferguson, *Poems,* p. 123

[29] *Poems of Sir Samuel Ferguson,* The Irish Library (Dublin, Cork and Belfast n.d. [1880]), pp. 116–123. Cf. Farag, p. 42.
[30] W. B. Yeats, "The Poetry of Sir Samuel Ferguson—II", in Frayne, I, p. 91.

But the similarity ends there, for in Tennyson's poem, and also, indeed, in Yeats's, another aspect is strongly emphasized, the king as a seeker. However, whereas Tennyson makes Ulysses set out in search of knowledge and new realms, even of death itself, Yeats's Fergus is above all a seeker of wisdom, a poet whose druidic knowledge and wisdom do not, however, produce personal happiness and harmony. In an interesting analysis of Yeats's two poems, Thomas L. Byrd Jr. in *The Early Poetry of W. B. Yeats: The Poetic Quest* claims that "Fergus and the Druid" (1892) and "Who Goes with Fergus?" (1899) "add another dimension to the theme of the poet as wanderer and seeker in the early works and show that Yeats's later ideas on the poet-seeker are contained in the earlier poems."[31]

The romantic Yeats was fascinated by an abdicating Fergus, less a king than a poet in search of the mystical wisdom of the Druids. In the character of Fergus, Yeats combines occult and Irish traditions in order to express his own bitter experience of love and his own aspirations as a poet. Neither a king nor a poet-druid can escape life's bitter truth. But Countess Kathleen, although tempted by Fergus's realm, rejects his imaginary world for the claims of reality. Her actions are prompted by her dedication to her people. She is the direct opposite to Fergus who renounced his kingdom for the sake of love.

Yeats retained "Who will go drive with Fergus now...?" (i.e. "Who goes with Fergus?") in all versions of *CC* up to and including the one in *Collected Works* (1908), but in 1912 he replaced it with another song sung by Aleel, "Lift up the white knee", which is perhaps as romantic as the Fergus poem, but which through the image of the white knee introduces an allusive erotic beauty which phrases such as "the white breast of the dim sea" in the poem on Fergus can also be said to convey. Act II, Part II (of the 1895 ed.), in which "Lift up the white knee" appears, was completely rewritten as Sc. II for the 1912 version (see list on p. 111 supra). Queen Maeve and her dancers are given a prominent place in the song, which undoubtedly changes this part of the play considerably. The mood is much wilder than in earlier versions. Oona for example openly dislikes Aleel, and refers to him as a pagan and an "empty rattle-plate" (*VPl,* p. 59). Aleel tries to impress Cathleen with a love story about a man who "Loved Maeve the Queen of all the invisible host,/ And died of his love nine centuries ago" (*VPl,* p. 55), thus introducing a form of demon lover theme; for at full moon Maeve leaves her invisible dancers and retires to the place where her once rejected lover died, "and for three days/ Stretches and

---

[31] (Port Washington, N.Y.; London: National Univ. Publ. Kennikat Press, 1978), p. 47.

sighs and wets her long pale cheeks" (*VPl*, p. 55). This Pre-Raphaelite image is used by Aleel in his attempt to make Cathleen love him, but in vain. During their walk in the wood (they have lost their way), Aleel plays on his lute, which is so old that it "remembers every foot/ That danced upon the level grass of the world,/ And will tell secrets if I whisper to it" (*VPl*, p. 57). The instrument is a link between the past and the present and its music expresses Aleel's longing for ideal love. The use of the magic harp in *SW* is certainly foreshadowed here. Aleel then sings his song:

> Lift up the white knee;
> Hear what they sing,
> Those young dancers
> That in a ring
> Raved but now
> Of the hearts that broke
> Long, long ago
> For their sake.

VPl, p. 57

This song further illustrates the love story just told by Aleel. The young dancers, Maeve's invisible host endowed with a long memory, dance on without heeding the hearts they broke ages ago, for there are always new lovers. Aleel, the singer, is interrupted by Oona, who says "New friends are sweet", but Aleel continues:

> But the dance changes,
> Lift up the gown,
> All that sorrow
> Is trodden down.[32]

VPl, p. 59

This poem expresses symbolically the idea of human beings and fairies being born several times, living innumerable lives like the Faery Child in *LHD*, who is older than the oldest animal in the world. The dance symbolizes the cycle of rebirth going on eternally. The never-ending dance of Maeve and her invisible dancers also symbolizes a deeply human situation, the mystery as well as mutability of love. The dancers have begun a new dance which will make them forget the sorrow they once caused, and invite Aleel and Cathleen to join in the dance.

As for the image of the white knee, Yeats could have come across it in a Fenian ballad, "Garw and Cuchulain", in which a character named Aedh

---

[32] In the 1912 ed., the first line and the last three lines of the poem are enclosed in quotation marks.

of the White Knee appears,[33] but he could also have come across this phrase in the part of *Lebor Gabála* which tells the story of Amergin of the White Knee, the first bard and druid of Ireland and one of the sons of Mil or Milesius, the legendary forefather of the Gaels.[34] On the other hand, it may be entirely his own invention.

The allusive dance of Maeve's fairy host expresses Aleel's innermost wish, his spiritual and physical longing for Cathleen. But it also reveals the cruelty with which Queen Maeve rejected a lover who died for her sake. Lifting up the white knee in a dance with her means death. Love and death are closely linked in this song to which the invisible host dances. It is a kind of esoteric dance of death in which mortals join with immortals—the erotic symbol being the white knee, which lends a pictorial strength to the poem. In her excellent study *Der Tanz im Drama: Untersuchungen zu W. B. Yeats' dramatischer Theorie und Praxis,* Isolde von Bülow examines the significance of the art of dancing, mainly for the Noh Plays and Yeats's later dance plays in the light of his dramatic theories.[35] She also touches on the importance of dancing for Yeats's early dramatic theory (pp. 66—70) and mentions that he uses the supernatural dance of the fairies as a motif in *The Celtic Twilight* and *The Secret Rose,* but that it is only with the story "Dust hath Closed Helen's Eyes" that "die Tanzkunst gleichwertig neben der Dichtkunst und der Weisheit als göttliche Gabe gennant wird" (p. 66; cf. *Mythologies,* p. 29). But only with the kind of initiation dance that occurs in *Rosa Alchemica* can Yeats's later use of the dance be said to be recognized, von Bülow states. The most important aspect here is the motif of ecstasy achieved through the dance. The shedding of the ordinary senses and the passing into a supernatural sphere are significant. On the stage, there is also an exchange between silence and speech, between the dance and the word. In my opinion, "Lift up the white knee", the song accompanied by the dance of the fairies, can be seen as an illustration of

---

[33] "Garw and Cuchulain", *Transactions of the Gaelic Society of Inverness,* 22 (1897—98), 297—298.

[34] Amergin composed a famous poem, "The Triumph Song of Amergin" beginning "I, the Wind at Sea", see George Sigerson, ed. and trans., *Bards of the Gael and Gall: Examples of the Poetic Literature of Erinn,* 2nd rev.and enl. ed. (London: Fisher Unwin, 1907), pp. 110—111. This song, which Sigerson considers to be "pan-egoistic", provides one of many examples of what seems to be metempsychosis in Irish literature. Robert Graves has incorporated a similar poem by Taliesin with Amergin's; see *The Faber Book of Irish Verse,* ed. John Montague (London: Faber and Faber, 1974), p. 45.

[35] Studien zur Englischen Literatur, 1. Ed. Johannes Kleinstück (Bonn: Bouvier, 1969).

Yeats's early dramatic theory of the combination of gesture with word to give expression to a deeply personal grief.[36]

"Lift up the white knee" changes the mood of the play and its approach to love and life, but through it Yeats also presents two points of view. The invisible world of Queen Maeve becomes a resort for the poet, whether he be Aleel or Yeats himself. There is a momentary union between the poet and his dream, and one might perhaps say that the dance itself symbolizes what Arthur Symons in his poem "The Dance" refers to as "the immortal moment":

> For the immortal moment of a passionate dance,
> Surely our two souls rushed together and were one.[37]

To Cathleen, however, this is all just an illusion. For a moment she may feel as if magically drawn to the poet's imaginary world, but her aim in life, to save her suffering people, is totally different from the poet's. The poem expresses the sweetness of love, but also conveys Aleel's disillusioned view that lovers change partners as easily as dancers. In spite of this rather common theme of the fickleness of love, the dominant mood of the poem is one of a mysterious dream full of the movement of supernatural dancers. It has the same kind of intense passion as the two Gaelic love poems quoted at the beginning of this chapter.

In 1895 Yeats also introduced another song, a lyric of six lines sung by Aleel in Act I. This song expresses another of love's many moods and tries to combine art with ritual. Having just warned the cottagers to "draw the door and the bolt" because of the two grey horned owls he has seen and heard outside, Aleel sings as he is going out:

> *Impetuous heart, be still, be still;*
> *Your sorrowful love may never be told;*
> *Cover it up with a lonely tune.*
> *He who could bend all things to his will*
> *Has covered the door of the infinite fold*
> *With the pale stars and the wandering moon.*[38]
>
> *Poems*, 1895, p. 77

The poet addresses his own heart begging it to "be still", to look for

---

[36] That Yeats expressed his own desperate love for Maud Gonne in *CC* was first stressed by T. R. Henn in *The Lonely Tower* (London: Methuen, 1950), p. 24. Henn stated that Yeats "started . . . *The Countess Cathleen*" as "the first projection of his own love and despair."

[37] *Poems*, 2 vol. (London: William Heinemann, 1902), p. 41. Isolde von Bülow (*Der Tanz im Drama*, p. 48n) points out that Symons's influence on Yeats's aesthetic theories has not yet been fully explored. To Symons as to Yeats, the dance is a significant symbol. In his Noh plays, the dance became such an important feature that Yeats called them *Plays for Dancers*.

[38] Cf. *VPl*, p. 129, where the poem is not italicized and not indented.

consolation in music. God himself has hidden the gates of heaven with the stars and the moon, and likewise the poet must hide his sorrow, and "cover it up with a lonely tune". With melancholy detachment Yeats here expresses his disillusion with love. Unhappy love cannot romantically look for comfort in the stars and the moon. Aleel's loneliness and love find an outlet in music. This poem has a certain kinship with another poem of disillusion which Yeats called "The Cold Heaven" and included in *The Green Helmet and Other Poems* (1912) and later also in *Responsibilities* (1914). Yeats told Maud Gonne that this poem "was an attempt to describe the feelings aroused in him by the cold detached sky in the winter" which made him think of "all the past mistakes that were torturing his peace of mind" (Jeffares, *Commentary Poems*, p. 146). "The Cold Heaven" is a poem dealing with metaphysical reflections on the state of the soul after death and its punishment by an unjust heaven:

> Suddenly I saw the cold and rook-delighting heaven
> That seemed as though ice burned and was but the
>   more ice,
> And thereupon imagination and heart were driven
> So wild that every casual thought of that and this
> Vanished, and left but memories, that should be out
>   of season
> With the hot blood of youth, of love crossed long ago;
> And I took all the blame out of all sense and reason,
> Until I cried and trembled and rocked to and fro,
> Riddled with light. Ah! when the ghost begins to
>   quicken,
> Confusion of the death-bed over, is it sent
> Out naked on the roads, as the books say, and stricken
> By the injustice of the skies for punishment?
>
> *Collected Poems*, p. 140

In "Impetuous heart" the sky closes the poet off from Heaven. In "The Cold Heaven" this feeling of isolation and alienation is even stronger; "the injustice of the skies" can strike the naked soul after death. Is the soul when parted from the body doomed to be a lonely wanderer on a road with a sky of burning ice above?[39] The soul itself is seen as a wanderer in search of justice.

[39] Bruce M. Wilson in " 'From Mirror after Mirror': Yeats and Eastern Thought", *Comparative Literature*, 34 (Winter 1982), pp. 28–46, quotes this poem as expressing the "tension between the creator and the creation" (p. 34). Wilson bases his article on Hiro Ishibashi's study *Yeats and the Noh: Types of Japanese Beauty and Their Reflection in Yeats's Plays*, in Yeats Centenary Papers, ed. Liam Miller (Dublin: Dolmen Press, 1968). In 1935 S. P. Swami and Yeats worked on a translation of the *Upanishads* published as *The Ten Principal Upanishads* (London: Faber and Faber, 1937; New York: Macmillan, 1937).

"Impetuous heart" also strongly recalls "The Everlasting Voices", one of the poems in WR:

> O sweet everlasting Voices, be still;
> Go to the guards of the heavenly fold
> And bid them wander obeying your will,
> Flame under flame, till Time be no more;
> Have you not heard that our hearts are old,
> That you call in birds, in wind on the hill,
> In shaken boughs, in tide on the shore?
> O sweet everlasting Voices, be still.
>
> Collected Poems, pp. 61−62

This poem written on 29 August 1895 (see Ellmann, *Ident.*, p. 287) and first printed in the *Northern Review* (January 1896), dates from about the same time as "Impetuous heart". The two poems are both admonitions, one to the heart, one to the everlasting voices, to "be still". Both also use the image of the heavenly fold from which the heart and the everlasting voices are excluded. There is no doubt that the "sweet everlasting Voices" are the fairy host, whose messages Yeats often imagined he heard and was longing to hear, as he says for example in his essay "The Golden Age" (*Mythologies*, pp. 104−105), in which he more or less identifies "the spirits" or fairies with "bodiless moods":[40]

A while ago I was in the train, and getting near Sligo. The last time I had been there something was troubling me, and I had longed for a message from those beings or bodiless moods, or whatever they be, who inhabit the world of spirits. The message came. . . . The fairies and the more innocent of the spirits dwelt within it [the earth], and lamented over our fallen world in the lamentation of the wind-tossed reeds, in the song of the birds, in the moan of the waves, and in the sweet cry of the fiddle. . . . It said that if only they who live in the Golden Age could die we might be happy, for the sad voices would be still; but they must sing and we must weep until the eternal gates swing open.

The voices must go on singing and the heart weeping until "the eternal gates swing open". Aleel's tormented heart seeks consolation in the harp and protection against evil in music.

When in 1913 Yeats introduced a new song for Aleel, "Were I but crazy for love's sake", a lyric in a more violent vein, he did not actually reject the earlier poem "Impetuous heart" (as Meir suggests, p. 76), but moved it to Sc. IV, a short scene from which at the same time he removed the sad spirits whom the Demons conjure up and force to carry bags of gold for them. In the new, tableau-like scene the Peasants and the Merchants were

---

[40] Cf. Mary Helen Thuente, *W. B. Yeats and Irish Folklore*, p. 133.

retained and after they have passed across the stage, *Aleel passes over the stage singing* (*VPl*, p. 129) the song "Impetuous heart". Coming as it does after the procession of Peasants and Merchants, but before the sale of the souls in Shemus Rua's house in Sc. V, the song here creates a totally new effect. Aleel's impetuous love is threatened by a sense of doom. The poem is undoubtedly a good conclusion to this short scene. Heaven is closed to Aleel, and a little later he sees "the brazen door" swing open to reveal his vision of Hell.

One might be surprised to find such an angry poem as "Were I but crazy for love's sake" replacing "Impetuous heart, be still, be still" in Sc. I of the 1913 and later versions. As Colin Meir states (p. 77), Aleel has become a realistic character by now, yet one might add, hardly a man of action, for his anger only makes him snap his fingers at Shemus:

> Were I but crazy for love's sake
> I know who'd measure out his length,
> I know the heads that I should break,
> For crazy men have double strength.
> I know—all's out to leave or take,
> Who mocks at music mocks at love;
> Were I but crazy for love's sake,
> No need to pick or choose.
> [*Snapping his fingers in Shemus' face*
> Enough!
>
> *VPL*, p. 23

Yeats here creates a mood emerging from a synthesis of madness, love and music. Aleel is possessed by a passion stronger than Shemus's greed for gold. He is the intense spokesman for art and love, and if he is insane, his madness does not spring merely from his frustration in love. This is certainly a new attitude in the play. What, one might ask, does Yeats aim at in this poem? Does not the crucial line "Who mocks at music mocks at love" indicate that the poem can be seen as a form of protest against the neglect of art which Yeats found all around him in Dublin? The peasant's mocking of music and Aleel's anger at this can be seen as a projection of Yeats's experience of Irish politics, and the Irish public controversies which he took part in, especially the Lane controversy between 1912–1913, which provoked Yeats to write many bitter poems. Aleel, although a more violent character than in earlier versions of the play, nevertheless strikes one as being a person almost as helpless as Kevin, but in a different way. He is unable to change the course of events, and this inability fills him with fierce anger. The poem is, however, radically different from the first poem on Fergus which Oona sings to Kathleen in Sc. II of the 1892 version.

Nor has it any of the religious allusions found in "Impetuous heart". Its mood is one of anger and can be seen as characteristic of the poems Yeats wrote during 1912–13. Love in the poem is a kind of frenzy comparable to madness, and in that respect Aleel has affinities with some of Shakespeare's Fools. The poem adds a realistic dimension to Aleel's character as well as to the play itself.

That Aleel's love for Cathleen, in its various moods, informs the songs of the play, has, I hope, been demonstrated so far in this chapter. The songs focus their attention on the poet, his love and his visionary or imaginary world, whereas "All the heavy days are over" or the "Song of the Seven Spirits" in the last scene of the first version is entirely concerned with Kathleen. "All the heavy days are over" was first published with the title "Kathleen" in the *National Observer* (October 31 1891), then included in *The Countess Kathleen* (1892) as "Song", and in *Poems* (1895) as "A Dream of a Blessed Spirit". In *Collected Poems* (p. 48) it has the title "The Countess Cathleen in Paradise".

In this poem old Oona envisions Kathleen's journey to Heaven. Carrying the lifeless body of the Countess and singing their song, the Seven Spirits descend from the oratory and place Kathleen *"with the head upon the knees of Oona"* (*VPl*, p. 162). The song is a dirge or lament written in quatrain form with alternate rhymes and in a Pre-Raphaelite manner. As Jeffares points out, the line "And her guides are angels seven" "is reminiscent of Rossetti" (*Commentary Poems*, p. 39). Also "the gold embroidered dress" and "the long hair" are details which remind us of Rossetti's paintings and poetry.[41]

As often in Yeats, the differences between the early version and the final one are considerable, and for convenience sake the two versions are here reproduced side by side:

Song	*The Countess Cathleen in Paradise*
All the heavy days are over;	All the heavy days are over;
Leave the body's coloured pride	Leave the body's coloured pride
Underneath the grass and clover	Underneath the grass and clover,
With the feet laid side by side.	With the feet laid side by side.
One with her are mirth and duty,	Bathed in flaming founts of duty
Bear the gold embroidered dress—	She'll not ask a haughty dress;
For she needs not her sad beauty—	Carry all that mournful beauty
To the scented oaken press.	To the scented oaken press.

[41] Miller, pp. 43–47, points out the influence on Yeats of "the illustrations made by Sir Edward Burne-Jones to the *Chaucer* which William Morris finished printing at the Kelmscott Press in 1896" (p. 44).

Hers the kiss of mother Mary,	Did the kiss of Mother Mary
The long hair is on her face,	Put that music in her face?
Still she goes with footsteps wary,	Yet she goes with footstep wary,
Full of earth's old timid grace.	Full of earth's old timid grace.
She goes down the floor of heaven,	'Mong the feet of angels seven
Shining bright as a new lance,	What a dancer glimmering!
And her guides are angels seven,	All the heavens bow down to Heaven.
While young stars about her dance.	Flame to flame and wing to wing.
VPl, pp. 162, 164	VP, pp. 124−125

This song is presented as a song sung by Seven Spirits seen by Oona, and both versions focus their attention on Kathleen/Cathleen although her name is not mentioned in the poem. The ceremonial burial of the Countess, who has become a blessed spirit, is stressed in both versions as is the timid grace with which she approaches Heaven. In the first version she is *"Shining bright as a new lance"*, seven angels guide her and the stars dance around her, whereas in the final version Yeats turned her into a glimmering dancer, who is transformed into music. Moreover, in the line "All the heavens bow down to Heaven", Yeats introduced a metaphor in which Cathleen herself has become Heaven. In a letter to Olivia Shakespeare (October 27, 1927), Yeats himself comments that "the dancer Cathleen has become heaven itself" (Wade, *Letters,* p. 731). That Yeats's poem also makes the Virgin Mary, "Mother Mary", a significant figure is quite in keeping with many religious folk songs which often show a special devotion to the Virgin Mother.[42] The cult of Mary, so characteristic of Roman Catholicism and also expressed in early Irish lyrics, has been, and still is, very strong among the Irish people. "The kiss of Mother Mary" in Yeats's poem is traditionally Irish in its appeal, whereas the line *"the long hair is on her face"* reminds one more of the long, yellow hair of the Pre-Raphaelite women depicted by Rossetti, for example in "The Blessed Damozel". For his songs Yeats drew on a rich tradition of living Irish folk songs, part of which Douglas Hyde made popular through his *Love Songs of Connacht*[43] and *Religious Songs of Connacht.*[44] The material had already been made known in 1890 and 1891 through a series of articles, first entitled "Gaelic Folk Songs", then "Poems of the Connacht Bards", in the *Nation*

---

[42] Seán Ó Súilleabháin, "Irish Oral Tradition", *A View of the Irish Language,* p. 50. Cf. Peter Allt, "Yeats, Religion, and History", *Sewanee Review,* 60 (Oct.−Dec. 1952), 624−658.

[43] *Being the Fourth Chapter of The Songs of Connacht* (Dublin and London, 1893; rpt. with Introduction by Micheál Ó hAodha, Shannon Ireland: IUP, 1969).

[44] *A Collection of Poems, Stories, Prayers, Satires, Ranns, Charms, etc.* 2nd ed. (London: Fisher Unwin; Dublin: Gill and Son, 1906).

and the *Weekly Freeman.* [45] As early as 1885 in an article in the *Dublin University Review,* Hyde had pointed out the importance of "the song and folklore of our peasantry . . ."[46]

There is also another song sung by another type of Spirit, lost souls introduced into the 1912 version and conjured up by the Demons, from hills and mounds, or from the sea and the lakes. These Spirits are dejected because they are forced to help the Demons carry the gold which has been stolen from Cathleen for whom they hold no malice. They arrive singing and dancing, but their song expresses sorrow:

> Our hearts are sore, but we come
> Because we have heard you call
>
> *Poems,* 1912, p. 63

they tell the Demons. The Second Spirit's words "Sorrow has made me dumb" (p. 63) recall the opening epigraph, an obvious attempt on Yeats's part to integrate it into the play. The Second Spirit repeats "Sorrow has made me dumb" three times, words which are also repeated by the Third Spirit. In a song-like speech, which shows that like human beings they eat and drink, they refer to the kindness the Countess has shown them and they also reveal their own feelings:

> Her shepherds at nightfall
> Lay many a plate and cup
> Down by the trodden brink,
> That when the dance break up
> We may have meat and drink.
> Therefore our hearts are sore;
> And though we have heard and come
> Our crying filled the shore.
>
> *Poems,* 1912, p. 64

The Demon-Merchants find these unwilling ghosts "the most troublesome of spirits" (Ibid., p. 66), but still manage to force them to carry the bags of gold. When leaving, the Spirits declare that they will never dance again. Their sorrow may symbolize a state of affliction in Nature itself produced by Cathleen's death. How effective these Spirits were on the stage is another matter. Their dance may have been attractive, but the words of the

---

[45] Seven Chapters on "Carolan and his Contemporaries", "Songs in Praise of Women", "Drinking Songs", "Love Songs", "Songs Ascribed to Raftery", and "Religious Songs" (two chapters) appeared, the first in *The Nation,* 48, Nos. 17–20, 22–35, 37–48, from Saturday, 26 April 1890 to Saturday, 29 November 1890, and were continued in the *Weekly Freeman* (1891). The only examples of the latter seem to have been the British Library copies of Vol. 1–6 for the years 1888–1891, which were destroyed during World War II.

[46] Quoted by D. Daly, *The Young Douglas Hyde* (Shannon: IUP, 1974), p. 55.

song could easily have created a comic effect instead of the intended serious one. In any case they were removed from the 1913 edition. It is, however, interesting to note that the song of these Four Spirits shows that Yeats was still at the time haunted by Morian Shehone's Lament.

The sorrowful lines of the four spirits also concern love, love of the Spirits for a human being, the Countess. Yeats had, however, not yet learned from the Noh drama how to dramatize relations between the living and the dead, as he did for example in *The Dreaming of the Bones* (written in 1917 and published in *Four Plays for Dancers* in 1921), a play in which a soldier escapes from the 1916 Easter Rising and meets the ghosts of Diarmuid and Devorgilla near Corcomroe Abbey in the West of Ireland.

Fairy Song and Fairy Music in *The Land of Heart's Desire*

If Cathleen rejected the world of Maeve and Fergus and the ideal world of Aengus, the Celtic god of love and beauty, seen by the poet Aleel as the only true reality, Maire/Mary in *LHD* is magically and inevitably drawn to the dream world (she has been reading about in an ancient book) whose call she hears again and again in the wind. *LHD* is a play permeated by fairy song and music. The play has a certain similarity to "The Rose of Shadow", one of the *Celtic Twilight* stories which first appeared in the *Speaker,* July 21 1894. Frayne (I, p. 328) points out that "Oona Herne resembles Mary Bruin, the heroine of *The Land of Heart's Desire* . . . One woman is called 'away' by the fairies, and the other is claimed by her demon lover." Like Mary, Oona in "The Rose of Shadow" breaks the unwritten laws and through her behaviour attracts the unseen powers. She brings in a sod from the grave of a notorious man, and this sod exhorts her in the dead man's voice to come with him "when the wind blows along the Mountain of Bulben and out to sea". Although frightened by this, she is unable to stop "listening to the storm in the fir-trees", and she starts singing a song which her father calls "an evil air", one which "Hanrahan the Red sang . . . and it has lured, and will lure, many a girl from her hearth and from her peace" (Frayne, I, p. 330). The dangerous and evil power of music expressed in the folklore of many countries informs this story. (One need only think of the evil power attributed to the fiddle or violin played by Swedish country fiddlers, who were thought to be inspired by the Devil himself in the shape of "Näcken", or "Strömkarlen", a water spirit in a man's shape.) The girl, thrown into a trance by the supernatural music she hears, sings on in spite of her father's warning. The fire goes out and her father and mother die of the icy cold filling the room during the girl's singing:

O, what to me the little room,
    That was brimmed up with prayer and rest?
He bade me out into the gloom,
    And my breast lies upon his breast.

O, what to me my mother's care,
    The home where I was safe and warm?
The shadowy blossom of my hair
    Will hide us from the bitter storm.

O, hiding hair and dewy eyes,
    I am no more with life and death!
My heart upon his warm heart lies;
    My breath is mixed into his breath. [47]

Frayne, I, p. 331

As in the song of the Seven Spirits in *CC*, Yeats used the quatrain form with alternate rhymes in Oona's little song, which shows that like Mary she has ceased to care for her home and her mother. She attracts the demon lover, who has already sent out his call to her in the voice of the wind blowing along the mountain and out to sea. He appears in "the shape of a man crouching on the storm. His heavy and brutal face and his partly naked limbs were scarred with many wounds, and his eyes were full of white fire under his knitted brows" (Frayne, I, p. 332).[48]

The similarities between *LHD* and this story dating from about the same time as the play are certainly remarkable, but the differences are even more significant. The fire symbolism, for example, shows a different pattern. The demon lover's eyes are filled with white fire, and yet his arrival is presaged by icy cold which kills everything. He comes in a violent storm whereas the Faery Child of *LHD* is brought by a more friendly wind. They are both spirits of the air, the brutal demon of the storm being a more formidable and frightening kind than the Faery Child who entices Mary away. In *LHD* the supernatural power is not malignant, at least not to

---

[47] This poem, with very slight changes in punctuation, and without italics and indented lines, appeared as "The Heart of Women" in *WR*, p. 20, and as "The Heart of the Woman" in *Collected Poems*, p. 67.

[48] The story "The Cradles of Gold" (first printed in *The Senate*, November 1896), dealing with Winnie Hearne, a peasant's wife who is taken by the fairy king but returned to her husband in the end, also contains "a wild air" called "The winds from beyond the world", a "cradle-song" or lullaby "which pious mothers had ever forbid their daughters to sing" (Frayne, I, p. 415). This poem was one of the "Two Poems Concerning Peasant Visionaries" which was first printed in *The Savoy* (April 1896), included as "A Cradle Song" in *WR*, and as "The Unappeasable Host" in *Collected Poems*, p. 65. It begins "The Danaan children laugh in cradles of wrought gold", and is not the same poem as "A Cradle Song" (1890) in *Collected Poems*, p. 45.

Mary, but in the story about Oona, the demon of the air is very similar to the frightful "Seabars" used in the early manuscript versions of *SW,* and in the early version of the story printed in the *Speaker* Yeats actually uses the word "Seabar" for demon.[49] The folklore, not least fairy beliefs, which Yeats collected, together with Lady Gregory, in the late 1890s and after, resulted not only in the *Celtic Twilight* stories but also in six long articles on folklore, one very aptly entitled "Away", published in the *Fortnightly Review* (April 1902) and comprising several stories of men, women and children who had been taken by the fairies (see Frayne, II, pp. 267–282).

Both *LHD* and "The Rose of Shadow" make conspicuous use of the power of supernatural song and music and make the wind or the storm the vehicle of this magic power. In Ireland there was, and still is, a strong belief in fairy music, and Yeats gives several examples of this in his articles and stories based on folklore. Fairy music entices people away to fairyland, and Yeats also found such stories in other countries, for example in India. In his review of T. F. Thistelton Dyer's *The Ghost World* (London, 1893), Yeats relates an Indian tale about the dangerous music of a river spirit: "Strange musical sounds were said to come out of the river at one place, and close to this place the Indians had set up an idol representing the water spirit who made the music" (Frayne, I, p. 287). After a priest had tried in vain to turn the people away from the magic music of the river, the water "was convulsed" and sent out such beautiful music that it drew first one person and then the whole tribe into the deep. Yeats adds that "the greatest poets of every nation have drawn from stories like this, symbols and events to express the most lyrical, the most subjective moods" (ibid.), and, indeed, Yeats himself made much beautiful poetry by drawing on similar Irish stories. He later tried to explain the existence of such spirits as the fairies and their "earth-resembling life" as being "the creation of the image-making power of the mind, plucked naked from the body, and mainly of the images in the memory".[50] The demon in "The Rose of Shadow" symbolizes the dangerous power of Nature working in the mind of a human being irresistibly drawn to the unknown. In *LHD* the fairy music and song first heard in the voice of the wind also symbolize the all-controlling power of Nature. As we learn from a description of fairy music *("Ceol-Sidhe")* by Lady Wilde in *Ancient Legends, Mystic Charms, and Superstitions of Ireland* (London, 1888) "the fairy music is soft and low and plaintive, with a fatal charm for mortal ears" (p. 29). In this context

[49] See Frayne, I, p. 331 n 7.
[50] W. B. Yeats, "Swedenborg, Mediums and the Desolate Places", in *Explorations*, p. 35.

Lady Wilde mentions a youth who heard a young girl in County Clare "chanting a melancholy song, without settled words or music". This girl had "once heard the fairy harp, and those who hear it lose all memory of love or hate, and forget all things, and never more have any other sound in their ears save the soft music of the fairy harp, and when the spell is broken, they die" (Ibid., pp. 29—30). Lady Wilde also relates that "On May Eve the fairy music is heard on all the hills, and many beautiful tunes have been caught up in this way by the people and the native musicians" (Ibid., p. 105). It is on May Eve that the young woman in *LHD* first hears the Faery Child as an alluring voice in the wind. Yeats makes this voice the *Leitmotif* of the play. In the previous chapters I have already dealt with the conspicuous use Yeats made of the wind in his plays, yet it should be stressed again that the wind brings with it the enticing music of the fairies. Maurteen Bruin, Mary's father, is the first to hear the sweet voice, and he says to the others:

> There's someone singing. Why it's but a child.
> It sang, 'The lonely of heart is withered away.'
> A strange song for a child, but she sings sweetly.
> Listen, listen!
>
> [*Goes to door.   VPl*, p. 194

While her father believes the singing to be simply that of an innocent child, Mary is afraid of the voice. It is Maurteen, not Mary, who brings the child in and bids her welcome; he takes her words, "There is one here that must away, away" not as a warning but as "dreamy and strange talk" (*VPl*, p. 196). The people of the house treat her kindly, warm her feet, give her bread and wine, honey and milk, and put shoes on her feet. However, the sight of the crucifix makes her shriek, and only when it is removed can she start dancing. She repeats the first three lines of the song she sang outside while Mary is beginning to hear the dancing of "The unholy powers":

> Other small steps beating upon the floor,
> And a faint music blowing in the wind,
> Invisible pipes giving her feet the tune.
>
> *VPl*, p. 201

The final stage directions inform us that

> [*Outside there are dancing figures, and it may be a white bird, and many voices singing:*]

> The wind blows out of the gates of the day,
> The wind blows over the lonely of heart,
> And the lonely of heart is withered away;
> (While the fairies dance in a place apart,

Shaking their milk-white feet in a ring,
Tossing their milk-white arms in the air;
For they hear the wind laugh and murmur and sing
Of a land where even the old are fair,
And even the wise are merry of tongue;
But I heard a reed of Coolaney say—
'When the wind has laughed and murmured and sung,
The lonely of heart is withered away.')[51]

VPl, p. 210

This song in its entirety occurs twice in the play, first before the Faery Child is brought into the house, and also at the end of the play as the final chorus of the fairies. Its first three lines and its last two lines also appear like a *Leitmotif* several other times in the play stressing the loneliness of the heart and its being withered away by the wind. The milk-white feet and the milk-white arms of the dancers are images symbolizing the love of the fairies for human beings and the desire of the mortals to reach the land of beauty and love, to which they are drawn by the magically enticing music, the song and dancing of the fairies. Perhaps a fairy-tale-like enchantment, but of universal appeal like Goethe's *Erlkönig*.

This play, epitomizing as it does Yeats's early fairy and dream world, was written at the request of his friend Florence Farr, stage manager of the Avenue Theatre in London, who wanted a role for her niece, the then only ten-year-old Dorothy Paget, whose first stage appearance was on 29 March 1894 as the Faery Child.[52] Often two plays were put on in the same evening, one as a curtain-raiser to the other. Yeats's play served as such to John Todhunter's *A Comedy of Sighs*. The success was far from being immediate, and Todhunter's play was a complete disaster. As stated by J. Hone, "the enemies of the intellectual drama, who crowded the gallery, derided [Todhunter's] ominously entitled play with loud laughter, which even the *Times* critic thought excusable. The critic cut Todhunter to pieces, adding, however, that a mood of mocking protest might have been excited by the 'small piece on an Irish theme which preceded it'."[53]

---

[51] The parentheses instruct amateur performers to omit lines so marked. The music composed by Florence Farr is reproduced in *The Collected Works*, III, p. [237]; see Appendix II below.

[52] *LHD* was, as pointed out by Miller, p. 12, "heralded by the appearance on the London billboards of the famous poster designed by Aubrey Beardsley", known today as one of his best pictures, but in 1894 ironically called "The Japanee-Rossetti girl" by Owen Seaman in some verses in *Punch* (see Miller, pp. 12–14). A detail of Beardsley's poster is reproduced by Miller, p. 13.

[53] Joseph Hone, *W. B. Yeats, 1865–1939* (New York: Macmillan, 1943), p. 114. *A Comedy of Sighs* does not seem to have been published.

This critic also scoffed at Yeats's instruction in the programme that "the characters are supposed to speak in Gaelic"—a piece of information which helped neither the audience ignorant of Gaelic nor the language movement, and added nothing to the mood of the play. Todhunter's play lasted until 14 April 1894 and was then replaced by Shaw's *Arms and the Man* a week later. Yeats's play served as a curtain-raiser to Shaw's anti-war play until May 12.[54] George Moore called Yeats's fairy play "an inoffensive trifle", which "neither pleased nor displeased" (quoted from Moore's *Ave,* by Hone, p. 115). In spite of the inauspicious first night and Moore's and Shaw's condescending judgement of the play, *LHD* met with unexpected popularity later: "Brought out as a separate edition, at two and sixpence, the play sold 10,000 copies in 1925", and Yeats, who himself called the play "a vague sentimental trifle" in a letter to Lady Gregory, was astonished to get £100 from the proceeds (Hone, p. 413n). About ten years after the first performance Yeats denounced the kind of poetry he wrote in *LHD* in a letter to AE [April 1904] (Wade, *Letters,* p. 434):

In my *Land of Heart's Desire,* and in some of my lyric verse of that time, there is an exaggereration of sentiment and sentimental beauty which I have come to think unmanly. . . . it is sentiment and sentimental sadness, a womanish introspection. . . . but I cannot probably be quite just to any poetry that speaks to me with the sweet insinuating feminine voice of the dwellers in that country of shadows and hollow images. I have dwelt there too long not to dread all that comes out of it.

Yeats himself realizes that as a result of his dislike of his former sentimental sadness, he may not be quite fair in his judgement of his own dream-world poetry and when he associates it with what he calls "womanish introspection" and a "sweet insinuating feminine voice", one feels that he enjoys denouncing his own sentimentalism. In *Plays and Controversies* (1923), however, he expresses a more balanced opinion:

This play contains more of my first experiments in blank verse than any other in my books . . . Many passages that pleased me when I wrote them, and some that please me still, are mere ornament without dramatic value. A revival of the play but a few days ago at the Abbey Theatre enabled me to leave out these and other passages and to test the play without them. I think that it gained greatly, became indeed for the first time tolerable drama . . .

Quoted in *VPl,* p. 212

---

[54] See Miller, p. 17.

134

Songs in *The Shadowy Waters*

The songs found in *CC* and *LHD* cannot be said to be based directly on any particular folk song, but rather on folk belief and Yeats's notions of what constitutes true folk poetry. *SW*, however, presents a somewhat different picture, for there we shall find that Yeats made use of both the traditional *caoineadh* or keening for the dead, and a particular ballad, although adapting both for his own dramatic purposes. It is necessary first to have a look at the revisions of the passages which follow immediately after the meeting of the two ships, for the differences between the versions of 1900, 1906 and 1911 will prove to be of great significance from our point of view.

In the 1900 version, the King of Lochlann and his crew are killed, but Queen Dectora and the King's crown are brought over to Forgael's ship. At first the captured Dectora promises the sailors riches of every kind if they help her to kill Forgael and bring her home to her own country. But enchanted by Forgael's music and beaten and torn by "the white wings" and "the silver claws" of a supernatural bird, the sailors take fright and when Forgael begins playing a different tune on his harp, they completely forget their murderous scheme and walk over to the Lochlann galley where they start drinking brown ale, and call to Aibric to come and tell them a story. After a while they return quarrelling to their own ship, and Aibric takes their sword from them.

They ask him to finish his story about "golden-armed Iolan and the queen / That lives among the woods of the dark hounds" (*VP*, p. 766), and this is how we first learn the name of Dectora's husband. Then Aibric and the sailors return to the foreign ship leaving Dectora and Forgael alone. In the early version of the play there is no wake, and no keen is raised for the murdered king, either by the sailors, or by Aibric or Dectora. In the 1906 version, however, the ale-feast only briefly referred to in the 1900 version is transformed into a wake, and consequently the passages in which the murder of Forgael is planned are considerably revised. To the sailors, the harp is "a crescent moon" from whose "holy fire" they shrink back in dread. Spellbound by the harp, they give up their murderous plan and start talking of a wake instead:

> *First Sailor* [*falling into a dream suddenly*]. But you were saying
>   there is somebody
> Upon that other ship we are to wake.
> You did not know what brought him to his end,
> But it was sudden.
> *Second Sailor.*   You are in the right;
>   I had forgotten that we must go wake him.

VP, p. 240

135

Perceiving the sudden change that has come over the sailors, Dectora says:

> He has flung a Druid spell upon the air,
> And set you dreaming.

VP, p. 240

The sailors complain that without ale and knowledge of the name of the dead person, they cannot have a wake:

> *Second Sailor.*   How can we have a wake
>   When we have neither brown nor yellow ale?
> *First Sailor.* I saw a flagon of brown ale aboard her.
> *Third Sailor.* How can we raise the keen that do not know
>   What name to call him by?
> *First Sailor.*   Come to his ship.
>   His name will come into our thoughts in a minute.
> I know that he died a thousand years ago,
> And has not yet been waked.

VP, pp. 240–241

The sailors have no recollection of having themselves just killed the king and think that the murder was committed a thousand years earlier. Yeats seems to use this device in order to make the past project itself into the present, thus relating the action of the play to the time of the sagas and bringing out the duality of time so characteristic of many Celtic tales: time in the Otherworld passes infinitely more quickly than in the real world, for a thousand years in this world may correspond to a few minutes or a few days in the Otherworld. In their dreamlike state the sailors begin to keen and one of them starts the keen by using the traditional cry of "Ochone":

> Ohone![55] O! O! O!
> The yew-bough has been broken into two,
> And all the birds are scattered.

VP, p. 241

All the sailors take up the keening refrain "O! O! O! O!" and then go back keening to the other ship, while Dectora, who is now planning to slay Forgael, snatches Aibric's sword from him. The sailors cry to Aibric to join them and let them know the name of the person they are waking. In his dreamy mood, Aibric at first thinks that they are keening King Arthur, but then he remembers:

> No, no—not Arthur. I remember now.
> It was golden-armed Iollan, and he died

---

[55] Yeats uses an old spelling.

136

Broken-hearted, having lost his queen
Through wicked spells. That is not all the tale,
For he was killed. O! O! O! O! O! O!
For golden-armed Iollan has been killed.

VP, p. 242

After this dirge Aibric joins the keening sailors on the other ship, and the wailing there is going on simultaneously with the actions of Forgael and Dectora. The sorrowful tune of the harp is accompanying the keening of Aibric and the sailors, and when Dectora lifts the sword to kill Forgael, his music makes her fall into a dreamlike state. The stage directions inform us that Dectora's "*voice becomes dreamy, and she lowers the sword slowly, and finally lets it fall. She spreads out her hair. She takes off her crown and lays it upon the deck*" (*VP*, p. 242). This clearly Pre-Raphaelite scene with Dectora spreading out her long hair and putting her crown on the deck of the ship is symbolical of her being completely dominated by the power of the enchanter Forgael and his magic harp. She does, however, raise a keen, a funeral elegy, over her dead husband, "golden-armed Iollan", in which she makes Aibric's sword serve both as a symbol of her husband's bravery in battle and as a heroic token to be placed beside him in the grave:

This sword is to lie beside him in the grave.
It was in all his battles. I will spread my hair,
And wring my hands, and wail him bitterly,
For I have heard that he was proud and laughing,
Blue-eyed, and a quick runner on bare feet,
And that he died a thousand years ago.
O! O! O! O!

VP, p. 242

Here Dectora herself, wringing her hands and uttering loud lamentations, is a traditional picture of grief, yet one feels that her sorrow is conditioned by a sense of decorum rather than by deep passion, not least because she thinks that the man she is mourning has been dead for a thousand years. Yet a different tune from the harp suddenly makes her realize that she had only just seen him being killed:

But no, that is not it.
I knew him well, and while I heard him laughing
They killed him at my feet. O! O! O! O!
For golden-armed Iollan that I loved.

VP, p. 242

Dectora is separated from her king and husband for ever, but her sorrow is moderate, unlike the excessive grief displayed by Deirdre on the death of Naoise and his two brothers. In Dectora's death-song Yeats shows the mutability of love, especially when he uses the device of letting one person, in order to deceive, take over the identity of another, that is Forgael asks Dectora if she does not realize that he is actually the person she is "weeping for", a statement which Dectora at first refuses to believe:

No, for he is dead
O! O! O! O! for golden-armed Iollan.

VP, p. 243

Thus ends Dectora's lament for her dead husband. At this stage in the play, there is a sudden peripety, however, for now she refuses to believe Forgael also when he states that he has, indeed, never been "golden-armed Iollan", but has all along been deceiving her by his magic into believing this. However, in the end Dectora is firmly convinced that she has loved nobody but Forgael "for a thousand years".

For Dectora's death-song Yeats undoubtedly drew on the very old tradition of having a wake and raising a keen for a dead person. Dectora's blank-verse lament is a mixture of a traditional keen performed by one or more keeners beside the corpse and a learned *marbhna* composed by a bardic poet for a dead chieftain.[56] In accordance with old custom, Dectora's death-song is also accompanied by music, the magic music performed by Forgael on his magic instrument. That he plays three different strains, that of sleep as well as those of sorrow and joy, is in accordance with Yeats's interpretation of the love story.

Dectora's lament is divided into three parts, each part ending with the repetition of the *gol* or cry "O! O! O! O!"[57] It is usual to distinguish

[56] See Breandán Ó Madagáin, "Irish Vocal Music of Lament and Syllabic Verse", in *The Celtic Consciousness*, ed. Robert O'Driscoll (Copyright Celtic Arts of Canada, 1981; Ireland; Dolmen Press; Scotland: Canongate Publishing, 1982), pp. 311–332, esp. 311 and 320; hereafter Ó Madagáin. His tape-recordings of dirges, among them a fragment of the well-known *Caoineadh Airt Uí Laoghaire* ("The Keen for Art O'Leary"), are equally interesting. Cf. *Éigse*, 18 (1980–81) 25–37.

[57] It is possible that the traditional *crónán*, or crónaun, described by P. W. Joyce as "consisting simply of the continued repetition of the two vowel sounds, *ee-oo ee-oo ee-oo* etc, which was prolonged *ad libitum*" (quoted by Ó Madagáin, p. 322) would be suitable as a finale to Dectora's death-song. Here, since it deals with one of Yeats's ecstatic bards, we might recall "The Binding of the Hair", a story first published in *The Savoy*, No. 1, Jan. 1896, pp. 135–138, and then slightly revised as the opening story in *The Secret Rose* (London: Lawrence & Bullen, 1897), pp. 1–10. The story, inspired by both a tale in *Lebor Gabála* and the story about Salome and the prophet St. John's head, tells of the fate of "the young and wise Queen Dectira, and of the old and foolish King Lua" (p. 1) and their famous bard Aodh, who owned a "five-stringed cruit", i.e. a harp, and often sang love songs to his Queen. He promised to sing a particular song also after a great battle in which, however, both he and the king were killed. Yet the bard kept his promise in what might be called a strikingly Celtic manner. His head hanging by its dark hair from a bush was ecstatically singing a song beginning "Fasten your hair with a golden pin" (published, under the title, "He Gives his

between the dirge-part of a keen, that is the words themselves, and the *gol*-part or the "Och-ochone" repeated by the keeners and all those present, at the end of the performance of the keen (see Ó Madagáin, p. 318). Yeats deviates somewhat from this pattern, but so do most *marbhnas* which often repeat the *gol* after every stanza.

Yeats included some music by Arthur Darley for Aibric's and Dectora's laments in *The Collected Works*, III (p. 231; see Appendix II below), and he also commented on this music as follows: ". . . Mr. Darley's music for *Shadowy Waters* was supposed to be played upon Forgael's magic harp, and it accompanied words of Dectora's and Aibric's. It was played in reality upon a violin, always pizzicato, and gave the effect of harp playing, at any rate of a magic harp. The 'cues' are all given and the words are printed under the music. The violinist followed the voice, except in the case of 'O!', where it was the actress that had to follow" (*Collected Works*, III, pp. 223–224).

What Yeats says here about the relation of the music to the words is characteristic of his idea of how verse should be recited: the music should be subordinated to the words.

A comparison between the 1906 and 1911 versions of *SW* will show that the latter retains Dectora's lament almost without any revisions, whereas the passage in which the sailors deliver their keen has been changed considerably. The earlier brief keen is turned into a regular ale-song and even the previous lines in which the sailors talk of having a wake and raising a keen have been altered, although not as much as the keen itself:

> *Second Sailor.* What way can we raise a keen, not knowing
>   what name to call him by?
> *First Sailor.* Come on to his ship. His name will come
>   to mind in a moment. All I know is he died a
>   thousand years ago, and was never yet waked.
> *Second Sailor.* How can we wake him having no ale?
> *First Sailor.* I saw a skin of ale aboard her—a pigskin
>   of brown ale.
> *Third Sailor.* Come to the ale, a pigskin of brown ale,
>   a goat-skin of yellow!
> *First Sailor* [*singing*]. Brown ale and yellow; yellow and brown
>   ale! a goat-skin of yellow!
> *All* [*singing*]. Brown ale and yellow; yellow and brown ale!
>   [*Sailors go out.*
>   *VPl*, p. 331

Beloved Certain Rhymes", in *Collected Poems*, p. 71). When the singing ended, crows—birds of the death goddess Morrígan—swept the head off the bush, so that it "rolled over at the feet of the queen" (*Secret Rose*, p. 10). In *The King of the Great Clock Tower* Yeats uses the theme of a poet's severed head singing to the dancing Queen.

As in the earlier version the sailors walk over to the other ship and ask Aibric whom they are waking, and he tells them in the same way as in the earlier version. But what is particularly interesting from our point-of-view is the ale-song of the sailors: "Brown ale and yellow; yellow and brown ale!" Here ale is not just a drink needed for the wake but becomes a ritual drink without which no keen can be raised for the dead king. In both versions, the magic harp music makes the sailors forget that they have violently murdered the king and his crew. Ale becomes a symbol of wordly joy, much as the phrase "Cakes and ale" in Shakespeare's *Twelfth Night* (Act II, iii, 114) is used as a traditional symbol of joy and festivity. Moreover, there is a sharp contrast between the rollicking drinking-song with which the sailors are keening the king they have just slain and their solemn keening in the earlier version. Besides, their merry ale-song forms an even more pronounced contrast to Dectora's solemn lament.

The ale-song of the sailors is much more realistic and in accordance with the true character of a wake than the corresponding passage in the 1906 version, where the solemnity of the sailors hardly agrees with the traditionally far from solemn business that a wake generally was. Séan Ó Súilleabháin records several references to excessive alcohol drinking at wakes and funerals in Irish seventeenth, eighteenth and nineteenth-century books. A result of the abuses was that "both the bishops and the clergy in general" made "every effort... to curb" them.[58] Story-telling—another as a rule less dangerous custom at wakes—is, as we have seen above, also reflected in Yeats's play.

The most interesting feature about the ale-song from our point of view is, however, that it derives from a ballad, several variants of which exist. Yeats also used one verse of this ballad for the pupils' song in *The Hour-Glass*. In *The Collected Works,* IV, he writes (p. 239): "One sometimes has need of more lines of the little song, and I have put into English rhyme three of the many verses of a Gaelic ballad:

> I was going the road one day
>   (O the brown and the yellow beer!)
> And I met with a man that was no right man
>   (O my dear, my dear).[59]

> 'Give me your wife', said he,
>   (O the brown and the yellow beer!)
> 'Till the sun goes down and an hour of the clock'
>   (O my dear, my dear).

[58] *Irish Wake Amusements* (Cork: Mercier Press, 1967; rpt., 1969), pp. 16–23.
[59] Cf. *VPl*, p. 608, under line.

140

'Good-bye, good-bye, my husband,'
(O the brown and the yellow beer!)
'For a year and a day by the clock of the sun'
(O my dear, my dear).[60]

However, Michael Yeats rejects Yeats's statement that the tune "is a traditional Aran air" and states that the original ballad is "a Gaelic song called 'Cuach mo L[i]on[n]dubh Buidhe', My Jug of Yellow Ale, which is still very popular in the Irish-speaking areas of Donegal" (p. 166).

The song "My Jug of Yellow Ale" which has been much discussed, inspired not only Yeats but also James Joyce and James Stephens. In a BBC talk, "The James Joyce I Knew", James Stephens told the story of how he once learned this song in Paris from Joyce, who claimed that his grandfather had taught it to him. James Stephens also sang the song itself in this programme.[61]

The song concerned is, as Yeats claimed, a Gaelic ballad, actually composed in a typical ballad quatrain stanza. Like most ballads it is anonymous and has a strong supernatural element. I use the word 'ballad' here like William Entwistle, "in the widest sense as meaning any short traditional narrative poem sung, with or without accompaniment or dance, in assemblies of the people."[62] Roger MacHugh, in "James Joyce's Synge-Song",[63] pointed out that Lady Gregory made available this ballad, entitled "An Gruagach Uasal", in *The Irish Homestead Christmas Number: A Celtic Christmas* (December 1901, pp. 19−20). Lady Gregory in a headnote to the text of the ballad states:

This ballad was taken down in Donegal by Mr. E. E. Fournier, as well as the music to which it was sung, and which the people told him was the music of the Sidhe.[64] Mr. Jack Yeats has made a drawing for it, and I have made a rough translation of it. "The Gruagach Uasal", literally the Noble Enchanter, is used for some strange, unearthly, unfriendly being.—

---

[60] Both words and music are printed in *Plays in Prose and Verse* (London, 1922). When claiming Aran origin for this tune, did Yeats's memory simply fail him, or did the Aran Islands perhaps symbolize the cradle of Irish folklore to him? "Ireland is always Connacht to my imagination", he once stated (*Explorations,* p. 231).

[61] *The Listener,* 36 (October 1946), 565. The song as James Joyce and James Stephens knew it is also printed in Ellmann's *James Joyce* (New York: OUP, 1959), p. 345. Cf. my Appendix I. 3.

[62] *European Balladry* (Oxford: Clarendon Press, 1939), pp. 16−17.

[63] *Envoy,* 3 (November 1950), 12−16.

[64] Edmund Edward Fournier d'Albe (1868−1933) was an English physicist who published not only works on physical and psychical research but also *An English-Irish Dictionary and Phrase-Book* (1903).

Since the newspaper concerned is not easily available, Lady Gregory's
English translation is reproduced here:

> *I was going the road one fine day.*
> *O! the brown and the yellow ale!*[65]
> And I met with a man that was no right man.
> O, love of my heart!

He asked was the young woman with me my daughter, and I said she was my
married wife.

He asked would I lend her for an hour or a day. "Oh, I would not do that, but I
would like to do what is fair. Let you take the upper path, and I will go by the road,
and whoever she will follow, let her belong to him for ever."

He took the upper path and I took the road, and she followed after him, he being
in his youth.

She stayed walking there the length of three quarters, and she came home after,
Mary without shame.

She asked me how was I in my health. "As is good with my friends and bad with
my enemies. And what would you do if I would die from you?" "I would put a
coffin of yellow gold on you."

When myself heard those fine words, I lay down and died there. And there were
two that went to the wood for timber, and they brought back a half board of holly
and a half board of alder.

They put me into the boarded coffin, and four yards of the ugliest sack about me,
and they lifted me up on their shoulders. "Throw him now into the best hole in the
street."

"Oh, wait, wait, lay me down, till I tell you a little story about women; a little
story to-day and a little story to-morrow, and a little story every day of the
quarter."

> And but that my own little mother was a woman,
> Oh, the brown and the yellow ale!
> I would tell you another little story about women,
> Oh, love of my heart![66]

The ballad relates an encounter between a stranger and an elderly man
accompanied by a young woman. In answer to the stranger's question, the
man says that the woman is his wife. Against his will, the old man is forced
to lend his wife to the Enchanter "for an hour or a day", and when she
returns, her husband dies of grief and is given an ignoble burial depicted by
himself. (Did he just pretend to be dead?)

This ballad exists in several versions with different titles and many
textual variations. The earliest printed example is, as far as I know, not

---

[65] My emphasis.
[66] For music and three verses of the text in Irish, see Appendix I. 1.

142

Lady Gregory's but a poem in Irish entitled "Oro! A lionn-dubh buidhe!" which appeared in *Irisleabhar na Gaedhilge: The Gaelic Journal*, 4, No. 42 (Dublin, July 1892), pp. 152–153. The Irish text (without an English translation) consists of 54 lines (counting the two slightly different refrain lines occurring in lines two and four).[67]

There is no doubt but that the ballad is the source of the Pupils' song in *The Hour-Glass*, three verses of which were reproduced above. But it has gone unnoticed that the first refrain line "O, the brown and the yellow ale!" served Yeats as a model for the ale-song of the sailors in *SW*. One of the sailors begins the song by singing "Brown ale and yellow; yellow and brown ale!" (*VPl*, p. 331) and then as they walk over to the other ship to start a wake for the dead king, they all sing "Brown ale and yellow; yellow and brown ale!" (*VPl*, p. 331). The drink used is ale as in Lady Gregory's English version of the ballad. (In the song in *The Hour-Glass* the word used is, however, "beer".) Ale might be a more suitable drink to use in an Otherworld play like *SW*, for Yeats often associated ale with the Otherworld and probably considered it proper for sailors who had been enchanted by the music of a magic harp, to get intoxicated on "ale from the Country of the Young", rather than on beer.[68]

Just as in the case of *CC*, where a mere half-line "The sorrowful are dumb for thee" from an anonymous Irish lament was made to serve as an epigraph which sets the sad note of the play, only one refrain line was needed to change the solemn mood of the sailors in the 1906 version of *SW* to the joyous mood of the 1911 version. What a masterly device on Yeats's part! Simply by varying the positions of the adjectives "yellow" and "brown", he also varies the rhythm of the ale-song and makes it imitate the undulating movement of the sea as well as the rollicking gait of the sailors. The tune itself is beautifully sad and should form an impressive contrast to the music of the magic harp.

Concluding Remarks

I should like to stress that the role of the songs in the three plays investigated in this study is as important as that assigned by Aristotle to music and song in Greek drama. It seems to me that a comprehensive investigation of song and music as used in Yeats's works, not least his plays, is a *desideratum*. Unlike Joyce, who had a beautiful tenor voice, Yeats had no

---

[67] See Appendix I. 2 for twelve lines of the Irish text of this ballad.

[68] "Song of Mongan", first published in *The Dome* (October 1898), and as "He Thinks of his Past Greatness . . .", in *Collected Poems*, p. 81, a poem beginning "I have drunk ale from the Country of the Young".

singing voice and claimed to be tone-deaf. He was, however, hardly as unmusical as he himself thought, for he had a true sense of the importance of music for the words of lyrical poems and for the songs he introduced into his plays, but considered it imperative that music should be subordinated to the words, which must all be heard.

For some time Yeats thought Florence Farr's speaking to her own accompaniment on a stringed instrument, "half psaltery half lyre", ideal. The instrument concerned is Alfred Dolmetsch's psaltery which has "all the chromatic intervals within the range of the speaking voice", as Yeats states in *IGE* (p. 16).

Yeats had high praise for Florence Farr's way of singing and said that "she spoke to a notation as definite as that of song, using the instrument, which murmured sweetly and faintly, under the spoken sounds, to give her the changing notes" (*IGE,* p. 12). In fact, he said, her singing differed not only from ordinary singing but also from the chanting in churches and ordinary reciting. Yeats was, however, realistic enough to understand that entire plays could not be performed in such a manner: "I do not say that we should speak our plays to musical notes, for dramatic verse will need its own method . . . but I am certain that, if people would listen to lyrical verse spoken to notes, they would soon find it impossible to listen without indignation to verse as it is spoken in our leading theatres", he said in 1902 (*IGE,* p. 19).

It should be clear from this chapter that Yeats used song and music for various purposes, to set a secret or mysterious tone, to change a tone or mood, to express passions such as love and anger, to create contrasts and turning-points in the plays, to introduce ritual elements, and so on. In *CC,* for example, the songs make the play either more romantic or more realistic according to which version we read. In *LHD* the voice of the wind changes into the song of the Faery Child and adds to the mysterious fairy quality of the play. In *SW* the music of the magic harp has total power over all the characters, Forgael included, and Dectora's death-song following on the sailors' ale-song adds another dimension to the acting version of 1911.

For the new art that Yeats wanted to create on the stage, music was essential, and he remarks that he sometimes had visions "of wild-eyed men speaking harmoniously to murmuring wires while audiences in many-coloured robes listened, hushed and excited" (*IGE,* p. 13). Undoubtedly Yeats's visionary characters Kevin/Aleel and Forgael could be said to be such "wild-eyed men", expressing like the Faery Child and the Countess Cathleen, the beauty and passion inherent in folk poetry, which the early romantic Yeats considered to be an expression of the passionate soul of the ancient Celt.

Afterword

To Yeats, folk thought and folk imagination were an enduring source of inspiration, and to neglect the role of folklore in Yeats's work would be to deprive it of one of its greatest mysteries. "The poet must always prefer the community where the perfected minds express the people, to a community that is vainly seeking to copy the perfected minds", Yeats wrote in 1903.[1]

In this study of the function of folklore elements in three of Yeats's early plays, *CC, LHD* and *SW*, three major categories of folklore have been dealt with; traditional stories or tales (Chapter I), popular belief (Chapter II), and popular poetry or folk songs—including ballads—(Chapter III). The role of music has also been touched on.

Although there is some overlap, it has been found that Yeats derived the subject-matter and some of the themes and motifs of his three plays from traditional stories or tales, whereas popular belief provided him with symbols, informed the dialogue and added to the mystery of the world depicted in his plays. Yeats's poems often arose from moods, and therefore it is hardly surprising to find that the lyrical songs written into the plays set the tone or mood of an act or a scene, or the mood of the whole play, and also make the play more realistic. The songs also help to heighten the conflict depicted in the three plays between the visible world and the invisible one, a conflict enacted by the powers of the unseen world and the chief protagonists of the plays, Maire/Mary, Cathleen, and Forgael.

Although a definite story, "The Countess Kathleen O'Shea", included in *Irish Fairy and Folk Tales,* forms the basis of *CC*, a number of other stories have also been indicated in this study, for example in Aleel's hell vision where there are elements from such disparate sources as Standish O'Grady's *Chain of Gold, Lebor Gabála, The Tragic Death of the Sons of Uisnech, The Death of Cuchulain,* the two *Battles of Moytura,* particularly the second, and folktale versions of the Lug-Balor myth.

LHD dramatizes the abduction of a newly-married bride to Fairyland. In Irish oral and literary sources there are thousands of stories telling of fatal

[1] *Essays and Introductions* (London: Macmillan & Co Ltd, 1961), p. 214.

meetings between mortals and fairies, or Otherworld beings, a motif cherished by many poets before Yeats. The Faery Child's enticing voice is first heard as a voice in the wind.

In *SW,* the chief protagonist, Forgael, is a mysterious voyager and enchanter whose magic harp helps him to avert violence, dominate everybody and make them fall into a trancelike sleep, burst into laughter, or shed tears. After a dream vision in which the Ever-living have promised him a woman of great beauty, he sets out in search of this woman, whom he hopes to find in an Otherworld of the Western sea. Yeats's own visionary experiences as well as elements from a number of Irish tales of voyages, adventures and visions, chiefly *The Voyage of Bran; of Maeldún; of St. Brendan; of the Uí Chorra, The Adventures of Connla,* and not least *The Dream of Óengus,* provided him with the structure and theme of a mysterious voyage and the vision of ideal love symbolized by the beauty of his dream woman. The name 'Aibric' derives from *The Fate of the Children of Lir.* Another famous Irish tale, *The Wooing of Étain,* can be found in a submerged form in all three plays, having in particular affected the pattern of rebirth.

The chief popular belief used in all three plays is the belief of the Irish country-people in the Otherworld and its inhabitants. In *LHD* the Otherworld is the fairy realm, and in *SW* a visionary world imagined to exist in or beyond the shadowy waters of the Western sea. In *CC,* Cathleen actually rejects both the Otherworld of the love god, and the poet Aleel's ecstatic love for her, and ends up in the Christian Paradise. In this play the two good Otherworlds vanquish the world of Evil of the Satanic traders in souls.

A number of symbols based on various folk beliefs, most of them in some way connected with the Otherworld, occur in the plays. In *CC,* many evil omens such as ghosts, some headless, some without mouths, some with bats' wings, or the uneasy barking of the dog, and the last hen's uneasy fluttering forebode the coming of the two Demons, appearing now as Oriental merchants, now as grey horned owls. The screeching of owls, the howling of the storm, and sudden thunderbolts are taken as forebodings of death by the peasants, as is of course the hammering of the underground joiner. Cathleen, finding consolation in Aleel's music, resorts to meditation and prayer. Like her, Mary Rua is a firm believer in God and the Holy Virgin and symbolizes the simple faith of ordinary country-people. Shemus Rua, on the other hand, being reduced to despair, curses not only rich and poor, but also Aleel's music, and brings the Demons in with his invocation of evil powers. He and his son Teigue become willing tools in the hands of the Demons. Yeats also uses a number of angels and good spirits as well as spirits of a more sinister kind conjured up by the Demons. The final battle in the air between the angels and the evil spirits symbolizes the defeat of the two Demons and is compared by Yeats to the battles which people believed that the Shee were fighting over a dying person, or to battles depicted in the mythological tales between the Titanic Fomorians and the powerful tribes of the Goddess Danu. Cathleen's death and the conveyance of her soul to Heaven symbolize God's grace. To the peasants, Cathleen remains "the white lily of the world" (*VPl*, p. 168).

In *LHD*, the murmuring wind symbolizes the fairies, who are thought to be especially dangerous on certain days, like May Eve, when newly-married brides like Mary, speaking of them too much or referring to them openly as fairies, and not as "the good people", runs a great risk of being abducted. Certain sacred flowers like primroses, or branches of sacred trees like the quicken or rowan tree, can be used as magic protection against evil powers, but for Mary, who has transgressed all taboos, and even given food, milk and fire to the fairies, such objects help to attract the fairies instead of averting them. Such folk beliefs enter quite naturally into the play and give added interest to the dialogue and the tapestry of symbols. The most conspicuous use of folk belief is perhaps the transformation of Maire/Mary's soul into a supernatural white bird with a crest of gold and silver feet—a symbol of her rebirth in Faery, the Happy Otherworld of the Shee.

The belief in an Otherworld of ideal love and beauty is strongly present in *SW*. The wind and the storm are important symbols of the Ever-living who have tossed Dectora's ship across the waves in the direction of Forgael's. Forgael is almost like a god, and with his harp given him by the White Fool, or the Fairy Fool, that is, the jester of the love god Aengus, he can spellbind everybody and dominate all Dectora's moods and actions. In the early versions Yeats used a number of symbols, such as eagle-headed Fomorians, spectral red, black, and white hounds, sea-birds and other birds, but in the later version, ash-grey sea-birds with human faces and human voices are the prime messengers and symbols of the Ever-living.

In the final choice between this world and the Otherworld, Dectora decides to accompany Forgael, but Aibric and the sailors return home on her ship. The harp and the sea-birds are symbols of the world of love and beauty in which Forgael and Dectora will be united for ever.

It can perhaps be said that the songs add another dimension to the plays. They are most numerous in *CC* where a number of them express love's many moods, passion, eroticism, disillusionment, despair and anger. The supernatural dancers symbolize the lover's dream of the impossible, his dream of a mysterious world in which, however, the dancers change partners as often as earthly lovers. Apart from these poems expressing Aleel's love for Cathleen, there are also two versions of "The Song of the Seven Spirits", one depicting Cathleen's passage to Heaven as a glimmering dancer, and even her becoming Heaven itself in the second version of the song. The little song of the four sinister spirits expresses their love for Cathleen and their grief at being forced to help the Demons. The epigraph "The sorrowful are dumb for thee", taken from an anonymous Irish lament, sets the sad mood of the play from the very start.

LHD is permeated with fairy music and fairy song, and the Faery Child's song "The wind blows out of the gates of the day", epitomizing the beauty and charm of Fairyland, is sung before the Faery Child's entrance, and also at the end of the play, as the final chorus sung by the whole host of fairies to the accompaniment of the music of the fairy pipers.

We have found that in *SW* Yeats made use both of the traditional keening for the dead and a popular ballad (loved also by James Joyce and James Stephens). In the early version, the sailors and Aibric raise solemn keens for the king they have just murdered. They use the traditional *gol* or cry, "Ohone! O! O! O! O!", as does Dectora in her lament over her dead king and husband. In the 1911 version, however, the solemn brief keen of the sailors is replaced by a rollicking ale-song, whose refrain "Brown ale and yellow; yellow and brown ale!" derives from the above-mentioned ballad entitled "The Noble Enchanter" *(An Gruagach Uasal),* collected by E. E. Fournier in Tory Island and translated and published by Lady Gregory in *The Irish Homestead Christmas Number* of 1902. The *Gruagach* is a noble but unfriendly and mysterious enchanter, who spirits a young wife away from her old husband. On his wife's return from the Otherworld, the old man dies of grief and is given a poor burial. The *Gruagach* causes the old man's death, and likewise Forgael is chiefly responsible for the murder of Dectora's husband, in whose honour, however, a keen is raised and an almost ritual wake celebrated before the departure of Forgael and Dectora for the Otherworld. The final mood of *SW* is not one of grief and sadness as in the ballad, but a nostalgically happy and mysterious one rising from the emotions of the two lovers, who follow the sea-birds to the world of the Ever-living.

In conclusion, I should like to say a few words about Yeats and his devotion to the theatre. As time passes, Yeats's plays are becoming more and more acknowledged by critics as plays for the theatre, not just as literary works. It should not be forgotten that a Dramatic Revival was an important part of the Celtic Revival or the Irish Literary Renaissance which Yeats initiated. Ernest Boyd in *The Contemporary Drama of Ireland* points out that "as far back as 1885 the dramatic form had appealed to

Yeats",[2] and we know that one of Yeats's distinct aims was to bring back poetry to the stage, to create a native drama and a theatre for the people. That this theatre finally went in a direction which did not greatly appeal to him, that he himself turned towards the aristocratic Noh drama for a model for his later plays, did not deter him from keeping up his interest in the Irish theatre. In *The Noble Drama of W. B. Yeats,* Liam Miller rightly states that much of Yeats's "own work was, perhaps, before its time", and he adds, "only now have we developed a theatre which can present the Noble Drama of W. B. Yeats to its deserved audience" (p. xii). The question is, have we? This question, and others, concerning the future fate of Yeats's plays on the stage could be asked. However, let me say that, if Yeats's plays are not produced as often in Dublin as one could wish, and very rarely, if at all, in London (where his fairy play *LHD* was first produced in 1894), the reason could hardly be that they provoke political or religious opinion as some of them once did. One thing is certain, Yeats himself rated his work for the Irish theatre very highly, as is evidenced by the speech he delivered to the Royal Swedish Academy when in 1923 he had been awarded the Nobel Prize for Literature. He begins as follows:

I have chosen as my theme the Irish Dramatic Movement because when I remember the great honour that you have conferred upon me, I cannot forget many known and unknown persons. Perhaps the English committees would never have sent you my name if I had written no plays, no dramatic criticism, if my lyric poetry had not a quality of speech practised upon the stage, perhaps even—though this could be no portion of their deliberate thought—if it were not in some degree the symbol of a movement. I wish to tell the Royal Academy of Sweden of the labours, triumphs and troubles of my fellow workers.[3]

In his speech he mentions Hyde's work for the language movement, and his own for the Literary Renaissance movement. He praises Martyn, Synge, Lady Gregory, and Annie Horniman for their work for the theatre. He praises the actors, the speech and the stories of the country-people living in the Kiltartan district where he and Lady Gregory learnt from the great oral tradition which in those days was still rich and flourishing. Towards the end of his speech he says:

...when I received from the hands of your King the great honour your Academy has conferred upon me, I felt that a young man's ghost [Synge's] should have stood upon one side of me and at the other a living woman in her vigorous old age [Lady Gregory].[4]

[2] (Dublin: The Talbot Press Ltd; London: T. Fisher Unwin, 1918), p. 53.
[3] *The Bounty of Sweden: A Meditation, and a Lecture Delivered before the Royal Swedish Academy . . . by William Butler Yeats* (Dublin Ireland: The Cuala Press, 1925), pp. 33—34.
[4] Ibid., pp. 48—49.

In Sweden Synge's two plays *Riders to the Sea* and *The Playboy of the Western World* are produced fairly often, as are some of Lady Gregory's, but Yeats's plays seem to have been all but forgotten by the Swedish theatre. However, during his stay in Stockholm in December 1923, Yeats saw a performance of his symbolic play *Cathleen Ni Houlihan* translated into Swedish by Hugo Hultenberg and included in *Irländska dramer av W. B. Yeats*, a selection which also contains translations of *The Pot of Broth (Soppkitteln)*, *The Hour-Glass (Timglaset)*, *On Baile's Strand (På Bailes strand)*, and *The Shadowy Waters (De mörka vattnen)*.[5] Karl Asplund's translation of *The Land of Heart's Desire* appeared in 1924,[6] and that by Teresia Eurén of *The Countess Cathleen* in 1923.[7] There are also authorised translations of *The Unicorn from the Stars*, and *The Player Queen*.[8] It would be interesting to see at least some of these plays and perhaps some of the Noh plays, for example *At the Hawk's Well* and *The Only Jealousy of Emer*, or the late play *Purgatory*, produced on some Swedish stage.

The chief aim of the present study of three of Yeats's early plays has been to show that Yeats managed in a remarkable way to make folklore a living organism in his own drama. The role of folklore for the Irish Dramatic Revival can hardly be overestimated, for also in, for example, Synge's and Lady Gregory's plays, native Irish tradition is a source of strength and beauty.

---

[5] Till svenska av Hugo Hultenberg (Stockholm: P. A. Norstedt & Söners Förlag, 1923).

[6] *Längtans land av W. B. Yeats* (Stockholm: P. A. Norstedt & Söners Förlag, 1924).

[7] *Grevinnan Cathleen. Legend i fem scener* (Stockholm: Thure Wahledows Förlag, 1923).

[8] *Enhörningen från stjärnorna. Drottningen. Två skådespel av W. B. Yeats.* Bemyndigad översättning (Stockholm: P. A. Norstedt & Söners Förlag, 1924).

Appendix I

Here follow three versions of the same ballad.

1
An Gruagach Uasal

bí mé 'lá bpeág gul a' bóčap,
  Só ṗa liorn ṫub buiṫe,
Aguṙ caraṫ 'n gṙuagač uaṙal óg ṫoṁ,
  Só ṗa gṙáṫ mo čṙoiṫe.

'D'iapṙ ṙé ṫoṁ féṁ an mġean ṫoṁ 'n óg-ṁṅaoi,
  Só ṗa liorn ṫub buiṫe,
Aguṙ ṫubaiṙc mé féṁ guṙb i mo bean póṙcaṫ
  Só ṗa gṙáṫ mo čṙoiṫe.

'D'iapṙ ṙé iaṙaċc uaṙ nó lá ṫoṁ,
  Só ṗa liorn ṫub buiṫe,
" Ó ċa ṫeánaim ṙin, aċ' ṫeánpaṫ mé an cóiṙ leac,'
  Só ṗa gṙáṫ mo čṙoiṫe.

Music and three of the fifteen quatrains of *An Gruagach Uasal,* collected by E. E. Fournier d'Albe in Tory Island and made available with an English translation (see p. 142 above) by Lady Gregory, in *The Irish Homestead Christmas Number,* December 1901, pp. 19–20. It was also printed in *Irisleabhar na Gaedhilge: The Gaelic Journal,* 12, No. 138, March 1902, p 43. Reproduced by permission of the British Library, London.

2   *Oro! A Lionn-dubh Buidhe!*

Bhí mise lá a siúbhal a' bhothair,
Oro! a lionn-dubh buidhe!
'S casadh orm a' gruagach láidir ;
Cuach mo lionn-dubh buidhe!
Chuir sé ceist orm an inghean dom an oig-
      bhean,
Oro! a lionn-dubh buidhe!
Dubhairt mé féin nár bh' í acht mo **bean** [bhean]
      phósta,
Cuach mo lionn-dubh buidhe!

● ● ● ● ● ● ● ● ● ●

Cuach andiu 's cuach amárach,
Oro! a lionn-dubh buidhe!
'S cuach beag eile go ceann trí ráithe,
'S a cuach mo lón-dubh buidhe!

The first eight lines and the last four lines of a Co. Tyrone version of the ballad taken down by J. J. Lyons from an Irish emigrant, Maggie Gordon in Philadelphia, "formerly of Dunamanagh, Co. Tyrone." See Énrí O'Muirgheasa, *Céad de Cheoltaibh Uladh* [A Hundred Ulster Songs], Dublin, 1915, pp. 250–251. This ballad was first printed in *Irisleabhar na Gaedhilge: The Gaelic Journal*, 4: No. 42, Dublin, July 1892, pp. 152–153. Reproduced by permission of the British Library, London.

There is also another version of the same ballad beginning "Cuach mo Lonndubh Buidhe", also printed in Énrí ÓMuirgheasa's *Céad de Cheoltaibh Uladh*, pp. 85–91, and notes, pp. 250–251. The first line is also used as the refrain of the ballad. (*Lonndubh* ought to be spelt *Lionndubh*.)

3   *O the Brown and the Yellow Ale!*

I was walking the road one fine day,
(O the brown and the yellow ale!)
When I met with a man who was no right man.
(O, O love of my heart!)

And he asked if the woman with me was my daughter
(O the brown and the yellow ale!)
And I said that she was my married wifie
(O, O love of my heart!)

And he asked would I lend her for an hour and a quarter
And I said I would do anything that was fair.

So you take the high road and I'll take the lower
And we'll meet again at the ford of the river.

I was waiting that way for a day and a quarter
When she came to me without any shame.

When I heard her tale I lay down and died
And she sent two men to the wood for timber.

A board of holly and a board of alder
And two great yards of a sacking about me.

And if it wasn't that me own little mother was a woman
(O the brown and the yellow ale!)
I could sing you another pretty song about women.
(O, O love of my heart!)

The version above is the ballad as James Stephens learned it from James Joyce and sang in a BBC programme (see Ch. III, n. 61). The version is taken down from a copy of a recording made available to me by the British Broadcasting Corporation and Mrs. Cynthia Stephens in 1955.

Appendix II

Music to one song in *The Countess Cathleen,* one song in *The Land of Heart's Desire,* and two songs in *The Shadowy Waters.* Grateful acknowledgement is made to Miss Anne Yeats and Senator Michael B. Yeats.

1   *Impetuous heart, be still, be still*

The Countess Cathleen: Music by F. Farr to "Impetuous heart, be still, be still", taken from W. B. Yeats, *Ideas of Good and Evil,* p. 17.

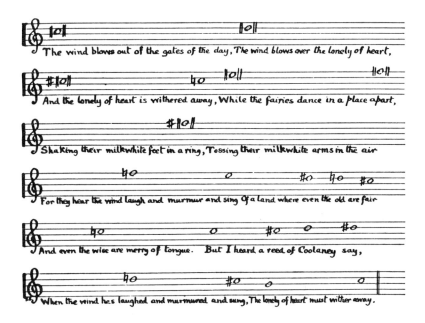

The wind blows out of the gates of the day, The wind blows over the lonely of heart,

And the lonely of heart is withered away, While the fairies dance in a place apart,

Shaking their milkwhite feet in a ring, Tossing their milkwhite arms in the air

For they hear the wind laugh and murmur and sing Of a land where even the old are fair

And even the wise are merry of tongue. But I heard a reed of Coolaney say,

When the wind has laughed and murmured and sung, The lonely of heart must wither away.

The Land of Heart's Desire: Music by Florence Farr to "The Wind blows out of the gates of the day" is taken from W. B. Yeats, *The Collected Works,* III, p. [237].

3   *[The Sailors' Song]*

I was going the road one day, O' the brown and the yellow beer, And I met with a man that was no right man, O my dear, my dear.

The Shadowy Waters: Music for the ale-song of the sailors the same music as for the Pupils' Song in *The Hour-Glass*. Taken from W. B. Yeats, *The Collected Works,* III, p. 232.

The Shadowy Waters: [Dectora's Lament]. Music composed by Arthur Darley. See W. B. Yeats, *The Collected Works*, III, p. 231.

Bibliography

A. Works of W. B. Yeats Quoted or Referred To

The Arrow. No. 2. 24 November 1906.

[*Axël*]. Preface to, dated 20 September 1924. Trans. by H. P. R. Finberg (London, 1925). Preface based on the early review "A Symbolical Drama in Paris." *The Bookman*, London, April 1894.

Beltaine: The Organ of the Irish Literary Theatre. Number One. London: At the Sign of the Unicorn, May 1899. Number Two. Number Three. 1900. Rpt. in One Volume With an Introductory Note by B. C. Bloomfield. Frank Cass Library of Little Magazines. No. 15. London: Frank Cass, 1970.

"The Binding of the Hair". In *The Savoy*, No. 1. January 1896, 135−138, and in *The Secret Rose*.

A Book of Irish Verse: Selected from Modern Irish Writers with an Introduction and Notes by W. B. Yeats. London: Methuen & Co., 1895. My ref. are to the rev. and enl. ed. London: Methuen, 1900.

The Bounty of Sweden. A Meditation, and a Lecture Delivered before the Royal Swedish Academy . . . Dublin, Ireland: The Cuala Press, 1925.

The Cat and the Moon and Certain Poems. Dublin: The Cuala Press, 1924. The play *The Cat and the Moon* first appeared in the *Criterion* and the *Dial*, in July 1924.

The Celtic Twilight. London: Lawrence and Bullen, 1893. 2nd ed. London: A. H. Bullen, 1902. New ed. New York, 1962.

The Collected Plays of W. B. Yeats. London: Macmillan, 1934; rev. ed. with additional plays, London, 1952. Several rpts.

The Collected Poems of W. B. Yeats. London: Macmillan, 1933. 2nd ed. with later poems added, 1950. Several rpts.

The Collected Works of William Butler Yeats in Verse and Prose. 8 vol. Stratford-on-Avon: Shakespeare Head Press, 1908.

The Countess Cathleen. London: T. Fisher Unwin, 1912; rpt. 1916, 1920, 1922, 1924. The 1924 vol. was bound together with *The Land of Heart's Desire*.

The Countess Kathleen and Various Legends and Lyrics. Boston: Robert Brothers; London: T. Fisher Unwin, 1892.

[*Cuchulain of Muirthemne*.] A Preface by W. B. Yeats. See Lady Gregory.

"The Desire of Man and of Woman." The *Dome*, June 1897.

Essays and Introductions. London: Macmillan & Co Ltd, 1961.

Explorations. Selected by Mrs. W. B. Yeats. London: Macmillan & Co Ltd, 1962.

Fairy and Folk Tales of the Irish Peasantry. London: Walter Scott, 1888. Also publ. as *Irish Fairy and Folk Tales*. Modern Library Ed. No. 44. New York: Boni and Liveright, n. d. [1918].

Four Plays for Dancers. London: Macmillan and Co., 1921.

[*Gods and Fighting Men*.] A Preface by W. B. Yeats. See Lady Gregory

The Green Helmet and Other Poems. Churchtown Dundrum: The Cuala Press, 1910. New York: Harold Paget, 1911.

The Hour-Glass: A Morality. London: Heinemann, 1903. Also: *Being Volume Two of Plays for an Irish Theatre.* London: A. H. Bullen, 1904.

Ideas of Good and Evil. London: A. H. Bullen, 1903.

If I Were Four-and-Twenty. Dublin: The Cuala Press, 1940.

In the Seven Woods: Being Poems Chiefly of the Irish Heroic Age. Dundrum: The Dun Emer Press, 1903.

Irish Fairy Tales. London: T. Fisher Unwin, 1892.

"King Goll, an Irish Legend." The *Leisure Hour,* Sept. 1887.

The Land of Heart's Desire. London: T. Fisher Unwin, 1894; rev. ed. Portland Maine: privately printed, 1903. Portland Maine: Th. B. Mosher, 1903; London: T. Fisher Unwin, 1912.

The Land of Heart's Desire . . . The Countess Cathleen. London: T. Fisher Unwin, 1924.

The Letters of W. B. Yeats. Ed. Allan Wade. London: Rupert Hart-Davis, 1954.

Literary Ideals in Ireland. See Eglinton, John.

"Michael Clancy, The Great Dhoul, and Death." *The Old Country: A Christmas Annual* (1893).

Mythologies. London: Macmillan & Co Ltd, 1959.

Per Amica Silentia Lunae. London: Macmillan and Co.; New York: The Macmillan Co., 1918.

Plays and Controversies. London: Macmillan and Co., 1923.

Plays in Prose and Verse Written for an Irish Theatre, and generally with the help of a friend. London: Macmillan and Co., 1922. New York, 1924.

Poems. London: T. Fisher Vnwin, 1895. Boston: Copeland and Day, 1895. 2nd Engl. ed., 1899. 3rd Engl. ed. 1901. 4th Engl. ed., 1904. 5th Engl. ed., 1908. 6th Engl. ed. rev., 1912. 7th Engl. ed., 1913. London: Ernest Benn, 1929; Dublin: Ireland: Cuala Press, 1935.

Poems, 1899–1905. London: A. H. Bullen; Dublin: Maunsel & Co., 1906. Contains a version of *SW.*

Poems and Ballads of Young Ireland. Dublin: M. H. Gill and Son, 1888. ". . . it seems probable that the actual editing was informal, under the general direction of O'Leary." (See Wade, No. 289.) Re-issues in 1890 and 1903.

The Poetical Works of William B. Yeats in Two Volumes. II: *Dramatical Poems.* New York and London, 1907. Rpt. 1909, 1911, 1912. [I: *Lyrical Poems.* New York and London, 1906. Several rpts.]

The Pot of Broth. London: A. H. Bullen, 1911.

Representative Irish Tales. Compiled, With an Introduction and Notes by W. B. Yeats. London: G. P. Putnam's Sons, 1891.

Responsibilities: Poems and A Play. Churchtown Dundrum: The Cuala Press, 1914. London: Macmillan, 1916. New York: Macmillan, 1916.

The Resurrection. First printed in *The Adelphi,* June 1927.

Rosa Alchemica. First appeared in *The Savoy,* April 1896.

The Secret Rose. London: Lawrence & Bullen, Ltd., 1897. In *The Collected Works of W. B. Yeats,* VII.

Selected Poems. New York: The Macmillan Company, 1921. Contains *LHD.*

A Selection from the Poetry of W. B. Yeats. Leipzig: Tauchnits, 1913. Contains *CC.*

The Shadowy Waters. In the *North American Review,* May 1900.

The Shadowy Waters. London: Hodder and Stoughton, 1900. 2nd ed. 1901.

The Shadowy Waters. Acting Version, as first played at the Abbey Theatre, 8 December 1906. London: A. H. Bullen, 1907.

Stories from Carleton. London: Walter Scott, 1889.

Stories of Red Hanrahan. Dundrum: The Dun Emer Press, 1905. In *Collected Works of W. B. Yeats,* V.

"Swedenborg, Mediums and the Desolate Places." Dated 14th October 1914. *In Visions and Beliefs in the West of Ireland,* pp. 295–339. See Lady Gregory. Rpt. in *If I Were Four-and-Twenty.*

The Tables of the Law and The Adoration of the Magi. London: Elkin Mathews, privately printed, 1897. London: Elkin Mathews, 1904. Reissued in 1905; Stratford-upon-Avon: The Shakespeare Head Press, 1914. See also under O'Driscoll, Robert.

"Tales from the Twilight." The *Scots Observer,* March 1 1890.

The Ten Principal Upanishads. Trans. and ed. by W. B. Yeats and S. P. Swami. London: Faber and Faber; New York: Macmillan, 1937.

"Two Poems Concerning Peasant Visionaries." *The Savoy,* April 1896.

Uncollected Prose by W. B. Yeats: I – First Reviews & Articles 1886–1896. Coll. and ed. John P. Frayne. London: Macmillan; New York: Columbia Univ. Press, 1970; *II – Later Reviews, Articles & Other Miscellaneous Prose 1897–1939.* Coll. and ed. John P. Frayne & Colton Johnson. London & Basingstoke: Macmillan, 1975. Associated Companies in New York, etc.

The Variorum Edition of the Plays of W. B. Yeats. Ed. Russell K. Alspach. London etc.: Macmillan, 1965; rpt. 1966.

The Variorum Edition of the Poems of W. B. Yeats. Ed. Peter Allt and Russell K. Alspach. New York: Macmillan, 1957.

A Vision. London: Macmillan, 1937. *A Reissue With the Author's Final Revisions.* New York: Macmillan, 1961. (1st. ed., 1925.)

[*Visions and Beliefs in the West of Ireland.*] With Two Essays and Notes by W. B. Yeats. See Lady Gregory.

The Wanderings of Oisin and Other Poems. London: Kegan Paul, Trench & Co., 1889.

The Wanderings of Oisin: Dramatic Sketches, Ballads & Lyrics. London: T. Fisher Unwin, 1892.

Wheels and Butterflies. London: Macmillan and Co., 1934. New York: Macmillan Company, 1935.

Where There Is Nothing. Being Volume One of Plays for an Irish Theatre. London, New York: Macmillan, 1903.

The Wind Among the Reeds. London: Elkin Mathews, 1899. New York and London: John Lane, 1899; 1902.

B. Swedish Translations of Works of W. B. Yeats Referred To

Enhörningen från stjärnorna. Drottningen. Två skådespel av W. B. Yeats. Bemyndigad översättning. Stockholm: P. A. Norstedt & Söners Förlag, 1924.

Grevinnan Cathleen: Legend i fem scener. Till svenska av Teresia Eurén. Stockholm: Thure Wahledows Förlag, 1923.
Irländska dramer av W. B. Yeats. Till svenska av Hugo Hultenberg. Stockholm: P. A. Norstedt & Söners Förlag, 1923.
Längtans land av William Butler Yeats. Till svenska av Karl Asplund. Stockholm: P. A. Norstedt & Söners Förlag, 1924.

C. Other Works Quoted or Referred To

Acallamh na Senórach. See Stokes, Whitley.
Alderson Smith, Peter. " 'Grown to Heaven Like a Tree': The Scenery of *The Countess Cathleen.*" *Éire: Ireland* (Fall 1979). St. Paul, Minnesota: IACI, 1979, 65–81.
Allingham, William. *Irish Songs and Poems.* London: Reeves and Turner, 1887.
Allt, Peter. "Yeats, Religion and History." *Sewanee Review,* 60 (Oct.–Dec. 1952), 624–658.
Alspach, Russell K. *Irish Poetry from the English Invasion to 1798.* Philadelphia: Univ. of Pennsylvania Press, 1959.
– "The Use by Yeats and Other Irish Writers of the Folklore of Patrick Kennedy." *Journal of American Folk-Lore,* 59 (October–December 1946), 404–412.
Annals of the Kingdom of Ireland by the Four Masters, from the earliest period to the year 1616. Ed. from MSS in the Library of the Royal Irish Academy and of Trinity College, Dublin, with a translation, and copious notes [and Indexes], by John O'Donovan. 7 vol. Dublin, 1848–1851.
Anon. "A Lament of Morian Shehone for Miss Mary Bourke." In Yeats's *A Book of Irish Verse.* London, 1895; rev. and enl. ed. 1900, pp. 242–245.
Arbois de Jubainville, Henri, d'. *Le cycle mythologique irlandais et la mythologie celtique.* Cours de Litt. Celtique, Tome II. Paris, 1884. Trans. Richard Best. *The Irish Mythological Cycle and Celtic Mythology.* Dublin, 1903.
The Atlantis: a Register of Literature and Science, conducted by members of the Catholic Univ. of Ireland. Vol. 1–4; Vol. 5, No. 1. London, Dublin, 1858–1870. The periodical was suspended during the years 1864–1870.
Barrington, Sir Jonah. *Personal Sketches and Recollections of his Own Times.* 3 vol. London: H. Coburn & R. Bentley, 1827–32.
– *Rise and Fall of the Irish Nation.* Paris: G. G. Bennis, 1833.
Barry, Joseph. *Songs of Ireland.* Dublin, 1845. 2nd ed. 1869.
Bergin, O. J. and R. I. Best, ed. "Tochmarc Étaíne." *Ériu,* 12 (1938), 137–196.
Best, R. I. (See under Bergin, O. J.)
– *Bibliography of Irish Philology.* Dublin: Dublin Institute for Advanced Studies, 1913.
– *Bibliography of Irish Philology 1913–1941.* Dublin: Dublin Institute for Advanced Studies, 1942.
Bjersby, Birgit. (See also under Bramsbäck, Birgit.)
– *The Interpretation of the Cuchulain Legend in the Works of W. B. Yeats.* Diss. Upsala 1950. Upsala Irish Studies, vol. 1. Ed. S. B. Liljegren, Upsala: Lundequistska Bokhandeln; Copenhagen: Munksgaard; Dublin: Hodges Figgis, 1950.
The Black Book of Carmarthen. Ed. J. G. Evans. Pwllheli, 1906.

Bliss, Alan. *Spoken English in Ireland 1600−1740*. Dolmen Texts 5. Dublin: The Dolmen Press, 1979.

The Book of Armagh. Ed. with introduction and appendices by John Gwynn. Dublin, 1913.

Boyd, Ernest. *The Contemporary Drama of Ireland*. Dublin: The Talbot Press Ltd.; London: T. Fisher Unwin, 1918.

Bramsbäck, Birgit. (See also under Bjersby, Birgit.)

− "Allusions to Yeats in *Stephen Hero* and *A Portrait of the Artist as a Young Man.*" In *Nordic Rejoycings 1982—in commemoration of the centenary of the birth of James Joyce*. [Ed. Johannes Hedberg.] The James Joyce Society of Sweden and Finland, 1982, pp. 9−25.

− "William Butler Yeats and Folklore Material." *Béaloideas: The Journal of the Folklore of Ireland Society,* vol. 39−41, 1971−73. Dublin: The Educational Company of Ireland, 1975, 56−68. Also in *Hereditas: Essays and Studies presented to Professor Ó Duilearga . . .* Ed. Bo Almqvist et. al. Dublin: The Folklore of Ireland Society, 1975, pp. 56−68.

Breatnach, P. A. "The Chief's Poet." *Proceedings of the Royal Irish Academy,* 83 C 3. Dublin: Royal Irish Academy, 1983, 37−79.

Briggs, Katharine. *A Dictionary of Fairies*. London: Allen Lane, 1976.

Brooke, Charlotte. *Reliques of Ancient Irish Poetry. Consisting of heroic poems, odes, elegies, and songs translated into English verse; with notes explanatory and historical; and the originals in the Irish character. To which is subjoined an Irish tale.* Dublin: George Bonham, 1789.

Brown, J. *Ireland in Fiction*. New ed. Dublin and London: Maunsel and Company, 1919.

Bülow, Isolde, von. *Der Tanz im Drama: Untersuchungen zu W. B. Yeats' dramatischer Theorie und Praxis.* Studien zur Englischen Literatur, 1. Ed. Johannes Kleinstück. Bonn: Bouvier, 1969.

Bushrui, S. B. *Yeats's Verse Plays: The Revisions 1900−1910*. Oxford: Clarendon Press, 1965.

Byrd, Thomas L. Jr. *The Early Poetry of W. B. Yeats*. Port Washington, N. Y., London: National Univ. Publications, Kennikat Press, 1978.

The *Cambrian Journal,* Part VI, June 1855. London; Tenby: The Cambrian Institute, 1855. Contains "The Story of Conn-Edda; or, the Golden Apples of Loch Erne", 101−115.

Cameron, Alexander. *Reliquiae Celticae*. 2 vol. Inverness, 1892.

Campbell, J. F., ed. *Leabhar na Feinne. Heroic Ballads collected in Scotland chiefly from 1512 to 1871.* London, 1872; rpt. Facsimile Ed. in Scottish Reprints. Intr. by D. S. Thomson. Shannon Ireland: IUP, 1980.

"Candida" [pseud. of Mrs. Frances Peck]. *Life in the Irish Militia, or Tales of the Barrack Room.* London: James Ridgeway & Sons, 1847.

Carleton, William. *The Black Prophet*. London, 1847; rpt. 1899 (ill. by J. B. Yeats); rpt. Shannon Ireland: IUP, 1972.

− *Tales and Sketches, Illustrating the Character, Usages, Traditions, Sports and Pastimes of the Irish Peasantry*. Dublin, 1845.

− *Traits and Stories of the Irish Peasantry*. First ed. 1830−33. Several subsequent editions.

Chatterton, Lady Henrietta Georgiana. *Rambles in the South of Ireland during the year 1838.* 2nd ed. [With Plates.] London, 1839.

Christiansen, Reidar Th. "Some Notes on the Fairies and the Fairy Faith." *Béaloideas: The Journal of the Folklore of Ireland Society*, Vol. 39–41, 1971– 73. Dublin: The Educational Company of Ireland, Ltd., 1975, 95–111. Also in *Hereditas* (Dublin, 1975), pp. 95–111.

Clark, David R., ed. "Half the Characters Had Eagles' Faces: W. B. Yeats' unpublished 'Shadowy Waters'." The *Massachusetts Review*, 6 (Autumn 1964 – Winter 1965), 151–180.

Clark, David R. and George Mayhew, ed. *A Tower of Black Polished Stones: Early Versions of The Shadowy Waters*. Dolmen Editions XI. Dublin: Dolmen Press, 1971.

Cohen, Hennig. "American Literature and American Folklore." *American Folklore*. Voice of America Forum Lectures, 2. Ed. Tristram Coffin (March 1968), pp. 269–278.

Comyn, David. "Laoidh Oisín ar Thír na nÓg" ("The Lay of Oisin on the Land of the Young.") Rev. ed. with a new literal trans. Dublin: Gaelic Union Publications, 1880.

Comyn, Michael. "Tír na nÓg, the Land of Youth, an Ossianic Poem." *Transactions of the Ossianic Society*, 4 (Dublin, 1859).

Conner, Lester. "The Importance of Douglas Hyde to the Irish Literary Renaissance." *Modern Irish Literature: Essays in Honor of William York Tindall*. The Library of Irish Studies, 1. Ed. Raymond J. Porter and James D. Brophy. New York: Iona College Press, Twayne, 1972, pp. 95–114.

Croker, T. Crofton. *Fairy Legends and Traditions of the South of Ireland*. 3 vol. Publ. anon. in 1825–1828. A new and complete ed. by T. Wright. With Illustrations by MacLise and Green. London, 1888; 5th ed. 1898.

– *Killarney Legends*. London, 1831. Abridged version of the *Legends of the Lakes*. 2 vol. London, 1829.

– *Researches in the South of Ireland*. London, 1824.

Cross, K. G. W. and R. T. Dunlop. *A Bibliography of Yeats Criticism 1887–1965*. London: Macmillan, 1971.

Cross, Tom Peete. *Motif-Index of Early Irish Literature*. Folklore Series, 7. Bloomington: Indiana Univ. Publications. 1952.

Cross, Tom Peete and Clark Harris Slover, ed. *Ancient Irish Tales*. London: George G. Harrap, n.d.

Curtin, Jeremiah. See under Ó Duilearga, Séamus.

– ed. "Balor of the Evil Eye and Lui Lavada, his Grandson." In *Hero-Tales of Ireland*. Boston, London, 1894, pp. 296–311.

– *Myths and Folk-Lore of Ireland*. Boston, London, 1890, and 1911.

– *Tales of the Fairies and the Ghost World, collected from oral Tradition in South-West Munster*. Boston, London, 1895.

Curtis, Edmund. *A History of Ireland*. 1936; rpt. London: Univ. Paper Books, Methuen, 1961.

Daly, Dominic. *The Young Douglas Hyde: The Dawn of the Irish Revolution and Renaissance 1874–1893*. Dublin: IUP, 1974.

Desai, Rupin W. *Yeats's Shakespeare*. Evanston: Northwestern Univ. Press, 1971.

Dillon, Myles. *Early Irish Literature*. Chicago: Univ. of Chicago Press, 1948.

Disraeli, Earl of Beaconsfield. *Vivian Grey*. Hughenden Ed. of *Novels and Tales*, 1. London, 1881.

Donne, John. "The Canonization." In *The Metaphysical Poets*. Ed. Helen Gardner. Penguin Poets D 38. Harmondsworth: Penguin Books, 1957; rev. ed. 1966; rpt. 1968.

Dorson, Richard. "Is Folklore a Discipline?" *Folklore*, 84 (Autumn 1973), 177–205.

Dottin, Georges. *The World of the Celts*. Trans. David Macrae. Genève: Minerva, 1977.

Dublin Penny Journal. 4. vol. Dublin, 1832–34.

Dublin University Magazine. 90 vol. Dublin, 1833–77.

Duffy's Fireside Magazine. A monthly miscellany containing original tales, etc. 4 vol. Dublin 1851–54.

Duffy's Hibernian Magazine. 3 vol. Dublin, 1860, 1861. N.S. 5 vol. Dublin, 1862–64.

Dunlop, R. T. See Cross, K.G.W.

Dyer, T. F. Thistelton. *The Ghost World*. London, 1893.

Edgeworth, Maria. *Castle Rackrent*. New York: Pratt, 1800; rpt. New York: Century, 1903; OUP, 1964; OU Paperback, 1969.

Éigse, 18 (1980–81), 25–37.

Eglinton, John, et al. *Literary Ideals in Ireland*. London and Dublin: T. Fisher Unwin and the *Daily Express* Office, 1899.

Ellmann, Richard. *The Identity of Yeats*. London: Macmillan, 1954.

– *James Joyce*. New York: OUP, 1959; rev. ed. 1982.

– *The Man and the Masks*. New York: Macmillan, 1948; London: Macmillan, 1949.

Encyclopaedia Britannica. 1964 ed. Article on "Catherine, Saint of Alexandria."

Entwistle, William. *European Balladry*. Oxford: Clarendon Press, 1939.

The Faber Book of Irish Verse. Ed. John Montague. London: Faber and Faber, 1974.

Farag, F. F. "Oriental and Celtic Elements in the Poetry of W. B. Yeats." In Maxwell, D. E. S. and S. B. Bushrui, ed. *W. B. Yeats 1865–1965: Centenary Essays*. Ibadan: Ibadan Univ. Press, 1965, pp. 33–53.

[Farewell, James, ed.]. *The Irish Hudibras, OR Fingallian Prince, Taken from the Sixth Book of VIRGIL's Aeneids, and Adapted to the Present Times*. London, 1689.

Ferguson, Sir Samuel. *Congal. A poem in five books, etc*. Dublin, London, 1872.

– *Lays of the Western Gael*. London, 1865.

– *Poems of Sir Samuel Ferguson*. The Irish Library. Dublin, Cork and Belfast, n.d. [1880].

Fournier d'Albe, Edmund Edward. *An English-Irish Dictionary and Phrase-Book*. With synonyms, idioms, and the genders of nouns. Dublin: Celtic Association, 1903.

Frazer, Sir James. *The Golden Bough: A Study in Comparative Religion*. 2 vol. London, 1890. 3rd enl. ed., 12 vol. London, 1907–1915.

Friend, Hilderic. *Flowers and Flower Lore*. 2 vol. London, 1883.

Funk & Wagnalls *Standard Dictionary of Folklore, Mythology and Legend*. New English Library. London. Ed. Maria Leach. New York: Funk & Wagnalls Publ. Co. (1949), 1972.

The Gaelic Journal. See *Irisleabhar na Gaedhilge*.

Gearrfhoclóir Gaeilge-Béarla. An Roinn Oidechais [The Department of Education]. Baile Átha Cliath: Richview Browne & Nolan Ltd., 1981.

163

Giraldus Cambrensis. *Topographia Hibernica (The Historical World of Giraldus Cambrensis Containing the Topography of Ireland, and the History of the Conquest of Ireland*. Trans. Thomas Forester. London, 1863.)

Goldgar, H. *"Axël* de Villiers de l'Isle-Adam et *The Shadowy Waters* de W. B. Yeats." *Revue de Littérature Comparée,* 24 (24ᵉ Année, 1950), 563−574.

Gregory, Lady Augusta. *Cuchulain of Muirthemne.* Preface by W. B. Yeats. London, 1902. 2nd ed., Coole Ed., 2. Gerrards Cross: Colin Smythe, 1970.

− *Gods and Fighting Men.* Preface by W. B. Yeats. London: Murray, 1904; 2nd ed., Coole Ed., 3. Gerrards Cross: Colin Smythe, 1970.

− *Our Irish Theatre.* Preface by W. B. Yeats. London and New York: G. P. Putnam's Sons, 1913.

− *Visions and Beliefs in the West of Ireland.* With Two Essays and Notes by W. B. Yeats (Copyright 1914). London and New York: G. P. Putnam's Sons, 1920. 2nd ed., Coole Ed., 1. Gerrards Cross: Colin Smythe, 1970. Toronto, 1976.

Griffin, Gerald. *The Duke of Monmouth.* Dublin, 1836. Another ed. London, 1857.

− "Hy-Brasail—The Isle of the Blest", a poem included in Yeats's *Irish Fairy and Folk Tales.*

− *Tales of the Munster Festivals.* New York: Pratt, 1827. Two more series in 1829 and 1832.

− *Talis Qualis; or, Tales of the Jury Room.* 3 vol. London, 1842. Another ed. London, 1857.

"An Gruagach Uasal" ("The Noble Enchanter"). Coll. E. E. Fournier d'Albe. Trans. and ed. Lady Gregory. *The Irish Homestead Christmas Number: A Celtic Christmas,* 7 Dec. 1901, pp. 19−20.

Guthrie, W. N. "Two Poets." The *Sewanee Review,* 9 (July 1901), 329−330.

Hall [Anna Maria and Samuel]. *Ireland: Its Scenery, Character, etc.* 3 vol. London n.d. [1841−43].

Hamel, G. van. *Immrama.* Medieval and Modern Irish Series, 10. Dublin: Stationery Office, 1941.

Hardiman, James. Coll. and ed. *Irish Minstrelsy, Or Bardic Remains of Ireland; with English Poetical Translations.* 2 vol. London, 1831.

Harper, George Mills. *Yeats's Golden Dawn.* London: Macmillan, 1974.

Hautala, J. "Folkminnesforskningen som vetenskapsgren" [Folklore as a Discipline]. In *Folkdikt och folktro* [Folk Poetry and Folk Belief]. Ed. Anna Birgitta Rooth. Lund: Gleerups, 1971, pp. 33−63.

Heffernan, William. "Caitilín Ní Uallacháin." In O'Sullivan, Donal. *Songs of the Irish,* pp. 141−142.

Hellquist, Elof. *Svensk etymologisk ordbok.* 3rd ed. 2 vol. Lund: Gleerups, 1948.

Henn, T. R. *The Lonely Tower.* London: Methuen, 1950.

Hereditas: Essays and Studies presented to Professor Séamus ÓDuilearga. Ed. Bo Almqvist et al. Dublin: The Folklore of Ireland Society, 1975.

Hirsch, Edward. " 'Contention is Better than Loneliness': The Poet as Folklorist." In *The Genres of the Irish Literary Revival.* Ed. Ronald Schleifer, pp. 11−25.

Hogan, J. J. "W. B. Yeats." *Studies* (March 1939), 35−48.

Hone, Joseph. *W. B. Yeats, 1865−1939.* London: Macmillan, 1942; New York: Macmillan, 1943; rev. ed. 1962. My ref. are to the 1943 ed.

Hühn, P. *Das Verhältnis von Mann und Frau im Werk von W. B. Yeats.* Bonn, 1971.

Hull, Eleanor. *The Cuchullin Saga in Irish Literature*. London, 1898.

– "The Hawk of Achill or the Legend of the Oldest Animals." *Folk-Lore*, 43 (1932), 376–409.

Hunt, Robert. *Popular Romances of the West of England*. London, 1896.

Hyde, Douglas. *Beside the Fire: A Collection of Irish Gaelic Folk Stories*. Irish text and English trans. by Hyde and notes by Alfred Nutt. London: Nutt, 1890.

– Gaelic Folk Songs", and "The Poems of the Connacht Bards". See Ch. III, n. 45.

– *Legends of Saints and Sinners*. London, Dublin n.d. [1915]; rpt. Shannon Ireland: IUP, 1973.

– *A Literary History of Ireland from Earliest Times to the Present Day*. The Library of Literary History. London: Fisher Unwin, 1899; 1901. Rev. ed. 1967.

– *Love Songs of Connacht*. Dublin and London, 1893; rpt. Shannon Ireland: IUP, 1969. Introduction by Mícheál Ó hAodha.

– *Religious Songs of Connacht: A Collection of Poems, Stories, Prayers, Satires, Ranns, Charms, etc.* 2nd ed. London: T. Fisher Unwin; Dublin: Gill & Sons, 1906.

– *Songs Ascribed to Raftery. Being the Fifth Chapter of the Songs of Connacht Now for the First time Collected Edited and Translated*. Dublin: Gill agus a Mhac, 1913.

Inis Fail, 11 (August 1905).

Irish Homestead Christmas Number: A Celtic Christmas. December 1901. Contains "An Gruagach Uasal" ("The Noble Enchanter").

The Irish Penny Journal. 1 vol. Dublin, 1840–41.

Irisleabhar na Gaedhilge: The Gaelic Journal, 4. No 42. Dublin, July 1892, 152–153. Contains "Oro! A Lionn-dubh buidhe!"

– 12. No. 138. Dublin, March 1902, 43. Contains "An Gruagach Uasal".

Ishibashi, Hiro. *Yeats and the Noh: Types of Japanese Beauty in Yeats's Plays*. Yeats Centenary Papers, ed. Liam Miller. Dublin: The Dolmen Press, 1968.

Jackson, Kenneth. *The International Popular Tale and Early Welsh Tradition*. Cardiff: Univ. of Wales Press, 1961.

Jeffares, A. Norman. *A Commentary on the Collected Poems of W. B. Yeats*. London, Melbourne, Toronto: Macmillan, 1968.

– ed. *W. B. Yeats*. The Critical Heritage Series. Gen. ed. B. C. Southam. London: Routledge & Kegan Paul, 1977.

– *W. B. Yeats: Man and Poet*. London: Routledge & Kegan Paul Ltd., 1949.

– and A. S. Knowland. *A Commentary on the Plays of W. B. Yeats*. London: Macmillan, 1975.

Jochum, K. P. S. *W. B. Yeats: A Classified Bibliography of Criticism: Including Additions to Allan Wade's Bibliography to the Writings of W. B. Yeats and a Section on the Irish Literary and Dramatic Revival*. Urbana, Chicago, London: Univ. of Illinois Press, 1978.

– "A Yeats Bibliography for 1981." *Yeats: An Annual of Critical and Textual Studies*, I. Ed. R. J. Finneran (1983), 155–173.

Johnson, Lionel. "The Red Wind." In W. B. Yeats, ed. *A Book of Irish Verse*.

Joyce, James. *A Portrait of the Artist as a Young Man*. Text, criticism and notes, ed. by Chester G. Anderson. New York: Viking Press, 1964; rpt. 1968.

Joyce, P. W., ed. *Old Celtic Romances*. London: David Nutt, 1879. 2nd rev. and enl. ed. 1894; rpt. Dublin: Talbot Press, 1961.

- *The Origin and History of Irish Names of Places*. 3 vol. Dublin, 1869, 1970, 1913.
- *A Social History of Ancient Ireland*. 2 vol. London, 1903; Dublin: M. H. Gill & Son, 1920.

Keating, Geoffrey. *The General History of Ireland . . . Collected by J.K. . . . translated from the original Irish language with . . . amendments* by D. O'Connor. Dublin, 1723; 2nd ed. Westminster, 1726. Another ed. Newry, 1817. Another ed. Dublin, 1854.

Kennedy, Patrick. *The Banks of the Boro*. Dublin, 1867.
- *The Bardic Stories of Ireland*. Dublin, 1871.
- *Evenings in the Duffrey*. Dublin, 1869.
- *The Fireside Stories of Ireland*. Dublin, 1870.
- *Legendary Fictions of the Irish Celts*. London, 1866.
- *Legends of the Mount Leinster*. Dublin, 1855. Written under the pen name Harry Whitney.
- "The Witches' Excursion." in *Legendary Fictions of the Irish Celts,* pp. 148–150. Rpt. in Yeats's *Fairy and Folk Tales of the Irish Peasantry,* pp. 179–182.

Kickham, Charles. *Knocknagow; or, the Homes of Tipperary*. Dublin: Duffy [1879]. 25th ed. Dublin: J. Duffy & Co., 1930.

Kinahan, F. "Armchair Folklore: Yeats and the Textual Sources of *Fairy and Folk Tales of the Irish Peasantry*." Proceedings of the Royal Irish Academy, 83 C 10. Dublin: Royal Irish Academy, 1983, 255–267.

Kinsella, Thomas, trans. and ed. *The Tain: Trans. from the Irish epic Táin Bó Cuailnge*. First publ. in a limited ed. by the Dolmen Press, 1969. Rpt. (Oxford, London, New York: OUP (in association with the Dolmen Press), 1970; rpt. 1974.

Krans, Horatio S. *William Butler Yeats and the Irish Literary Revival*. Contemporary Men of Letters Series. London: Heinemann, 1905.

"Lageniensis" (pseud. for John O'Hanlon). *The Poetical Works*. Dublin, 1893.

Lang, Andrew. *Custom and Myth*. London, 1884; 1885; new ed. 1898, 1904.
- *Myth, Ritual and Religon*. London, 1887; new ed. 1899.

Larminie, William. "Legends as Material for Literature." In John Eglinton et al., *Literary Ideals in Ireland*.
- *West Irish Folk-Tales and Romances*. Coll. and trans. by W. Larminie. London, 1893.

Lebor Gabála Érenn (The Book of the Taking of Ireland). Ed. and trans. R. A. Stewart Macalister. ITS, 34, 35, 39, 41, 44, etc. London 1938–41.

Lebar (Lebor) na hUidre: A collection of pieces in prose and verse, in the Irish language. . . . Dublin, 1870. Also referred to as *The Book of the Dun Cow*.

Lespès, Antoine-Joseph-Napoléon (Léo). Wrote under the pseud. Timothée Trimm, Mme Vieuxbois. *Les Matinées de Timothée Trimm*. Illustr. H. de Montaut. Libraire du Petit Journal. Paris n.d. [1865].

Lysaght, Patricia. "*An Bhean Chaointe:* The Supernatural Woman in Irish Folklore." *Éire: Ireland* (Winter 1979). St. Paul, Minnesota: IACI, 1979, 7–29.

The Mabinogion. Trans. G. Jones and J. Jones. London, 1949.

Macalister, R. A. Stewart. See under *Lebor Gabála*.

MacHugh, Roger. "James Joyce's Synge-Song." *Envoy,* 3 (November 1950), 12–16.

MacLeod, Fiona (William Sharp). *The Dominion of Dreams. Under the Dark Star*.

London: Heinemann, 1895. Uniform Ed., 1910.

- *The Immortal Hour*. The *Fortnightly Review* (1900).
- "The Later Work of W. B. Yeats." The *North American Review* (Oct. 1902).
- *Poems and Dramas*. London: Thomas B. Mosher, 1901; London: Heinemann, 1923.
- "The Washer of the Ford." In *At the Turn of the Year: Essays and Nature Thoughts*. Edinburgh: Turnbull and Speirs, 1913, pp. 147–216.

Mangan, J. C. *The Poets and Poetry of Munster: a selection of Irish songs of the poets of the last century,* with poetical trans. by the late James Clarence Mangan. With the original music and biographical sketches by J. O'Daly. Dublin, 1849.

Maxwell, Constantia. *History of Trinity College, Dublin, 1591–1929*. Dublin, 1946.

Maxwell, D. E. S. and S. B. Bushrui. ed. *W. B. Yeats 1865–1965: Centenary Essays*. Ibadan: Ibadan UP, 1965.

Meir, Colin. *The Ballads and Songs of W. B. Yeats: The Anglo-Irish Heritage in Subject and Style*. London and Basingstoke: Macmillan, 1974.

Melchiori, Giorgio. *The Whole Mystery of Art*. London: Routledge & Kegan Paul, 1960.

Meyer, Kuno, ed. *The Voyage of Bran Son of Febal to the Land of the Living; An Old Irish saga edited and translated by Kuno Meyer. With Essays upon the Irish Vision of the Happy Otherworld: and the Celtic Doctrine of Re-birth: by Alfred Nutt*. 2 vol. I. Grimm Library, 4; London, 1895. II. Grimm Library, 6. London, 1897. See also under Nutt, Alfred.

Miller, Liam. *The Noble Drama of W. B. Yeats*. Dublin: The Dolmen Press, 1977.

Mirecourt, E. de (pseud. for Ch. J. B. Jacquot). *Timothée Trimm*. Histoire contemporaine, 16. Paris, 1867.

Munch-Pederson, Ole. "Crazy Jane: A Cycle of Popular Literature." *Éire: Ireland* (Spring 1979). St. Paul, Minnesota: IACI, 1979, 56–73.
- "Some Aspects of the Rewriting of W. B. Yeats's 'Red Hanrahan's Song About Ireland.' " *Orbis Litterarum: International Review of Literary Studies,* 36 (1981), 155–172.

Murphy, Gerard. *Saga and Myth in Ancient Ireland*. Irish Life and Culture, 10. Dublin: Publ. for CRC by Colm O Lochlainn, 1955.

Müller, d'Eduard. "Two Irish Tales. I. Aislinge Oengusso." *RC,* 3 (1877), 342–350; and "II. Scéla Aillill agus Étaine." *RC,* 3 (1877), 351–360.

Nathan, Leonard E. *The Tragic Drama of W. B. Yeats*. New York and London, 1965.

The *Nation,* 48, nos. 17–20, 22–35, 37–48, from 17 May 1890–20 November 1890. (Contains Douglas Hyde's articles "Gaelic Folk Songs", a title changed to "Poems of the Connacht Bards" in no. 20.) Continued in the *Weekly Freeman*.

Nutt, Alfred. "The Celtic Doctrine of Re-birth." In *Bran* II. See Meyer, Kuno.
- "The Irish Vision of the Happy Otherworld." In *Bran* I. See Meyer, Kuno.

O'Curry, Eugene. *On the Manners and Customs of the Ancient Irish*. 3 vol. Ed. W. K. O'Sullivan. London, New York, Dublin, 1861–1873.

Ó Duilearga, Séamus, ed. *Irish Folk-Tales*. Coll. by Jeremiah Curtin. Dublin: The Talbot Press, 1960.
- See Wilde, William.

O'Driscoll, Robert, ed. *The Celtic Consciousness*. Copyright, Celtic Arts of Canada, 1981; Ireland: The Dolmen Press; Scotland: Canongate Publ., 1982.
- "*The Tables of the Law:* A Critical Text." *Yeats Studies: an international*

journal, 1. Ed. Robert O'Driscoll and Lorna Reynolds. Shannon Ireland: IUP, 1971, 87–118.

O'Grady, Standish Hayes. *Silva Gadelica*. 2 vol. London, 1892.

O'Grady, Standish James. *The Chain of Gold*. London: T. Fisher Unwin, 1895; rpt. 1921.

– *Early Bardic Literature: Ireland*. London, 1879.

– *Finn and His Companions*. London, 1892.

– *History of Ireland*. 2 vol. London, 1878–80.

– *The Story of Ireland*. London, 1894.

O'Looney, Brian. "Laoidh Oisín ar Tír na nÓg." *The Transactions of the Ossianic Society*, 4. Dublin, 1859.

Ó Madagáin, Breandán. "Irish Vocal Music of Lament and Syllabic Verse." In *The Celtic Consciousness*, ed. Robert O'Driscoll. Canada, 1981; Scotland and Ireland, 1982, pp. 311–332.

Ó Muirgheasa, Énrí. *Céad de Cheoltaibh Uladh* [A Hundred Ulster Songs]. Dublin, 1915.

O'Rahilly, T. F. *Early Irish History and Mythology*. 1946; rpt. Dublin: Dublin Institute for Advanced Studies, 1971.

Osterling, Anders. *Horisonter*. Stockholm: Albert Bonniers Förlag, 1939.

O'Sullivan, Donal. *Songs of the Irish*. Dublin: Browne & Nolan, 1950.

Ó Súilleabháin, Seán. "Irish Oral Tradition." In *A View of the Irish Language*, ed. Brian Ó Cuív. Dublin: Stationery Office, 1969, pp. 47–56.

– *Irish Wake Amusements*. Cork: Mercier Press, 1969; rpt. 1969. Trans. by the author from the original Irish *Caitheamh Aimsire ar Thórraimh* (1961).

– (O'Sullivan, Sean), ed. and trans. *Folktales of Ireland*. Foreword by Richard M. Dorson. London: Routledge & Kegan Paul, 1969.

O'Sullivan, Sheila. "W. B. Yeats's Use of Irish Oral and Literary Tradition." *Béaloideas*, 39–41, 1971–73 (Dublin: The Educational Company of Ireland, 1975), 266–279. Also in *Hereditas*. Dublin, 1975, pp. 266–279.

Parkinson, Thomas. *W. B. Yeats Self-Critic: A Study of his Early Verse*. Berkeley: Univ. of California Press, 1951.

Pauly, Marie-Hélène. "W. B. Yeats et les Symbolistes Français." *Revue de Littérature Comparée*, 20 (1940–46), 13–33.

Peck, Frances. *The Bard of the West; Commonly Called Eman Ac Knuck or Ned of the Hills: An Irish Historical Romance*, London and Dublin, 1818. New ed. Dublin 1842. 6th ed. Dublin 1869.

– *The Welch Peasant Boy. A Novel*. 3 vol. By the Author of *The Maid of Avon* [Mrs Peck]. London: Printed at the Minerva Press, for Lane, Newman, and Co., 1808. (The British Library copy is bound in one volume.) Cf. "Candida"

Poems and Ballads of Young Ireland. Dublin: M. H. Gill and Son, 1888. Gen. ed., John O'Leary.

Pokorny, J. "Conle's abenteuerliche Fahrt." *(Echtra Connla.)* ZCP, 17 (1927), 193–205.

Rhŷs, Sir John. *Celtic Folklore: Welsh and Manx*. 2 vol. Oxford: Clarendon Press, 1901.

– *Lectures on the Origin and Growth of Religion as Illustrated by Celtic Heathendom*. The Hibbert Lectures, 1886. London, 1886.

– *Studies in the Arthurian Legend*. Oxford, 1881.

Rodenberg, Julius, alias Levy. *Die Insel der Heiligen*. Berlin, 1860.

Rooth, Anna Birgitta, ed. *Folkdikt och Folktro*. [Folk Literature and Folk Belief.] Lund: Gleerups, 1971.

Rosenberg, Bruce A. "Irish Folklore and 'The Song of Wandering Aengus.' " *PQ*, 46 (October 1967), 527–535.

Ross, Anne. *Pagan Celtic Britain*. London: Routledge & Kegan Paul, 1967.

Saltair na Rann. Ed. Whitley Stokes. Oxford, 1883.

Saul, George, B. *Prolegomena to the Study of Yeats's Plays*. Philadelphia: Univ. of Pennsylvania Press, 1958.

– *Prolegomena to the Study of Yeats's Poems*. Philadelphia: Univ. of Pennsylvania Press, 1957; rpt. New York: Octagon Books, 1971.

– "The Winged Image." In *In . . . Luminous Wind*. Dublin: Liam Miller, 1961.

Saurat, Denis. *Victor Hugo et les dieux du peuple*. Paris, n.d. [1948].

Schweisgut, Elsbeth. *Yeats' Feendichtung*. Diss. Darmstadt: K. F. Bender, 1927.

Seanchas Mór. Ancient Laws of Ireland. Ed. W. Hancock et al. Dublin: Alexander Thom, 1865.

Shaw, Francis, ed. *The Dream of Óengus: Aislinge Óenguso. An Old Irish text critically restored and ed. with Notes and Glossary*. Dublin: Browne & Nolan, 1934.

Shaw, G. B. *Arms and the Man*. In *Plays Pleasant and Unpleasant*. 2 vol. London: Grant Richards, 1898; rpt. Penguin Books, 1946. Several reprints.

Shorter Oxford English Dictionary. 1959 ed.

Sidnell, Michael J. Photographic copy of a typed essay on the MS versions of "The Countess Cathleen". MS 12 076. National Library of Ireland.

– "Manuscript Versions of Yeats's *The Countess Cathleen*." *Papers of the Bibliographical Society of America,* 56 (1962).

– "Yeats's First Work for the Stage." In *Centenary Essays* (1965), pp. 167–188. See Maxwell, D. E. S.

Sidnell, Michael J., George P. Mayhew and David R. Clark, ed. *Druid Craft: The Writing of The Shadowy Waters. Manuscripts of W. B. Yeats transcribed, edited and with a commentary*. I. *Manuscripts of W. B. Yeats*. Amherst: Univ. of Massachusetts Press, 1971.

Sigerson, George, ed. *Bards of the Gael and Gall: Examples of the Poetic Literature of Erinn*. 2nd rev. and enl. ed. London: T. Fisher Unwin, 1907.

Slover, Clark Harris. See Cross, Tom Peete.

Stephens, James. "The James Joyce I Knew." *The Listener,* 36, Oct. 1946.

Stewart, W. Grant. *The Popular Superstitions and Festive Amusements of the Highlanders of Scotland*. Edinburgh, 1823.

Stokes, Whitley. *Acallamh na Senórach (The Colloquy of the Old Men). Irische Texte*. Ed. Wh. Stokes und E. Windisch. Vierte Serie, 1 Heft. Leipzig, 1900.

Swami, Shri Purohit. *The Ten Principal Upanishads*. Put into English by Shri Purohit Swami and W. B. Yeats. Preface by W. B. Yeats. London: Faber and Faber, 1937.

Sydow, C. W. von. "Prosafolkdiktningens kategorier." [The Categories of Prose Folk Literature]. In *Folkdikt och folktro*. Ed. Anna Birgitta Rooth. Lund: Gleerups, 1971, pp. 110–111.

Symons, Arthur. *Poems*. 2 vol. London: Heinemann, 1902.

Thompson, Stith. *The Folktale*. New York: The Dryden Press, 1964.

Thuente, Mary Helen. *W. B. Yeats and Folklore*. Dublin: Gill and Macmillan, 1980. Totowa, New Jersey: Barnes & Noble Books, 1981.

Thurneysen, Rudolf. *Die irische Helden- und Königsage bis zum siebzehnten Jahrhundert*. Halle: Max Niemeyer, 1921.

Timothée Trimm. See Lespès.

Todhunter, John. *A Comedy of Sighs*. Performed 1894. (Published?)

Transactions of the Gaelic Society of Inverness, 22 (1897–98), 297–298. Contains "Garw and Cuchulain", a Fenian poem.

The *Universal Irish Song Book: A Complete Collection of Songs and Ballads of Ireland*. New York: P. J. Kenedy, 1886.

Ure, Peter. *Yeats the Playwright*. London: Routledge & Kegan Paul, 1963.

Utley, Francis Lee. "A Definition of Folklore." *American Folklore*. Voice of America Forum Lectures, 2. Ed. Tristram Coffin. March 1968, pp. 3–14.

Vickery, John B. " 'The Golden Bough': Impact and Archetype." *Virginia Quarterly Review*, 39 (Winter 1963), 37–57.

Wade, Allan. *A Bibliography of the Writings of W. B. Yeats*. London: Rupert Hart-Davis, 1951. 3rd ed. London, 1968.

Walker, Joseph. *Historical Memoirs of the Irish Bards*. London, 1786.

Walsh, Edward. *Irish Popular Songs*. Dublin, 1847. 2nd ed. 1883.

The *Weekly Freeman*. 6 vol. (1888–1891). The volumes of the journal in the British Library were destroyed during World War II.

Wilde, Lady Jane Francesca ("Speranza"), ed. *Ancient Cures, Charms, and Usages of Ireland*. London, 1890.

– *Ancient Legends, Mystic Charms, and Superstitions of Ireland*. To which is appended A Chapter on "The Ancient Race of Ireland" by the late Sir William Wilde. London, 1888.

Wilde, Sir William. *Irish Popular Superstitions*. Dublin, 1852. Rpt. Irish Folklore Series, ed. Séamus Ó Duilearga. Shannon Ireland: Irish UP, 1972; Paperback ed. Dublin: Irish Academic Press, 1979.

Wilson, Bruce M. " 'From Mirror after Mirror': Yeats and Eastern Thought." *Comparative Literature*, 34 (Winter 1982), 28–46.

Yeats, Michael. "W. B. Yeats and Irish Folk Song." *Southern Folklore Quarterly*, 31 (June 1966), 153–178.

The *Yellow Book of Lecan, a collection of pieces (prose and verse) in the Irish language, compiled during the eleventh and twelfth centuries* . . . With Introduction . . . by Robert Atkinson. Dublin, 1896.

Zeuss, Johann Caspar. *Grammatica Celtica*. 2 vol. Lipsiae, 1853.

Österling, Anders. See Osterling.

Index

(Titles of songs in the three plays found under Yeats, W. B., *Works: CC, LHD*, and *SW*.)

Abduction. *See* fairies
Abbey Theatre, 2ln *et passim*
Acallamh na Senórach, 79
Adene (Edain), linked with Fergus, 38
Adventures of Connla, 34, 145
AE (G. Russell), 73, 83, 134, 145
Aedh, 23
Aengus, 32, 34, 35, 39, 40–42, 49, 50, 50n, 73, 74, 101 *et passim*
Aislingi, 46
Alcestis, 18
Alchemical Rose, 65
Ale, 31, 135, 139–43
Ale-feast, ale-song, 31, 135, 136, 139, 140, 148, 155
Aleel, spokesman for art and love, 125. *See* Yeats, W.|B., *Works: CC*
Allegory, political, 108
Allingham, W., 11; *Songs and Poems*, 11n; 27, 104
Almqvist, Bo, vii
Amadán-na Breena, amadán na bruidhne, 76n
Amait, 76n
Amergin, 118; "of the White Knee", 121n; "Triumph Song", 116
Ancient Irish Tales, ed. Cross and Slover, 26n, 51n *et passim*
Angels, stern-looking, 18
Animals, supernatural, associated with Celtic mythology and Finn, 77–78
Annals of the Four Masters, 10, 49n
Arawn, king of Annwn, 81
Arbois de Jubainville, H. d', *Essai d'un Catalogue*, 12; *Le Cycle Mythologique Irlandais*, 12, 43n, 48n
Ardroe the Wise, 65
Aristotle, 143
Arnold, M. "The Forsaken Merman", 45n
Arthur, King, 136
Arthurian legends, 98
Ash-grey, grey, signifying death, 98
Asplund, Karl, 150
Atlantis, The, 11
Axël, 100, 100n
Avenue Theatre (*LHD* first performed), 133

Ballad, definition, 141
Ballads, 102

Ballads and Poems of Young Ireland, 11
Balor, 23, 24, 25, 26, 145
Banim, J., 10
Banim, M., 10
Banshee, 98n
Barach, 24
Bard of the West, The, 114–16
Barrington, Sir J., *Recollections; Rise and Fall of the Irish Nation*, 9n
Barry, J., *Songs of Ireland*, 113n
Battle of Ventry, The, 52n
Battles of Moytura, 26, 27, 145
Battles of the Shee, 147
Battles over the dying, 52
Battles over the souls of the dead, 26
Beardsley, A., 133
Belief, popular, traditional, 13; in *CC, LHD, SW*, 49–101 *et passim*
Beggars, 91, 94
Beltaine, 21n
Best, R., 12, 42n, 43n
Biblical, 22
Bilingualism, 8
Bird lore and associated beliefs in *CC, LHD, SW*, 85–101
Bird (soul into), 86–87, ash-grey, with human heads and voices, 97, 98; birdlike quality of Faery Child, 87, man-headed, 98; messengers of the Ever-living, 147; moral message from, 99; "shadows, illusions", 100; sea-(ordinary), 97–98; supernatural, 135 *et passim;* white, 69, 86, white with silver feet and crest of gold (rebirth), 86, 147
Black Book of Carmarthen, The, 81
Black Jester, 40–41
"Blinded man" carrying "lamed man" to well, 51
Bliss, A., *Spoken English in Ireland, 1600–1740*, 23n
Book of Armagh, 60
Bourke, Mary, 113–114
Boyd, E., *Contemporary Drama of Ireland*, 148
Brahmaism (concept of consumed heart), 38, 40
Bramsbäck, B., "William Butler Yeats and Folklore Material", 2
Bran, 44, 48
Bran I and II, 43n, 48n, 49n, 58n

Brendan, St., 25
Breatnach, P. A., "The Chief's Poet", 107n
Bride, newly-married, 59, 63, 65 et passim
Briggs, K., Dictionary of Fairies, 93n
Brooke, Ch., Reliques of Irish Poetry, 10, 115n
Brown, S., Ireland in Fiction, 10
Bülow, I. von, Der Tanz im Drama, 121, 122n
Burns, 103
Bushrui, S., 30n, 31, 33, 34, 34n, 35n, 84
Butterfly (soul into), 86
Byrd, Th. L. Jr., Early Poetry of W. B. Yeats, 119

Cabbalistic belief re purple, 65 n
Cailitin (Gaile Dána), 24
"Caitilín Ní Uallacháin" ("Cathleen Ni Houlihan"), song, 105, 105n
Callanan, J. J., 104
Cambrian Journal, The, 51n
Carleton, W., 5; The Black Prophet, 92; Tales and Sketches, 10
Carrion crow, 91
carroghe, 107n
Cathbad, 117
Catherine of Alexandria, Saint, 18n
Cath Maige Tuired, 26n
Celtic emotion, 114
Celtic Revival (Irish Literary Renaissance), 13, 148
Cenél Eoghain, 46n
Ceol-sidhe, 131
Changeling, 88, 89
Chatterton, Lady H. G., Rambles in the South of Ireland, 9
Christiansen, R. Th., 60n
Clark, D., 30n et passim
Coffin, T., 4n, 13n
Cohen, H. (on literature and folklore), 13
Coleridge, S., 53
Colgan, Father J., 49, 49n
Comyn, M., 11, 79n
Conchubar, 24, 99
Conflict (struggle) between the visible and the invisible worlds, 48, 72, 145 et passim
Conn-Eda, 51n
Connacht, 4, 141
"Countess Cathleen in Paradise". See Yeats, W. B., Works: CC
"Countess Kathleen O'Shea, The", 7, 10n, 16—18, 145
Countess Kathleen/Cathleen, The. See Yeats, W. B., Works: CC
Croker, C., Fairy Legends . . . of the South of Ireland, 6, 9, 33n; Researches in the South of Ireland, 28n
Cronán, 138n
Cross, K. G. W. (and Dunlop, R. T.), 1—2n

Cross, T. P., Motif-Index of Early Irish Literature, 56n
Crucifix (removed), 132
"Cuach mo Lionndubh Buidhe", 152
Cuchulain, 24, 34, 35, 80, 89
Cummen Strand, 110
Cwn Annwn, 81, 82n
Curse (unjustified, reverts), 94
Curtin, J., 6n, 9; "Balor of the Evil Eye and Lui Lavada, his Grandson", 26, 26n
Curtis, E., History of Ireland, 106—07

Dagda, the, 32, 73, 101 et passim
Dalua, 75—76; ("The Amadan"), 75
Daly, D., The Young Douglas Hyde, 128, 128n
Dance of death, 121
Dancers (of the woods), 54
Dandy-Dogs, 82n
Dante, 25
Danu (goddess), 43, 46, 52, 147
Darley, A., 139, 156
Death of the Children of Lir, The (story), 19n
Death of Cuchulain, The (play), 25; (story), 27, 145
Dectora. See Yeats, W. B., Works: SW
Deer, hornless, 77—79, 82 et passim
Deichtire, 34
Deirdre, 99
Deirdre, 24, 99
Demon lover, 119, 130
Demons, 49, 90—94, 124, 146; as Merchants, 109, 128 et passim. See also Yeats, W. B., Works: CC
"Devil and his Dandy-Dogs, The", 82n
Dillon, M., Early Irish Literature, 34, 52n
Dinneen, P., Foclóir Gaedhilge agus Béarla, 107n
Dinnschenchas, 72n
Dirge, 113, 126
Dolmetsch, A. (psaltery), 144
Domhnall Óg, 103, 103n
Donne, J., 41
Dormarth, 81
Dorson, R., 4, 7n
Dottin, G., The World of the Celts (trans.), 23n
Dream of Macsen, 43n
Druid, 116, 117—19
Druidess, 24
Dublin and London Magazine, 11
Dublin Penny Journal, 11
Dublin University Magazine, 11
Dublin University Review, 128
Dulla(g)hans, 94n
Dunlop, R. T., 1—2n
Dyer, Thistleton T. F., The Ghost World, 5n

Eagle, 40, 77, 88

Eagle-cock, 87
Ebric (Aibric), 35n
Echaid the Ploughman, 43
Ecstasy, 121
Edgeworth, M., *Castle Rackrent,* 10
Edain (Étain, Edaine, Adene), 32, 34–37, 42, 43n, 45, 46n, 72, 74, 101 *et passim*
Eglinton, J., 1n
Eiblín a Rúin, 5
Éigse 18 (1980–81), 138n
Eithne Inguba, 89
Elizabeth I (harp fell into disrepute), 107–08
Elizabethans, the, 104
Ellmann, R., 21n, 30n, 34n, 124, 141n *et passim*
Eman ac Knuck (*Eamonn an Chnuic*), character in *The Bard of the West,* 114–15
Eochaid, King, 36–37
Epigraph to *CC,* 111, 112, 113–14
Erin (a beautiful lady), 108
Étain. *See* Edain
Étar, 36
Eurén, T.
Ever-living, the, 31, 44, 49, 71, 72, 99, 100, 148 *et passim*

Faber Book of Irish Verse, 121n
Faery Child, *See* Yeats, W.B., *Works: LHD*
Fairies, adbuction (kidnapping), 145–146; avoid speaking of, 60; "bodiless moods", 124; bride, 48; earth-resembling life, 131; gifts of fire, food, etc. to, 62 *et passim;* sea, 44–45, 45n; shape and size, 62, stealing bride, 28; stealing children, men and women, 88; theories about, 60–61, 131; *See also:* Shee, *Sidhe*
Fairy, belief in power of hawthorn, 66; (*see also* quicken, rowan); changeling, 88, 89; dancers, 39, 99, 119, 120 *et passim;* enchantments, 27–28, 86; Fool, 73–76, 84, 101 *et passim;* joiner, 58, lore, 2; luring away to fairyland, 27 *et passim;* music, 131–32; piper(s), 28, 148; tale, definition of, 14; tribes, 48; white, associated with, 86, white bird, *see* bird
"Fairy Palace of the Quicken Tree, The" (Fenian tale), 66
Farag, F. F., "Celtic and Oriental Elements . . .", 40n
[Farewell, J.], *The Irish Hudibras,* 23n
Farr, F., 31n, 32, 42, 133, 144
Fate of the Children of Lir, The, 35
Fenian Cycle, 15, 66
Fergus, King, 24. *See* Yeats, W. B. *Works: CC, characters*
"Fergus O'Mara and the Air-Demons", 81
Ferguson, Sir S., "The Fairy Thorn", 7, 10, 11, 104; "The Abdication of Fergus Mac Roy", 118; *Poems,* 118n

Fiachra, 65
Finn, 15, 66, 77, 83
Finneran, R. et al., ed., *Letters to W.B. Yeats,* 76n
Finvara, 65
Fire (symbolism, etc.), 62, 64–65, 129–30, 135, 147
Fjellström, Phebe, 15n
Flame(s), dancing, etc., 59, 64–65
Floral decorations, 63–64
Flynn, Paddy, 8
Folk belief and magic, 68
Folklore, definitions, 3–4, 11; emphasis in the present study on the role it plays in Yeats's creative writing, 15; indigenous West-of-Ireland, 15; neglected field in Yeatsian research, 1; Yeats's sources, 1–13 *et passim*
Folk-Lore, 11
Folk-Lore Record, 11
Folk poetry, traditional, 13 *et passim;* popular, 102–105; and music, 102–143
Folk tale, definition, 14
Folk thought and folk imagination, 145
Fomor, the, 52
Fomorians ("Fomoroh", "Fomorah"), 24, 25, 26, 33, 34, 147
Fool, Dark (*Amadan Dhu*), 75–76
Fool of Aengus, 74, 101 *et passim*
Fool, White, or, Fairy Fool, 73–76, 84, 101 *et passim*
Fournier d'Albe, E. E., *An English-Irish Dictionary and Phrase-Book,* 141n
Frazer, Sir J., *The Golden Bough,* 12, 12n
Frayne, J. P., 5n, 6n, 7n, 8n, 9n. 32–34 *et passim*
Free Booters, 115n
Friend, H., *Flowers and Flower Lore,* 65, 65n, 26, 67, 67n
Fuamnach, 35, 36
Funk and Wagnalls *Standard Dictionary of Folklore, Mythology and Legend,* 3

Gaelic, 8, 34
Gaile Dána, 24
"Garw and Cuchulain" (Fenian ballad), 120, 121n
Ge, 51
Ghosts, 53, 90–92, 128 *et passim*
Giraldus Cambrensis, 9, 70, 107n
Gol, 138
Goll, 25, 26, 106
Gonne, M., 86, 122n
"Good People", the, 60, 147 *et passim*
Graves, R., 86–87, 121n
Gregory, Lady, 7, 11, 26n, 28, 29, 37n (spelling of Irish names); 41, 42, 46, 47, 73, 98–99, 105, 106, 141–43 *et passim*
Griffin, G., 7, 11, 31, 69–70
"Gruagach Uasal, An" ("The Noble Enchanter"), 141–42, 151

Gwyn ap Nudd, 81

Hall [A. M. and S.], *Ireland: Its Scenery, Character, etc.,* 9
Hamlet, 33
Hanrahan, 23, 108, 110, 129
Hardiman, J., 5n, 9, 107n
Harp, magic, etc., 31, 32−35, 41, 44, 73, 74, 76, 83, 99, 100−02, 106, 107, 108, 110, 124, 135, 137−40, 143, 144, 147
Hautala, J., "Folkminnesforskningen som vetenskapsgren", 3
Hawk, of Achill, 88n; 89
Hawk-Guardian, 89
Head, severed, 23n, 36, 138n
Hearne, Martin, 23
Heart Lake, the, 28
Heaven, 147 *et passim*
Heffernan, W. (William Dall O'Heffernan), 10n, 11, 105
Hell, 22, 23, 23n, 25, 27; (world of Evil), 49, 101, 125; (realm of Demons), 83
Hell vision, Aleel's, 22−27
Hellqvist, E., *Svensk etymologisk ordbok,* 93
Hen, 90, 91
Henn, T. R., *The Lonely Tower,* 122n
Hereditas, vii, 2
Heron, 24
Hesperides, the
Hirsch, E., "The Poet as Folklorist", 33n
Historical Cycle, 15
Hogan, J. J., 2
Hone, J., *W. B. Yeats, 1865−1939,* 133n
Horniman, A., 149
Hound, white, 76, 79n; phantom: "pearly white save one red ear", 77, 78, 79, 80, 82, 84
Hounds, demon, spectral, 77−78, 79−82; different-coloured, 84, 85 *et passim;* hell, 81
Hounds of Annwvyn, 80
Hühn, P., *Das Verhältnis von Mann und Frau im Werk von William Butler Yeats,* 43n, 68
Hull, E., *The Cuchullin Saga,* 12; 13
Hultenberg, H., 150
Hunt, R., *Popular Romances of the West of England,* 82n
Hyde, D., 8n, 49n, 76n; *Beside the Fire,* 6, 9, 10; "Gaelic Folk Songs", 127; *Literary History of Ireland,* 8n; *Legends of Saints and Sinners,* 76n; *Love Songs of Connacht,* 6, 7, 10, 127; "Poems of the Connacht Bards", 127; *Religious Songs of Connacht,* 10, 127; *Songs Ascribed to Raftery,* 105; *Story of the Bush, 106, 108n; 149 et passim*

Immrama, 46; ed. van Hamel, 49n
Immortality, 70 *et passim*

Inis Fail, 84n
Irish, spoken (Hyde on), 8n
Irish Theosophist, The, 7n
Ishibashi, H., *Yeats and the Noh,* 123n
ITS, 12 *et passim*

Jackson, K., 43n
Jacobite poetry, 108
James I of Scotland, 107
"Japanee-Rossetti girl", 133n
Jeffares, A. N., 30n, 50n, 106n, 110n *et passim*
Jochum, S., 2n
Johnson, L. ("The Red Wind"), 110n
Joyce, J., 54n, 143
Joyce, P. W., *Old Celtic Romances,* 9, 66; *Irish Names of Places,* 10, 33n, 52n, 93n; *Social History of Ancient Ireland,* 10, 19n, 48−49

Kathleen/Cathleen (Yeats's spelling), 15; legend, 18
Keating, G., *General History of Ireland, The,* 10
Keats, J., 5, 27, 104
"Keen for Art O'Leary, The", 138
Keening (keeners), 28, 135−140
Kennedy, P., 26n; "Witches' Excursion, The", 20n
Kickham, Ch., *Knocknagow,* 11
Kinahan, F., "Armchair Folklore . . .", 3
Kinsella, Th., 117
Knee, white, 119−122
"King Goll, an Irish Legend", 106n
Knowland, A. S., 30n
Krans, H. S., 31n
"Kubla Khan", 79

Ladon, 51
"Lageniensis" (Canon John O'Hanlon), 50n, 55
"Lamed man", 51
"Lament for Morian Shehone for Miss Mary Bourke" (anon.), 111−14, 143
Land of Heart's Desire, The. See Yeats, W. B., *Works: LHD*
Lane controversy, 125
Lang, A., *Custom and Myth,* 3n, 12; *Myth, Ritual and Religion,* 12
"Laoidh Oisín ar Thír na n Óg", 79n
Lawless, Emily, 11
Leabhar na Feinne, ed. J. Campbell, 10
Lebor Gabála, 21, 26, 27, 138n, 145
Lebor na hUidre (Book of the Dun Cow), 39
legend, definition, 14
Leisure Hour, The, 7n
Lespès, Léo, *Les Matinées de Timothée Trimm,* 16
Lever, Ch., 11
"Lift up the white knee". See Yeats,

W. B., *Works: CC*
Lochlann, king of, 135
Longfellow, 103
Love, 99, 116, 117, 118, 119, 120, 121, 122, 123 *et passim*
Lover, S., 10, 11
Lucifer, 28n
Lug, 24, 26, 27, 145
Lysaght, P., *"An Bhean Chaointe . . ."*, 98n

Mabinogion, The, 81
Macbeth, 53
MacLeod, Fiona (William Sharp), 31n, 40, 66–67, 73–74, 75, 76, 77n
Macpherson, J., *Fingal*, 37
Maeve, 48 *et passim*
Mag Mell, 49, 50
Maiden (woman, young, with a golden apple in her hand, riding a horse), 77–80, 82 *et passim*
Man (young, riding a horse, pursuing a maiden), 77–80, 82 *et passim*
Mangan, J. C., 11; *Poets and Poetry of Munster*, 11n; 27, 104
Marbhna, 138
"Marchands d'Ames, Les", 16, 16n
Marlowe, *Doctor Faustus*, 21
Mongan, 23 *et passim*
Martyn, E., 149
Mary, cult of, 127
Maxwell, D. F. S., 35n
Maxwell, C., 114n
Mayhew, G. P., 30n
Mc Hugh, R., 141
Meir, C., 104, 124, 125
Melchiori, G., *The Whole Mystery of Art*, 22n
Merrow, 45
Meyer, K., *Bran* I, II, 12, 12n *et passim*
Michael Robartes, 23
Midir (Midhir, Midher), 34–37, 40, 41, 42, 43, 44, 45
Milesians, 26
Miller, L., *The Noble Drama of W. B. Yeats*, 21n, 30n, 126n, 133
Mirecourt, E. de, *Timothée Trimm*, 16n
Mongan, 79n
Monsters, dog-headed, eagle-headed, 77 *et passim*
Moods, 6, 113, 118, 119, 121, 122, 123, 124, 125, 126, 128, 131, 145 *et passim*
Moon, crescent, 135
Moore, G., 83, 134
More, H., 61
Moreen Shehone, 115
Morna, 37
Morrígan (Morrígu, or Badbh), 25
Morris, W., 100, 126n
Mountain-ash, 67
Munch-Pedersen, Ole, 2, 110

Murphy, G., *Saga and Myth in Ancient Ireland*, 49
Music, Irish, flourished, 107, 108; madness, love and, 125; Yeats on, 139; song and music, Ch. III
"My Jug of Yellow Ale", 141, 152

Näcken (Strömkarlen, music, evil power), 129
Naoise, 24
Nasturtium, red, 66, 69
Nathan, L. E., 30n, 44n
Nation, The, 128n
Nature, dangerous power, 131
Nera's Adventures, 48, 62
Nessa, 117, 118
Niamh, 80, 85
Nirvana, 84
Nobel Prize for Literature, 149
Noh drama, 149 *et passim*
Nordic Rejoycings 1982, 54n
November Eve (Hallow E'en), 62
Nuala, 65
Nutt, A., 12; essays on Otherworld and rebirth, 43n

O'Connor, Ketty, 16, 17, 18n
Ó Corráin, A., 107n
O'Curry, E., 12, 36, 43n, 108n
O'Donnor, Ketty, 16, 18n
O'Driscoll, R., 66n, 138n
Ó Duilearga, S., vii, 6n
O'Grady, S. H., *Silva Gadelica*, 12, 79n
O'Grady, S. J., 8n, 25, 26, 45; *Early Bardic Literature*, 11; *Finn and his Companions*, 11; *History of Ireland*, 11; *Story of Ireland*, 50n
O'Heffernan, W. *See* Heffernan
Oisin, Oisín, 48, 70, 78, 80, 85, 106
Old Celtic Romances, 78 *et passim*
Ó Madagáin, B., "Irish Vocal Music . . ."
Ó Muirgheasa, É., *Céad de Cheoltaibh Uladh*, 152
O'Rahilly, Egan, 11 *O'*
O'Rahilly, T. F., *Early Irish History and Mythology*, 24
Orchil, 23, 24, 25, 26
"Oro! A Lionn-dubh Buidhe!", 143, 152
O'Shea, Kathleen, 16
Osterling, A. (Österling), "Den unge Yeats och den gamle", 1, 2
Ó Súilleábháin, S. *See* O'Sullivan, Sean
O'Sullivan, Owen Rua, 10n, 11, 105; "Le h-ais na Suire", 108
O'Sullivan, Sean, 7n, 103, 105
O'Sullivan, Sheila, "W. B. Yeats's Use of Oral and Literary Tradition", 2
"O the Brown and the Yellow Ale" (J. Stephens's rendering of the ballad as he learnt it from J. Joyce), 152–53
Otherworld, the (Eden, Paradise, Tír na n

Óg, etc.), 23, 27, 29, 31–34, 39, 44, 46–51, 59, 65, 69, 72, 79, 86, 87, 89, 99, 100, 101, 117, 126, 146, 137 *et passim*
"Our hearts are sore". *See* Yeats, W. B., *Works: CC*
Owen Aherne, 23
Owls, horned (demons), 53, 77, 90–95, 96, 146
Oxen, black, 22

Paget, Dorothy, 133
Parkinson, Th., 30n, 32
Patrick, Saint, 79, 80
Poe, E. A., 53
Poems and Ballads of Young Ireland, 115n
Poet/Musician in *CC,* 105–10
Pollexfen, 98n
Pooka (Phooka, Phuca, *Púca*), 93, 93n
Poyning's Parliament 107
Pre-Raphaelite (manner, scene, etc.), 126–127, 137
"Priest's Soul, The", 7
Primroses, 63–65, 67
Pwyll, king of Dyuet, 81
Pwyll Pendeuic Dyuet, 81

Quest, 47, 84 *et passim*
Quicken bough, 63, 66–69, 147

Rafferty, T., 46n
Raftery, Anthony, 11, 106
rapparee, 115
RC, 11, 43n, 48n *et passim*
Rebirth, 35, 36, 37, 39, 43n, 44–47, 87–88, 117–18, 120, 121–22 (in Paradise); 146
Red Branch Cycle, 38
Reliquiae Celticae, ed. A. Cameron, 10; *Celtic Heathendom,* 12
Rhys, E. P., 39
Rhŷs, J., 43n, 59, 81
Robbery, 95
Rodenberg, J., *Die Insel der Heiligen,* 8n
Rooth, A. B., *Folkdikt och Folktro,* 3, 15n
Rosenberg, B. A., "Irish Folklore and 'The Song of Wandering Aengus' ", 2
Ross, Anne, *Pagan Celtic Britain,* 77
Rossetti, D. G., 127
Rowan, 63, 66–69, 147
Royal Swedish Academy, 149
Rupin, W. D., *Yeats's Shakespeare,* 33n
Russell, G., 83. *See* AE

Sagas, Irish: traditional division, and later division into cycles, 15
Salome, 138n
Saltair na Rann, 110n
Saul, G. B., 30, 30n, 35n, 85
Saurat, D., 65n
Savoy, The, 130n
"Scél Baile Binnbérlaig", 73n
Schweisgut, E., *Yeats' Feendichtung,* 2

Sea, the, 34 *et passim* isea lore, 46
Seabars (Siabhras, etc.) 33, 33n, 83, 131 *et passim*
Séidan, 54n
Setanta, 80
Shadowy Waters, The. See Yeats, W.B., *Works: SW*
Shakespeare, W., 5
Shaw, F., ed., *The Dream of Óengus,* 44n
Shaw, G. B., *Arms and the Man,* 134
Shee (*Sidhe, Sidhi, Sidi*), 38, 48, 49, 54n, 70 *et passim*
Shee-geehy, 55
Shelley, P. B., 5, 27, 103, 104
Sheogue, 58 *et passim*
Sheoques, 88
Ship(s), 31, 32, 33, 70, 71, 95, 135, 147
Sidnell, M. J., 30n, 35n, 37n
Sigerson, G., *Bards of the Gael and Gall,* 121n
Sluagh-Gaoith, Aes-Sidhe, Slua-shee, Sluagh Sidhe, 54, 55
Songs (list of, in *CC*), 111
Song and music, 102 *et passim* in Ch. III
Sons of Uisnech, Tragic Death of, 145
Soul, a lonely wanderer, 123; money for a, 97; plastic power, 61
"Soul Cages, The" (story), 86n
Souls, of dead sailors, 97; selling, 95 *et passim*
Sowlths, 57
Spirit (river), 131
Spirits (sorrow of), 128
Statutes of Kilkenny, 106
Stephens, J., 141n, 153
Stewart, W. G., *The Popular Superstitions of the Highlanders of Scotland,* 67n
Storm, magic, etc., 52, 53, 54–57, 70–71, 101, 114, 130, 131 *et passim*
St. Patrick's Purgatory, 23n
"Stut Ozel", and the Wild Hunter, 92n
Suibne Geilt, 106
Swallow, lonely, 54
Swans, 36, 74, 77
Swedenborg . . ., 131n
Swedenborgian (ghost), 91
Swift, J., 106
Sword, 136, 137 *et passim*
Sydow, C. W., von, 14n, 15
Symons, A., 58; "The Dancer" (poem), 122; dance and "the immortal moment", 122
Synge, J. M., *Riders to the Sea,* 22, 149

Taboos (trangressions), 148
Taidhbhse, 57n
Táin Bó Fráich, 73n
'Tale', definition, 14
Tales, traditional prose, 13, 14–46
Tasks, 51–52
Tennyson's "Ulysses", 118

Ten Principal Upanishads, The (trans by W. B. Yeats and S.¦P. Swami), 123n
Tethra, King of, 34; people of, 34
Tevish (Thivish), 57, 58n
Thoms, W. J., 3
Thompson, Stith, 3, 14, 14n, 15
Thuente, M. H., *W. B. Yeats and Irish Folklore,* 2, 115n, 124n *et passim*
Thurneysen, R., 36n, 42n
Time, duality of, 136
Tochmarc Étaíne, 36n
Todhunter, J., *A Comedy of Sighs,* 133
Tonn Cliodhna (a wave), 72
Tradition, "written and unwritten", 103 *et passim*
Tragic Death of the Sons of Uisneach, The, 27
Transactions of the Gaelic Society, 11
Transactions of the Ossianic Society, 11–12
Túatha Dé Danann, 3n, 27, 61, 70 *et passim*
Tynan, K., 58–59
"Two Irish Tales . . .", 43n, 44n
Tyrone, fishing off, 46, 46n

Unicorn, 77
Universal Irish Song Book, The, 113n
Ure, P., 20n, 30n, 44
Utley, F. L., 4

Vedanta (*Tamas, Rajas, Sattva*), 84
Vickery, J. B., " 'The Golden Bough': Impact and Archetype", 12n
Vivian Grey, 92n
Virgin (Mary), the, 91, 93, 127
Visionaries, 23, 24 *et passim*
Voyages (of *Bran, Maeldún, St. Brendan, the Uí Chorra*), 34 *et passim*

Wade, A., *A Bibliography of the Writings of W. B. Yeats,* 19n, *et passim; Letters,* 42 *et passim*
Wake, 135–140
Walker, J., *Irish Bards,* 107
Walsh, E., *Irish Popular Songs,* 10, 10n
Watson, W., 58
Wave (high), 71–72, 135, 138–40
Whip, idle, 82n
Weekly Freeman, The, 103, 104
Wilde, Lady, *Ancient Cures . . .* 6, 9; *Ancient Legends . . .* 10, 131, 132
Wilde, Sir W., *Irish Popular Superstitions,* 10, 53n, 55, 60, 61, 62, 63, 67
Wilson, B. M., " 'From Mirror after Mirror': Yeats and Eastern Thought", 123–39
Wind, 53, 54, 59, 64, 71, 72; (different-coloured winds), 110; 131, 132, 133, *et passim*
Woman, ideal image of, 68 *et passim*

Yeats, Jack B., 7
Yeats, M. B., viii, 2, 10n, 104, 141
Yeats, Anne, viii, 141
Yeats, W. B. (Items like the Ever-living, Fairies, Otherworld, Seabar, Storm, Wind, are found under their initial letters in Index.) Folklore, collecting more methodically, 9, 63; manner of collecting, 8; collecting with Lady Gregory, 131; material (sources), 1–13 *et passim;* Irish politics provoked Yeats to bitter poems, 125; Nobel Prize for Literature, 149; poetry, bring back to stage; speech to Royal Swedish Academy, 149–50; spelling of Irish names, 37n; theatre, devotion to, 148–49; *on:* Arthurian Legends, 80; *Eiblín a Rúin,* 5–6; folk, the, 4–5, folk-art, 4–5; folklore, 4–5; folklore and literature, 1, 4, 13 *et passim; LHD* and its "world of shadows", 134; literature, native Irish, 5, 6; music, relation to words, 139; poetry, popular, 102–105; poetry, music, and magic, 105; tradition, native, 5; style, 104; *SW* as a fairy tale, 31n; "Trees of Knowledge and of Life", 5
Works:
Arrow, The, 31n; At the Hawk's Well, 89
Baile and Aillinn, 41, 73, 74; "Binding of the Hair, The", 138n; *Book of Irish Verse, A,* 111, 114; *Bounty of Sweden, The,* 149; "By the Roadside", 5;
Cathleen Ni Houlihan, 47, 150; *Celtic Twilight, The,* 5, 7, 27, 44 *et passim;* "Circus Animals' Desertion, The", 97; "Cold Heaven, The", 123; *Collected Plays, The,* 21, 30n, 44 *et passim; Collected Works,* 32 *et passim; Collected Works in Verse and Prose,* 19n *et passim; Countess Cathleen, The,* 15–27, 29, 35, 37–40, 47, 48, 49–59, 85–89, 90, 97, 102, 105–28, 135, 144, 145, 146, 147, 148, 150, 155. *Characters:* Aleel, 20–24, 26–27, 35, 37, 47, 50–54, 105–10, 116, 119, 120–26, 129 *et passim;* Demons (Merchants, traders in souls), 15, 19, 20, 21, 52, 53, 57, 90, 94, 96–97 *et passim;* Demons (Owls), 53, 91–93, 94, 95, 96; Cathleen/Kathleen, 15, 19, 21, 23, 26; 37, 38, 47; 50–54, 56, 97, 116, 117, 119, 122–128 *et passim;* Kevin, 20, 22, 23: 58, 105–06, 108–10, 116; Mary Rua, 59, 60, 62, 89, 90–96; Old Man, 21; Neal, an old peasant, 52; Shemus Rua, 20, 25, 59, 66, 90–95, 109, 110, 125; Teigue Rua, 20, 90–93, 146. *Songs:* "All the heavy days are over", 111, 126–28; "Countess Cathleen in Paradise", 126–27; Epigraph: "The sorrowful are dumb for thee", 111, 112, 113–14; "Impetuous heart, be still, be still", 111; 119–24; "Lift up the white knee", 111, 119–22;

"Our hearts are sore", 111, 128–29; "Song", 126–27; "Were I but crazy for love's sake", 111, 124–25; "Who will go drive with Fergus now . . .?", 111, 116–18. *Versions:* 18–19, 19n.; *The Countess Kathleen and Various Legends and Lyrics,* 19n; "Cradle Song, A", 130n; "Cradle Song, The", 72; "Cradles of Gold, The" (story), 130n;
Death of Cuchulain, The (play), 25; *Deirdre,* 35; "Desire of Man and of Woman", 79n "Dust hath Closed Helen's Eyes", 121
"Everlasting Voices, The", 124;
Fairy and Folk Tales of the Irish Peasantry. See *Irish Fairy and Folk Tales.*
"Fergus and the Druid", 117–19; 121n; "Fiddler of Dooney, The", 106, *Four Plays for Dancers,* 129
Green Helmet and Other Poems, The, 123
"Harp of Aengus, The", 41; "He Gives his Beloved Certain Rhymes", 138n; "Heart of Women, The" ("Heart of the Woman"), 130n; "Host of the Air, The", 28; *Hour-Glass, The,* 7, 140, 143
Ideas of Good and Evil, 102, 103, 104, 105, 144, 145; "I have drunk ale from the Country of the Young", 143n; "In Memory of Alfred Pollexfen", 98n; *In the Seven Woods,* 110n; "Invoking the Irish Fairies", 7, 43n; "Irish Fairies", 7; "Irish Fairies, Ghosts, Witches, etc.", 28; *Irish Fairy and Folk Tales (Fairy and Folk Tales of the Irish Peasantry),* 3, 6, 7, 7n, 10, 15, 16, 17, 19, 21, 27, 28, 45, 49, 69, 70, 93 *et passim;* "Irish National Literature", 6, 7; "I walked among the Seven Woods of Coole", 41
"Kathleen-Ny-Houlihan", ("Kathleen the Daughter of Hanrahan", "Song of the Red Hanrahan"), 110n; "Kidnappers", 27; "King Goll, an Irish Legend", 106n; *King of the Great Clock Tower, The,* 79n, 139n
Land of Heart's Desire, The (LHD), 25–35, 49, 59–69, 70, 72, 86–92, 97, 100–02, 129–34, 135, 145, 146, 147, 148, 149 *et passim. Characters:* Bridget Bruin, 29, 59–60, 62; Faery Child, 29, 62, 64–65, 67–69, 87–89, 130–133, 144, 148, 155; Father Hart, 29, 64, 87, 88, 132; Maire/Mary, 29, 39, 47, 59–69, 100, 129, 130, 132, 133; Maurteen Bruin, 29, 63, 64, 67, 132; Shawn Bruin, 29, 59; flowers and trees, sacred: *see* primroses; quicken; fairy song and music, 120–34; *song:* "The wind blows out of the gates of the day", 132–133, 148, 155 (F. Farr's music)
"Madness of King Goll, The", 25, 26;

"Message of the Folk-lorist, The", 5; "Michael Clancy, the Great Dhoul, and Death", 7; "Mongan Laments . . .", 79n; *Mythologies,* 5 *et passim*
Only Jealousy of Emer, The, 89;
Plays and Controversies, 19, 134; *Plays for an Irish Theatre,* I and II, 47; *Poems,* 19, 122 *et passim; Poems, 1899–1905,* 30 *et passim; Poetical Works of W.!B. Yeats,* 19, 111; "Poetry of Sir Samuel Ferguson", 118
"Queen and the Fool, The", 74, 76
"Red Hanrahan's Song about Ireland", 110; *Representative Irish Tales,* 7; *Responsibilities, The,* 123; *Resurrection, The,* 80; *Reveries over Childhood and Youth,* 98; *Rosa Alchemica* (initiation dance and motif ot ecstasy), 121; "Rose of Shadow, The", 129–31
"Sailing to Byzantium", 86; *Selected Poems,* 19; *Selection from the Poetry of W. B. Yeats,* 19; *Secret Rose, The,* 110n, 121, 139; *Shadowy Waters, The (SW),* 7, 29–35, 41, 69–86, 97, 99, 102, 135–43, 146, 148. *Characters:* Aibric, 31, 32, 35, 135–37, 139, 147; Aleel (a poet in early versions), 33, 35; Dectora, 30–35, 41, 43, 44, 70–72, 83–84, 99, 101, 135–39, 140, 144, 156; Forgael, 29–35, 41, 43, 44, 47, 69, 70–74, 82–85, 99, 101, 135–39, 145, 146, 147; Iol(1)an (spoken about, but not speaking himself), 31, 33, 136–38; Sailors, 31, 32, 33, 44–46, 70, 83, 97, 135–37, 139–40, 143, 155. *Songs:* Dectora's Death Song or Lament, 137–139, 140, 156; Sailors' song, 135–36, 139–40, 155; use of ballad, 135, 136, 139, 140–43; use of keen, 135–136. *Versions and stage productions,* 30, 30n *et passim*
"Song of Red Hanrahan", 110n; "Stolen Bride, The", 28; *Stories from Carleton,* 7; *Swedenborg, Mediums and the Desolate Places,* 131n
Tables of the Law and The Adoration of the Magi, The, 65, 66; "Two Kings, The", 35, 36; "Two Poems Concerning Peasant Visionaries", 130
"Unappeasable Host, The", 62, 130n; *Uncollected Prose* (Frayne I, II), 5, 131 *et passim; Unicorn from the Stars, The,* 22–23
Variorum Edition of the Plays, 16n *et passim*
Variorum Edition of the Poems, 30n *et passim; Vision, A,* 42
Wanderings of Oisin, The, 15, 76, 77, 78, 79, 80, 81; "What is 'Popular Poetry'?", 102–05; *Wind Among the Reeds,* 28, 110 *et passim*
Yellow Book of Lecan, The, 39

178